Although Walt Whitman is known primarily by the last edition of *Leaves of Grass* (1891–1892), almost all of the important poems were composed before 1860. After this date, Whitman adopted a less personal voice and often revised or deleted passages in the early poems that revealed the personal origins of his poems. Stephen A. Black combines psychoanalytic, historical, and literary methods to study the development of Whitman's poetic process during his most productive period.

The first three editions of *Leaves of Grass* reveal evidence of psychological conflict, suggesting that poetic composition was the crucial emotional activity of Whitman's life during the period. The writing of these poems, the author contends, involved journeys into the turmoil of the poet's unconscious. The poems do not chronicle events: they are themselves the events.

"Stephen Black's argument is an original one, and his book ought to have a significant impact on Whitman studies." *—Frederick Crews, University of California, Berkeley*

Stephen A. Black is Associate Professor of English at Simon Fraser University.

Whitman's Journeys into Chaos

O give me some clew!
O if I am to have so much, let me have more!
O a word! O what is my destination?
O I fear it is henceforth chaos!

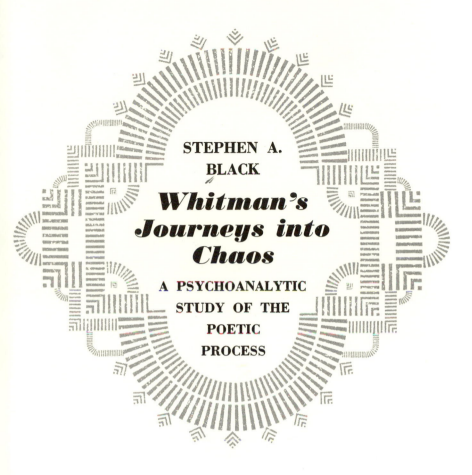

STEPHEN A.
BLACK

Whitman's Journeys into Chaos

A PSYCHOANALYTIC STUDY OF THE POETIC PROCESS

Princeton University Press

Princeton, New Jersey

Library of Congress Cataloging in Publication Data will
be found on the last printed page of this book

Publication of this book has been aided
by the Andrew W. Mellon Foundation

This book has been composed in Linotype Caledonia

Printed in the United States of America
by Princeton University Press,
Princeton, New Jersey

Acknowledgments

IT IS my pleasure to name and thank some of the numerous people who have helped me complete this book. Evan Alderson, Robert H. Dunham, Carol T. Hall, Richard M. Ludwig, Temple Maynard, William Messenger, and Edwin H. Miller read the typescript and made valuable suggestions for its improvement. John Cody, M.D., also read the typescript and made a thousand valuable comments about my use of psychoanalytic theory and my application of the theory to Whitman and his poetry. Frederick C. Crews, in letters and conversations, is responsible for persuading me of the value of psychoanalytic theory for literary studies; his scholarship, like John Cody's, has been an example I have tried to follow. Edwin Lipinski, M.D., has spent many hours clarifying my understanding of psychoanalysis, as has my friend and colleague, Michael Steig.

Many others—colleagues, teachers, students, friends— have helped me in important if indirect ways: Robin Blaser, Dan Callahan, Arthur Efron, Nelson Gray, James Hall, Edgar Harden, Verona Manders, Gerald Newman, Sheila Roberts, Paul Sanders, Roger Stein, and Jerald Zaslove. Barbara McDaniel provided editorial help. I am especially indebted to Margaret Frick Watt, whose honors essay in 1965 led to the beginning of my work on Whitman. Claire Rodger typed numerous versions of the manuscript with patience, accuracy, and good cheer. The President's Research Grant Committee and the Dean of Arts of Simon Fraser University have awarded me three generous grants to assist this work. *PMLA* and *Walt Whitman Review* have kindly permitted me to incorporate different versions of essays first published in their pages. Thanks also to the

Andrew W. Mellon Foundation for a grant to assist the publication of this book. Finally, my warmest gratitude to R. Miriam Brokaw and Carol Orr for the unflagging interest and unfailing courtesy which led this book to and through the presses.

SAB

June 1974

Contents

A Note to the Reader

UNLESS otherwise indicated, all quotations from Whitman are taken from the earliest published versions of the poems and prose. Quotations from the last *Leaves of Grass* are taken from the *Comprehensive Reader's Edition* of *Leaves of Grass*. Because of Whitman's use of periods for internal punctuation in poetic lines, I have indicated ellipses in poetic quotations by asterisks.

After the first chapter I have tried to avoid the technical concepts and jargon of psychoanalysis or have explained in my text or notes such concepts and words as I have used. The reader who wishes to refresh his knowledge of psychoanalytic theory may find useful the excellent summary by H. Kohut and P.F.D. Seitz, "Concepts and Theories of Psychoanalysis," in *Concepts of Personality*, ed. J. M. Wepman and R. Heine (1963), or Charles Rycroft's *Critical Dictionary of Psychoanalysis* (1971).

Whitman Chronology

1819   Born 31 May, West Hills, Long Island.
1821   (Age 21 months) Sister Mary Elizabeth born 3 February.
1823   (Age 4) Sister Hannah Louise born 28 November.
1825–1830   (Age 6-11) Attends public school, Brooklyn. Infant sister born 2 March and dies 14 September 1825.
1827   (Age 8) Brother Andrew born 7 April.
1829   (Age 10) Brother George born 28 November.
1830–1831   (Age 11-12) Works for lawyer, then doctor; leaves school.
1831–1832   (Age 12-13) Begins to learn printing trade.
1833   (Age 14) Family moves from Brooklyn to West Hills; brother Jeff born 18 July.
1835–1836   (Age 16-17) Writes earliest surviving story, "My Boys and Girls"; brother Edward born 9 August 1835; works as printer.
1836–1838   (Age 17-18) Teaches in several Long Island schools; edits own newspaper, Huntington *Long Islander*. Family living in Brooklyn again.
1839–1841   (Age 19-21) Teaches in various Long Island schools; works as journalist and compositor in New York City; begins publishing fiction.
1842   (Age 23) Edits *The Aurora* and *The Tattler*; publishes temperance novel, *Franklin Evans*.
1843   (Age 24) Edits *The Statesman*.
1844   (Age 25) Edits *The New York Democrat*; later works for New York *Mirror*.
1846–1847   (Age 27-28) Edits Brooklyn *Daily Eagle*.
1848   (Age 29) Leaves (perhaps fired from) *Daily*

Eagle in January. Travels with Jeff to New Orleans to edit *Crescent*; remains in New Orleans from February to May, then returns to Brooklyn; edits Brooklyn *Freeman* through summer, 1849.

1850-1854 (Age 31-35) Apparently works as carpenter, bookseller in Brooklyn. Almost no information about this period. Sister Hannah elopes, 1852, with future husband.

1855 (Age 36) Publishes first *Leaves of Grass* about 4 July; father dies about 11 July; receives congratulatory letter from Emerson 21 July.

1856 (Age 37) Publishes second *Leaves of Grass* in September (which is distributed, like first edition, by phrenologists Fowler and Wells); visited by Alcott and Thoreau.

1857 (Age 38) Writes to Mrs. Tyndale 20 June of "completion" of third *Leaves of Grass*; begins period of presumed crisis; begins editorship of Brooklyn *Times*. Crisis continues through 1858.

1859 (Age 40) Brother Jeff marries 23 February; Whitman resumes long interrupted work on third *Leaves of Grass*; leaves *Times* in the spring; Valentine-Barrett MS inscribed by midsummer; Rome Brothers typescript set in August.

1860 (Age 41) Begins organizing poems into "clusters"; in February receives letter from Thayer and Eldridge offering to print third *Leaves of Grass*; travels to Boston to meet Emerson and supervise typesetting of third *Leaves of Grass* (which is published in late March).

1861 (Age 42) Civil War begins; brother George enlists.

1862 (Age 43) Goes to Virginia when George wounded.

1863-1864 (Age 44-45) Works for Army paymaster and as volunteer nurse in military hospitals; brother Andrew dies 3 December 1863; friendships with

O'Connor and Burroughs begin. May 1864 begins to suffer headaches, dizziness, and depression, which lead to return to his mother's home in June for period of seven months. Commits brother Jesse to insane asylum in December.

1865   (Age 46) Employed as clerk in Department of the Interior in February but fired in June when Secretary Harlan learns about *Leaves of Grass*; *Drum-Taps* published as booklet, independent of *Leaves of Grass*; begins tenure as clerk in Attorney General's office in July; begins friendship with Peter Doyle.

1866   (Age 47) Publishes *Sequel to Drum-Taps*; O'Connor prints vitriolic defense of Whitman, *The Good Gray Poet*, inspired by Harlan affair.

1867   (Age 48) Publishes fourth *Leaves of Grass*; begins to gain English audience after favorable review by William Rossetti; Burroughs publishes biography, *Notes on Walt Whitman as Poet and Person*. Publishes fourth *Leaves of Grass* with *Drum-Taps* and *Sequel* incorporated.

1868   (Age 49) Rossetti publishes *Poems of Walt Whitman* in England.

1869   (Age 50) Mrs. Anne Gilchrist, widow of Blake's biographer, reads *Leaves of Grass*.

1870   (Age 51) Completes "Passage to India." Various crises in Whitman family include death of older brother, Jesse, in insane asylum, and beginning of brother Jeff's wife's fatal illness.

1871   (Age 52) Publishes fifth *Leaves of Grass*. Receives first of several letters from Mrs. Gilchrist proposing marriage; correspondence with J. A. Symonds begins.

1872   (Age 53) Quarrels with O'Connor, ending their friendship; Swinburne attacks Whitman.

1873   (Age 54) Suffers paralyzing stroke 23 January; moves from Washington to Camden to live with

brother George; mother dies of heart attack 23
May.

1874 (Age 55) Publishes "Prayer of Columbus," most despairing and perhaps strongest of late poems.

1875 (Age 56) Publishes sixth ("Centennial") *Leaves of Grass* (dated "1876") with an important preface; partially recovers from paralysis.

1876 (Age 57) Mrs. Gilchrist moves with her children from England to Philadelphia, still hoping to marry Whitman; they become good friends.

1877 (Age 58) Friendships begin with Carpenter, Dr. Bucke; Burroughs publishes second biography, "The Flight of the Eagle," with help from Whitman.

1879 (Age 60) Makes first trip west of Mississippi, to St. Louis, Colorado, Nevada.

1880 (Age 61) Travels to Boston, Ontario, and up the St. Lawrence with Dr. Bucke.

1881 (Age 62) Seventh *Leaves of Grass* published by Osgood in Boston.

1882 (Age 63) Society for Suppression of Vice bans *Leaves of Grass* in Boston; Osgood sells plates to Rees Welch (later David McKay) in Philadelphia, who sells 3,000 copies in one day; meets Pearsall Smith.

1883 (Age 64) Dr. Bucke publishes biography (approved, supervised, and partly written by Whitman).

1884 (Age 65) Buys Mickle Street house in Camden; begins friendships with Traubel, Harned, Williams, Donaldson, Ingersoll.

1885 (Age 66) Suffers "sunstroke" and increased paralysis.

1886 (Age 67) Receives financial assistance from English and American friends.

1887 (Age 68) Portrait sculpture by Sydney Morse; paintings by Herbert Gilchrist, J. W. Alexander, Eakins.

1888   (Age 69) Suffers another paraylzing stroke; Traubel raises funds for doctors; publishes *November Boughs* and eighth *Leaves of Grass*.

1890   (Age 71) Writes to Symonds denying homosexuality, claiming "six children"; brother Jeff dies 25 November.

1891   (Age 72) Contracts pneumonia in December.

1892   (Age 73) "Death-Bed" edition of *Leaves of Grass*. Dies 26 March.

Whitman's Journeys into Chaos

Introduction

THIS book is neither a biography of Whitman nor an interpretation of *Leaves of Grass*; instead it is a psychoanalytic investigation of Whitman's poetic processes as they developed between 1855-1865. The "chaos" to which my title refers existed in Whitman's unconscious, where his fantasies and poetic impulses originated; the journeys into this chaos are the poems.

The methods of psychoanalysis enable one to be systematic rather than random in drawing inferences about a poet's unconscious life; when one finds general patterns of fantasies and assumptions, the possibilities of making specific errors of interpretation are reduced. One may expect the patterns to repeat themselves over a period of years, even when the form of the assumptions or fantasies has changed. If more external information existed about the crucial decade in Whitman's poetic career, one could draw a more factual picture of the relation between the poet's activities and his mental life; but even with little historical information, there is, in the first three editions of *Leaves of Grass* (1855, 1856, 1860), a treasurehouse of material from which inferences may be drawn. Considered with the fiction of his youth, the poems of Whitman's middle years directly or indirectly express the psychological determinants that governed the way Whitman perceived and understood his experience.

My reader may be puzzled momentarily by the dates which limit this study: 1855-1865. Since we are so accustomed to knowing Whitman through the last *Leaves of Grass* (1891-1892), we may forget that nearly all the important poems were composed before 1860. Of the post-1860 poems only the Lincoln elegy, a few of the Civil War poems, "Passage to India," and "Prayer of Columbus" have received or deserved much attention. Whitman himself insisted that he wanted the world to know him by his last *Leaves of Grass*. This wish conformed to the ideals he had nourished through the thirty-seven years that followed the first *Leaves of Grass*; he meant his request to show that he celebrated and was satisfied with himself in 1892 when he was about to die. It is understandable that scholars have tended to accept Whitman's wish, but great disadvantages result from the elevation of the last edition, not the least of which is the consequent inaccessibility and devaluation of the early editions. Moreover, after 1860, as Whitman tended to adopt an increasingly abstract, less personal, poetic voice, he often deleted or revised passages that connected the early poems with their originating psychological impulses. (Whitman's habit of endlessly revising to bring early poems into alignment with later moods and attitudes has contributed to the misleading assumption that the poems are chronicles of events in the poet's psychological history. In their original versions the most important poems do not record events; the poems *are* the events.) A study of Whitman's creative processes must consider as fully as it can the impulses with which the poems began, and it therefore must proceed from material as close to the impulses as possible. Fortunately, the early versions have survived, along with a limited amount of manuscript material from the crucial period between the second and third editions, 1856-1860.

Various scholars have addressed themselves to certain questions that concern me in this study. Thomas E. Crawley, in *The Structure of "Leaves of Grass"* (Austin, Texas, 1970), has briefly discussed the early editions on the way to his defense of the formal structure of the last edition. E. Fred Carlisle, in *The Uncertain Self, Whitman's Drama of Identity* (East Lansing, 1973), has come to conclusions quite different from my own about Whitman's identity crisis (I discussed Mr. Carlisle's book in *Walt Whitman Review*, 1973). I have found it necessary to repeat some observations made in Roger Asselineau's survey of the evolution of Whitman and his book, and I am constantly indebted to Gay Wilson Allen's many studies of Whitman's life. But the book to which I owe most is Edwin Haviland Miller's *Walt Whitman's Poetry: A Psychological Journey* (Boston, 1968). Professor Miller's book, a psychoanalytic interpretation of Whitman's poetry, uses biographical material to support readings of the poems. Although to some extent my study of Whitman's poetic processes is complementary to Miller's work, I have found myself in frequent disagreement not only with Miller's interpretations of poems, but also with his view of the man Whitman. For example, Miller is convinced that Whitman was overtly and actively homosexual and generally conscious of the sexual meanings of his poems. I shall argue (as did Jean Catel, *Walt Whitman, la naissance du poète*, Paris, 1929) that Whitman was chiefly autoerotic in his sexual expressions. I believe that Whitman tended to keep hidden from himself both his homosexual impulses and his sexual confusions. Miller believes that the psychological conflicts evident in the poems tended to "find some kind of resolution or release." But in my view Whitman's poems usually end with the conflicts unresolved, the anxieties little relieved. Perhaps our most important difference lies in the relation thought to exist between the poems and Whitman's psychological life. Unlike Professor Miller and all preceding psychological interpreters of Whitman, I do not regard the poems as records of past events but regard the composition of the poems as the crucial psychological activity of Whitman's life between 1855-1865.

1

**In Search
of
Whitman**

Some Theoretical Considerations

LIKE Freud, Ernest Jones, Ernst Kris, and many others, I begin with the premise that the artistic process originates in and often expresses personal conflicts that may be, in whole or in part, unconscious.[1] This premise suggests that if one can discover the patterns that recur in an artist's fantasies—his assumptions, his view of the world, and his modes of responding to experience—one should be able to approach that artist's work with reasoned expectations about the artist's intentions and about his probable habits of thought and imagination. The scholar so armed should be in a unique position to discern patterns in a work of art that are more or less hidden from those whose perspective does not include a psychological understanding of the artist. Yet when the scholar wishes to study an artist from the past, he may have great difficulties in obtaining the

[1] Freud made the first psychoanalytic formulation of this premise in *The Interpretation of Dreams* and later elaborated it in *Jokes and Their Relation to the Unconscious* (*Standard Edition*, IV and VIII). See also, among others, Jones, *Hamlet and Oedipus* (New York: Norton, 1949); Kris, *Psychoanalytic Explorations in Art* (New York: Schocken, 1964); Crews, *The Sins of the Fathers: Hawthorne's Psychological Themes* (New York: Oxford, 1964); Miller, *Walt Whitman's Poetry: A Psychological Journey* (Boston: Houghton Mifflin, 1968); Cody, *After Great Pain: The Inner Life of Emily Dickinson* (Cambridge, Mass.: Harvard, 1971).

9

kinds of information he needs to discover unconscious patterns.

With literary artists the scholar may mitigate the difficulties if he regards the artist's use of language as a source of indirect psychological information, supplemental to whatever biographical information happens to exist. From the standpoint of psychoanalysis, regard for language seems to be a legitimate extension of the use of language in the clinical context (Freud's early patients called his treatment the "talking cure"). From the standpoint of literary scholarship, the procedure may not so readily be granted legitimacy. The psychoanalytic critic must not equate the psychological content inferred from literary language with literature or with the meaning of a literary work or with the effect that work has on its audience. One of the first tests of a psychoanalytic interpretation is the critic's ability to resist being tempted into reductiveness.

Psychoanalytic clinicians regard language as a system of symbols in which words are distinguishable from other kinds of symbols. Charles Rycroft, who extends and modifies discussions of symbolism and language begun by Freud, Jones, Lawrence Kubie, and Marion Milner,[2] says that, like other kinds of symbols, words function in the service of both the primary and secondary processes.[3] Words

[2] *Imagination and Reality* (London: Hogarth, 1968), pp. 42-113. See Rycroft's references, pp. 136-39, for bibliography.

[3] According to psychoanalytic theory, the primary and secondary processes (the two modes by which psychological functions occur) operate as follows:

In the *primary process*, energy is directed or discharged toward imagoes (memory traces of objects that in the past provided actual satisfaction of wishes or impulses); the imagoes are then experienced as hallucinations. In the primary process, the originating wish or impulse does not usually become conscious. Primary process occurs in

(a) sleep—as dreams;

(b) psychosis—as a defensive denial of reality;

(c) infancy—as hallucinatory wish-fulfillment;

(d) neurosis—as a partial withdrawal from reality that is compensated by wish-fulfilling fantasies.

In the *secondary process*, energy is directed and discharged toward the psychic apparatus, which

serve as links not only between a person and the world of external objects, but also between a person's consciousness and his unconscious. Furthermore, language shares the general characteristics of symbolism described by Rycroft: "Symbolization is a general tendency or capacity of the mind, one which may be used by the primary or the secondary process, neurotically or realistically, for defense or self-expression, to maintain fixation or to promote growth" (p. 53).

To summarize, thus far I have proposed that an artist's meanings and intentions may be understood if perceived in the context of psychological patterns and predispositions, and that these patterns may be inferred not only from biographical knowledge but also from the artist's use of linguistic symbols. Linguistic symbols may reveal patterns of

---

(a) perceives external reality;

(b) controls physical systems that can effect changes in the external world and allow the wish to become conscious and be satisfied in relation to an external object.

Via the *primary process*, a particular impulse is gratified immediately, but partially and temporarily. (The thirsty dreamer may continue sleeping for a while if he dreams of drinking, but his actual thirst will not be fully satisfied unless he wakes and drinks.)

Via the *secondary process*, a particular impulse *may* be permanently and completely satisfied (as by an actual drink).

Via the *primary process*, no actual contact with an object occurs. The primary process is fundamentally autistic, satisfactions being achieved by means of cathecting imagoes.

Via the *secondary process*, both subjective and objective cathexes occur. However, Rycroft (pp. 43-47) argues against Freud's assumption that there is inherent mutual opposition between the primary and secondary processes, as well as against the assumption that primary processes are invariably maladaptive. In the most striking of his several arguments on this hand, he speculates that in infancy real satisfaction may occur "while the infant is under the influence of the primary process, in which a real experience is subjectively a hallucination" (p. 47). Whitman's poetic movement between his unconscious and the object world seems to me parallel to the infantile experience Rycroft describes. I hypothesize that such infantile experiences may predispose the future adult toward greater than usual tolerance of his regressions, a tolerance that I believe is a necessary feature in "creative" or "talented" people.

11

unconscious processes as well as patterns of response to objects in the external world.[4] By studying a literary artist's writings we may come to understand the psychological processes; when we understand something about the psychological processes we may return to the writings and understand them better. If at first glance this procedure seems circular, one must consider that the circle is closed only if one assumes that psychological processes and intentions are identical with literary processes and intentions, an assumption the interpreter must avoid.

A psychoanalytic understanding of symbolization, however, may lead beyond an enlarged comprehension of a literary work to an understanding of the process by which the work was created. The importance of understanding the creative process lies in what I believe to be the ultimate inseparability of the three subjects of this book: the life of an artist (especially his unconscious life), the artist's work, and the process by which his work is done. We can understand any two of these subjects only to the extent that we understand the third. (As I will try to demonstrate, an under-

[4] See Robert Waelder, "The Principle of Multiple Function, Observations on Over-Determination," *Psychoanalytic Quarterly* 5 (1936), 45-62. Norman Holland, *Poems in Persons* (New York: Norton, 1973), summarizes Waelder's argument for lay readers: "Waelder sees the ego as mediating among four structures or functions that act on it: id and superego, reality and the repetition compulsion. These four forces acting on the ego show a neat symmetry. The id pushes for the expression of sexual and aggressive drives; the superego tries to inhibit them. The repetition compulsion tends to keep the ego doing what it did before, while reality (because it constantly changes) constantly demands new solutions from the ego. These four forces press on the ego, and in that sense the ego passively mediates among them. But the ego also assigns itself the task of testing and probing the four forces, and in this sense the ego actively seeks out problems and solutions. *Every psychic act results from the ego's actively and passively seeking an optimum balance of the forces impinging on it*" (pp. 45-46; Holland's emphasis). Holland goes on to claim that Waelder's essay "shows why the various attempts to look at artistic creativity as a function of 'neurosis' have been clumsy and misinforming" (p. 47). The logic that leads Holland from Waelder to the position described in my note 5, below, does not appear inevitable.

standing of the creative process leads to new understandings of works created by that process.)

Psychoanalysis has offered several important hypotheses toward a description of the creative process. Most hypotheses begin with the premise noted above: that the artistic process originates in and often expresses personal (usually unconscious) conflicts. At this point the hypotheses tend to diverge, for some theorists claim that the psychological aim of creativity is to enhance adaptation, to strengthen ego defenses, or to promote general psychological integrity.[5] Others seem willing to let the question of psychological consequences remain open. Since symbolization is obviously a fundamental aspect of any artistic process, Rycroft's general description of symbolization (quoted above) should be considered in the present context. Rycroft's emphasis on the potential inherent in symbolization for either adaptive or maladaptive effects suggests that even within the work of a single artist there may be no consistency in the psychological aim or effect of the creative process. Sometimes the process may lead to enhanced ego defenses and an enlarged or altered experience with the external world; but sometimes creativity may exacerbate neurotic conflicts and anxieties, thereby leading to rigidity or even threatening to inhibit the creative process itself.[6]

[5] An extreme variation of this position is adopted by Holland in *Poems in Persons*. Holland believes that writers can *only* write in ways that confirm or strengthen existing ego defenses. By extension it would seem impossible for a writer to alter, while writing, his pattern of response to either unconscious imagoes or to external objects; similarly, it would seem impossible for therapeutic change to occur in either a clinical or a creative context. Holland's view is strongly opposed to the views of Kris and Jacobson (see below) on which my arguments rest. (See note 19, Chapter 3.)

[6] Kris (pp. 308-18) and Lawrence S. Kubie, *Neurotic Distortion of the Creative Process* (New York: Noonday, 1958, 1961), emphasize the importance of the preconscious in symbolization (the system preconscious being those functions and materials of the ego which are not conscious at a given time but which are accessible to consciousness by an act of will). Kubie presents the following theory of the creative process: creativity becomes possible when there is "the continuous

Whatever the effect of the artistic process, most theorists agree that creativity lies within the province of the ego, the part of the psyche whose chief functions are to organize defenses against internal or external perils and to "test reality" (that is, to distinguish between mental images and external perceptions). Genetically, the ego is a portion of the id (the original, undifferentiated psyche of infancy) that becomes more highly organized than and finally discrete from the id. But the discreteness of the ego is not absolute. In the artistic process, as Edith Jacobson (reflecting on a conversation with Ernst Kris) has said, the artist lets his ego "immerge into the id and emerge again, and thus, by oscillating between closeness to the id and distance from it, to use the id in the service of the ego."[7] I propose that the service rendered the ego by regression is not necessarily therapeutic. Instead, the ego initiates the creative process in response to instinctual and superego demands. It may be that the ego's initiation of creative regression parallels the processes that

and spontaneous flow of associative material, on all three levels simultaneously: i.e., on *conscious* levels, where the current of fantasy is slow, intermittent, limited, and verbally sharply differentiated and precise; on *preconscious* levels of allegory [symbolism], where the current is turbulent, free, and swift, tossing up all manner of strange and unexpected shapes out of the churning depths; on *unconscious* levels, where again the current is slower, stylized, rigid, condensed, stereotyped, unmoving, uncreative, and underground. It is out of the parallel flow of these three streams and their incessant interweaving that the creative processes and the processes of illness evolve" (p. 103).

[7] *The Self and the Object World* (New York: International Universities Press, 1964), p. 80, n. 4. Jacobson continues, summarizing a conversation with Kris: "In further comments on this problem, Kris expressed his assumption that the capacity for sublimation was connected with a particular ability of creative people to draw and absorb psychic energy through manifold avenues from the deepest energic flux of the id, and to direct it into the channel of creative activity. This ability, I believe, presupposes a particular energic fluidity and elasticity in such persons, permitting rapid processes of drive transformation, drive fusion, and drive neutralization. This drive elasticity would account for the capacity for such continuous fluctuations between id closeness and id distance during the creative process" (pp. 80-81).

occur when the ego initiates complex object relations (as when a person seeks friendship or love). Kris's well-known phrase describing the creative process—"regression in the service of the ego"—affords me the title for this book about Walt Whitman, whose poems, I will try to show, were often journeys into chaos.

TWO

A Biography of an Imagination:
I

THE FULLEST and most nearly direct information available about Whitman's imagination in the years before the first *Leaves of Grass* exists in the fiction written in the poet's adolescence. In the two dozen examples that survive, there is not a single effective characterization, nor a credible plot, nor an instance of answerable prose style. Yet this work shows something important about the evolution of Whitman's ego defenses. The same psychological conflicts that in 1855 generated the first *Leaves of Grass* motivated the fiction published between 1841 and 1848. In other words, a clear line of psychological continuity links Whitman's earliest known literary writing to his mature work. The stories, sketches, and reminiscences tend to reveal with naïve simplicity the subtle and complex psychological patterns and conflicts underlying *Leaves of Grass*. The later stories hint at some of the habits of symbolization fundamental to the mature poetry.

From his sixteenth year Whitman tried to write fiction (along with setting type, teaching school, and editing the Huntington *Long Islander*). In 1841, aged twenty-two, he moved to New York City, taking with him a number of manuscripts.[1] One completed novel, fragments of two other novels, and twenty-one stories and sketches exist. In later years Whitman expressed fond contempt for his youthful work, claiming he wrote it only to make money. But the need for money does not adequately explain why he tried to write fiction, nor why he wrote the particular things he wrote, nor yet why he wrote so badly. Except in a few plot-less sketches (e.g. "The Tomb Blossoms" and "Richard Parker's Widow"), Whitman's experiments in fiction fail in their attempts to exploit stock responses and conventional sentimentalities. Many critics have noticed that Whitman's ineffective characterizations and improbable plots lack fictive credibility.

Yet merely to say that Whitman had no talent for writing fiction does not seem enough. At twenty-two Whitman was an experienced newspaperman whose editorials were as sophisticated as the work of his fellow editorialists. If some other factor had not been involved, Whitman the storyteller could surely have imitated more successfully the styles and methods of other writers of popular fiction. When critics dismiss the fiction as trite, they miss the point of how really bad it is and what is wrong with it. The fiction fails because when Whitman employed stock situations and devices of characterization his own unconscious attitudes and assumptions intruded upon the material. Unconscious forces conflicted with the intent to be conventional; Whitman's narcissism confused the fictional world he was trying to create.

A case in point is Whitman's second published story, "Wild Frank's Return." It may be that the resounding incredibility of this story's conclusion can be explained only in psychoanalytic terms. Like Walt Whitman himself, Wild Frank is a second son, his mother's favorite. Frank quarrels with his older brother, Richard, about who owns Frank's

---

[1] Gay Wilson Allen, *The Solitary Singer* (New York, 1967), p. 44. The early writings appear in Thomas L. Brasher's volume in the *Collected Writings, The Early Poems and the Fiction* (New York, 1963). See Edwin H. Miller's perceptive discussion of Whitman's fiction, *A Psychological Journey*, pp. 48-50.

17

mare, Black Nell. Their father decides on behalf of Richard, his favorite, "and added a harsh lecture to his other son. The farmer was really unjust."[2] Frank runs off to sea and stays away two years; when he returns, he unaccountably stops to visit Richard before returning to his parents' farm. Richard lends him a horse—Black Nell—to ride home, and Frank goes on his way. When Frank is but two miles from home he is overtaken by a sudden urge to nap in the shade of a mighty oak. Anyone else would have tied his horse to the tree, but not Frank, who "took from his little bundle * * * a piece of strong cord, four or five yards in length, which he tied to the bridle, and wound and tied the other end, for security, over his own wrist."

A thunderstorm arises that somehow fails to awaken Frank but that frightens the horse. Black Nell bolts, dragging her rider to a bloody death. The horse runs home to the parents' farm, and the story ends:

"The clattering of a horse's hoofs came to the ears of those who were gather'd there. It was on the other side of the house that the wagon road led; and they open'd the door and rush'd in a tumult of glad anticipations, through the adjoining room to the porch. What a sight it was that met them there! Black Nell stood a few feet from the door, with her neck crouch'd down; she drew her breath long and deep, and vapor rose from every part of her reeking body. And with eyes starting from their sockets, and mouths agape with stupefying terror, they beheld on the ground near her a mangled, hideous mass—the rough semblance of a human form—all batter'd, and cut, and bloody. Attach'd to it was the fatal cord, dabbled over with gore. And as the mother gazed—for she could not withdraw her eyes—and the appalling truth came upon her mind, she sank down without shriek or utterance, into a deep, deathly swoon."

The gory ending does not clearly follow from the rest of the story. For some reason the author seems sadistically to attack the family, and especially the mother, by making

[2] *Specimen Days & Collect* (Philadelphia, 1882-83), p. 354; see, also, Brasher, p. 63.

them witness this scene. The mother has been mentioned only once before in the story: "The farmer's wife was a quiet woman, in rather tender health; and though for all her offspring she had a mother's love, Frank's kiss ever seem'd sweetest to her lips. She favor'd him more than the rest—perhaps, as in a hundred similar instances, for his being so often at fault, and so often blamed."

Whitman takes remarkable steps to have Frank dragged to death by that fatal cord. Usually, in popular fiction, when a character is dragged to death by a horse, the rider's foot has caught in the stirrup when he has been thrown. But Whitman's unconscious apparently would not permit him to end a trite story by a trite device. There is something seductive about the mother's preference for Frank's sweetest kiss, and something umbilical about that fatal cord. It seems to me that the secret motive for writing this story was to punish a mother for her son's Oedipal impulses. In this light Black Nell becomes a symbol for a mother who was imagined to be both innocent and destructive. Black Nell was the subject of the quarrel between the brothers that sent Frank off to sea; she remembered "her early master" when he returned but capriciously dragged him to death during the storm.

A futile wish for a father's love, the death of a child, the covert attack on a seductive mother—these are the same elements that were to generate one of Whitman's finest poems, "As I Ebb'd with the Ocean of Life," eighteen years later. But what a difference between the story and the poem! In fiction, making an effort toward realism, Whitman tries to hide his feelings and assumptions behind reportorial objectivity. The power of the feelings, which eventually gave power to the poetry, overwhelms the fiction's pretense to objectivity and expresses itself in aristically unintegrated "accidental" symbols like the rope and the mare. The author's presence in the story is all the more obtrusive for his absence. The brilliant poem has nothing in common artistically with the preposterous story, yet the two grew out of the same psychological compost. In the years between the two works Whitman learned to be simultaneously more direct and more indirect in his approach to such material. In poetry Whitman could establish his relation to the elements of his art: he was safe behind his conviction that he uttered the fantasies of all men and that his expressions liberated long dumb voices and united his fellows in spiritual democracy. Further, the "fierce old mother" and "friable" fish-shaped father of "As I Ebb'd" were not so fierce or friable when perceived through a screen of symbols as they appeared in the cooler logic of fiction. In "As I Ebb'd," the poet, his feelings, and his unconscious self are the unmistakable and direct subjects. It took Whitman almost two decades to learn to deal artistically with such material.

Other stories published between 1841-1844 also foreshadow significant vectors of Whitman's artistic development; for example, they indicate that the ideals of spiritualized male comradeship on which "Calamus" would later be based had existed in Whitman's late adolescence.

Whitman's last two works of fiction show that important changes have occurred in his literary processes. A sketch called "Some Fact-Romances," published in December 1845, has little literary merit but is interesting because, for the first time, Whitman wrote from personal experience without moralizing or sentimentalizing and without contriving a plot that pretends to justify unaccountable actions or gratuitous violence. Its five brief scenes resemble narratives interpolated into the longer poems, like the stories of the battle of Goliad and the old-time frigate fight in "Song of Myself" and the romance about Whitman's mother and the red girl in "The Sleepers."

If Whitman published any more fiction between the end of 1845 and the middle of 1848, it has been lost. The last story Whitman is known to have printed, "The Shadow and the Light of a Young Man's Soul," appeared in *The Union Magazine* in June 1848.[3] Here Whitman reverted to the patent moralizing and improbability of his earlier tales, but

[3] Brasher, p. 327, n. 1. The story is printed on pp. 327-30.

he added something new: the elemental symbolism, which was to become fundamental to *Leaves of Grass*, found its way into Whitman's writing. In *Leaves of Grass* a consistent group of symbols represents the most important things in Whitman's world and enables the poet's unconscious attitudes toward these things to be indirectly expressed. Water represents mother and the maternal; earth, the father; fire, sexual and aggressive impulses; and air, the poet's songs, his links with the rest of the elements.[4] In "The Shadow and the Light of a Young Man's Soul," a fire impoverishes the widow Dean when it destroys the insurance company where she has invested her life's savings; she and her sons must move from the city to the country. The older boy, Archibald, "unstable as water," is lazy and subject to depressions, but he is also honest, generous, and willing to work at something other than menial labor. His mother finds him a job teaching in a country school and makes a separate home for herself and her other son. Gradually, "the untainted air and water" of the country purge the vices of the city from Archie's veins. Then Archie meets an old woman whose life has been ruined because her father has lost the family farm (a piece of earth) through "extravagance and dissipation."

"Archie felt the narrative of this old maid's doings as a rebuke—a sharp-pointed moral to himself and his infirmity of purpose. Moreover, the custom of his then way of life forced him into habits of more thorough activity; he had to help himself or go unhelped; he found a novel satisfaction in that highest kind of independence which consists in being able to do the offices of one's own comfort, and achieve resources and capacities 'at home,' whereof to place happiness beyond the reach of variable circumstances, or of the services of the hireling, or even of the uses of fortune. The change was not a sudden one: few great changes are. But his heart was awakened to his weakness; the seed was sown;

---

[4] A parody or imitation of Wordsworth, "New Years Day, 1848," possibly written by Whitman, incorporates the elemental symbolism; see Brasher, p. 49, for text.

Archie Dean felt that he *could* expand his nature by means of that very nature itself. Many times he flagged; but at each fretful falling back, he thought of the yellow-faced dame, and roused himself again."

From this point on, the problems which had marked Archie's previous life are no longer visible: "He met his fortunes as they came, face to face, and shirked no conflict. Indeed, he felt it glorious to vanquish obstacles. For his mother he furnished a peaceful, plentiful home; and from the hour of [his younger brother's] death, never did his tongue utter words other than kindness, or his lips, whatever annoyances or disappointments came, cease to offer their cheerfullest smile in her presence."

On the surface, "The Shadow and the Light of a Young Man's Soul" seems tritely to exemplify a chief axiom of the Protestant ethic: that honest work and freedom from urban vices lead to economic independence and a "mature" sense of one's responsibility to life. But with the benefit of hindsight we can perceive hints of psychological activity in this tale that Whitman has not previously revealed. Vague as they are, the two passages just quoted suggest that Whitman has undergone a considerable struggle to make changes in "his nature" in accord with new perceptions of personal inadequacies—which is to say, newly adopted ego ideals. These ideals are generally clear: he wants to remove his personal happiness from vulnerability to whims of fate or other people; he wants to live independent of, but at peace with, his mother, which he can do by not expecting her to provide for his comfort. This story was published fifteen years after Whitman first left home, but in those years the early emotional dependence on his mother had not abated. In this story Whitman half-consciously connected his dependency on his mother with the "infirmity of purpose" that marked Archie Dean's life. Archie's feeling of maternal dependence was symbolically transferred to the old woman he met in the country from whom he could more easily free himself than from his actual mother.

The issue of dependency is part of a larger problem.

22

Whitman's biographers have shown that the poet's steps toward independence were not especially effective. From the poetry we know that for him "independence" was synonymous with "aloneness." "Live Oak, with Moss," the manuscript prototype of "Calamus," shows with great clarity how painful Whitman's aloneness was to become, and yet how unable he would be to give up aloneness as a defense. Lying beneath this paradox is Whitman's crisis of identity, manifest in Archie Dean's story through the same symbols that were to occur in *Leaves of Grass*: the earth, air, fire, and water. In the city Archie is "unstable as water"; in the country, where Archie is separated from his mother, the water is "untainted." The old woman he meets in the country has been dispossessed of her land by her father's "extravagance and dissipation," and Archie's mother has been similarly dispossessed by a fire. In Whitman's symbolism both agents have the same root: masculine perversity is the cause of instability. In the terms of Whitman's unconscious ego ideals, the addition of earth (the farm; non-sexual masculinity) to the fire-water-air mixture seems to promise a solution to the crisis of identity that Whitman projects onto Archie Dean.

In "The Shadow and the Light of a Young Man's Soul," Whitman took a short step toward articulating the vision that was to permeate *Leaves of Grass*, yet that step did not make this tale a whit more successful than the earlier efforts. Part of the reason may be discerned from yet another fiction, "Lingave's Temptation," the date of which cannot be ascertained.[5] Lingave is a young poet who is given to musing: " 'I am a genius, they say,' and the speaker smiled bitterly, 'but genius is not apparel and food. Why should I exist in the world, unknown, unloved, press'd with cares, while so many around me have all their souls can desire?' " and " 'What is it to us [i.e. geniuses] that the mass pay us not that deference which wealth commands? We desire no

[5] Brasher, p. 331, describes a clipping of the original in the Feinberg collection from which the date and origin cannot be known; Whitman reprinted the story in *Specimen Days & Collect*, pp. 366-68.

applause, save the applause of the good and discriminating —the choice spirits among men. Our intellect would be sullied, were the vulgar to approximate to it, by professing to readily enter in, and praising it. Our pride is a towering, and thrice refined pride.' "

Lingave's temptation amounts to his being offered a job by "a *money-maker*" (Whitman's italics) who needs "a writer of power, a master of elegant diction, of fine taste, in style passionate yet pure, and of the delicate imagery that belongs to the children of song." Lingave promises to think over the offer and retires to his Spartan pallet. During the night, Virtue struggles with Temptation and wins by means of superior rhetoric: " 'Be and continue poor, young man,' so taught one whose counsels should be graven on the heart of every youth, 'while others around you grow rich by fraud and disloyalty. * * * If you have, in such a course, grown gray with unblench'd honor, bless God and die.' "

I cannot find the least hint in this story that Whitman offers Lingave as an object of satire. On the other hand, there is not much visible similarity between Whitman and Lingave. Whitman had been making money by hack writing since his late teens, and he ostentatiously identified himself with the very "mass" Lingave despises. Very few (least of all the poet himself) have accused Whitman of "elegant diction" or "fine taste." With its blatant anti-democratic sentiments, the story seems anomalous when we consider that even at the height of Whitman's power his poetic purposes were characteristically crossed. In the preface to the first *Leaves of Grass* and in two of the most important poems of the second edition (eventually called "By Blue Ontario's Shore" and "Song of the Broad-Axe"), Whitman was to define a difficult task for the American poet: to surpass the highest achievements of all previous bards while remaining merely one of the average unending procession. The conflicting demands of these two sets of ideals seem often to distract Whitman's attention from the moment-to-moment making of poetry by placing disproportionate importance on every utterance. Each word associatively dredged from

24

the underworld is justified only as far as it contributes to both the bardic and populist ideals.

Later we will see that conflicts in Whitman's values had much to do with the problems of completing the third *Leaves of Grass*. "Lingave's Temptation" suggests that fantasies of being a genius, in 1855-1856 as earlier, inhibited Whitman's actual genius and contributed to specific artistic failures. As I will demonstrate, Whitman's psychological aim, in the forties as well as in the fifties, was the restoration of infantile convictions of omnipotence. The unconscious forces attending this intention often inhibited Whitman's creative processes.

Whitman's creative processes, as they developed in *Leaves of Grass*, depended on factors inherently inimical to credible fiction, but fundamental to the mode of poetry he evolved. Free association enabled him simultaneously to explore his unconscious world and to limit the responsibility he felt for the things discovered. His system of symbolization had essentially the same effect. Symbolizing enabled him to confront certain feelings about himself and about his relations with his family, but the symbols did not necessarily threaten to disrupt his conscious view of himself and his world. Finally, the explorations he was compelled to make were justified by the benefit he felt his poems conferred on all mankind. When these conditions were not present, as they were not in his fictional efforts, Whitman's work failed dreadfully, but when they existed he could write as if he believed his declaration,

> Creeds and schools in abeyance, * * *
> I harbor for good or bad—I permit to speak,
> Nature, without check, with original energy.

"My Boys and Girls"

When Whitman was about sixteen (1835-1836) he wrote a prose sketch he called "My Boys and Girls."[6] The earliest

[6] Published much later in *The Rover*, 20 April 1844; reprinted in Brasher. Following Allen (p. 31), Brasher dates the composition of

surviving example of Whitman's work, this sketch is important because it presents the central fantasy around which
the poet's life and much of his work were to be organized,
the fantasy of himself as father to his brothers and sisters.
"My Boys and Girls" is a plotless series of impressions of
twelve children, seven of whom can be identified as Whitman's younger brothers and sisters. (One is a sister who
died in infancy in 1825; Whitman excluded his older
brother, Jesse.) The other five children are boys who were
probably friends of the Whitman children. "My Boys and
Girls" begins: "Though a bachelor, I have several girls and

---

this sketch as 1835 because Mary Whitman is described as "in her
fourteenth year." Apparently neither Allen nor Brasher considered that
Mary's fourteenth year occurred between 3 February 1834–3 February
1835, the year following her thirteenth birthday. On the other hand,
the description of the infant I identify below as Edward Whitman
makes it appear that Whitman also erred in describing Mary's age.
Allen and Brasher seems not to notice the description of the infant
in the first paragraph. This unnamed infant is said to be Louisa's
brother; he is therefore Whitman's brother as well. The infant is
described as follows: "A fat, hearty, rosy-cheeked youngster, the girl's
brother * * * . Never was there such an imp of mischief! Falls and
bumps hath he every hour of the day, which affect him not, however.
Incessant work occupies his mornings, noons and nights; and dangerous is it, in the room with him, to leave anything unguarded,
which the most persevering activity of a stout pair of dumpy hands can
destroy." The infant described in the quoted passage might be Jeff,
born 18 July 1833, but this seems unlikely since the next paragraph
describes Jeff by name as a quiet child learning to read. Edward was
born 9 August 1835. If the infant described is Edward, he must have
been prodigious to be so effective in his mischief at four or five months
of age. On the other hand, the story may have been written a year
later than the date I propose, but, if so, the age Whitman gives as
Mary's is patently wrong. If Jeff was three-and-a-half and Edward a
year-and-a-half, Mary would have been about sixteen, not fifteen, and
the year would have been 1837. I cannot guess why Whitman would
have reduced Mary's age unless he sought to justify his uneasiness
about her sexuality by making her seem sexually precocious. Compare the description of another sister named "Mary" in Whitman's
incomplete novel, "The Half-Breed" (Brasher, pp. 270-71), who is
described as sexually "capricious and headstrong."

boys that I consider my own." Whitman first tells of his favorite sister, Hannah Louisa (called "Louisa" in this sketch), whom he refers to as his "niece." He describes Louisa's infant brother (Edward Whitman), mentions teaching "Jeff" to read, and plays with the presidential names of Andrew, George, and Jeff (Andrew Jackson, George Washington, and Thomas Jefferson Whitman). He gives more detail about Mary, his independent oldest sister, than about any of the other children:[7]

"One of my children—a child of light and loveliness— sometimes gives me rise to many uneasy feelings. She is a very beautiful girl, in her fourteenth year. Flattery comes too often to her ears. From the depths of her soul I now and then see misty revealings of thought and wish, that are not well. I see them through her eyes and in the expression of her face.

"It is a dreary thought to imagine what may happen, in the future years, to a handsome, merry child—to gaze far down the vista, and see the dim phantoms of Evil standing about with nets and temptations—to witness, in the perspective, purity gone, and the freshness of youthful innocence rubbed off, like the wasted bloom of flowers. Who, at twenty-five or thirty years of age, is without many memories of wrongs done and mean or wicked deeds performed?"

The first paragraph implies that Mary was beginning to develop sexually. Beyond the conventional speculations in the second paragraph about innocence being tempted into evil, there are implications that the author is fighting some "evil" thoughts of his own, awakened by or projected toward his sister.

Whitman changes the subject abruptly, next describing four young boys named only by initials. The tone of this

[7] Apparently the most gracefully independent of the children, Mary married at eighteen and thereafter had limited contact with the rest of the family. If there was distance between the poet and his sister, it may have been because Mary needed less "fathering" from Walt than did the younger children.

paragraph somewhat resembles that of the "Calamus" poems (1860), which led readers to surmise that Whitman was homosexual:

"Right well do I love many more of my children. H. is my 'summer child.' An affectionate fellow is he—with merits and with faults, as all boys have—and it has come to be that should his voice no more salute my ears, nor his face my eyes, I might not feel as happy as I am. M., too, a volatile lively young gentleman, is an acquaintance by no means unpleasant to have by my side. Perhaps M. is a little too rattlesome, but he has qualities which have endeared him to me much during our brief acquaintance. Then there is J.H., a sober, good-natured youth, whom I hope I shall always number among my friends. Another H. has lately come among us—too large, perhaps, and too near manhood, to be called one of my *children*. I know I shall love him well when we become better acquainted—as I hope we are destined to be."

Whitman moves without transition from the "uneasy feelings" evoked by Mary to easier feelings about these four boys. This adolescent sketch foreshadows the split in Whitman's affections that divides his later work. In the third *Leaves of Grass* (1860) Whitman segregates his poems about "woman-love" ("Enfans D'Adam") from poems about masculine camaraderie ("Calamus"). Apparently it was always easier for Whitman to spiritualize (that is, desexualize) his feelings about friends who resembled his brothers and father than about friends who resembled his sisters and mother. His fantasies of relationships with women awaken his anxieties about incest; Whitman retreats from these anxieties into less demanding and less threatening "Calamus" fantasies of spiritual-paternal relationships with young men. The underlying factor in Whitman's anxieties seems to have been how much he felt himself in control of whatever intimacy involved him.

The model for control derived from Whitman's youth. From early in his life, Whitman imagined himself in partnership with his mother, their joint endeavor being to provide a stable shelter for the younger Whitman children. Whitman imagined himself filling the role of dominant supporting male in his mother's household, a role vacated by his taciturn father and unsuited to his troubled older brother, Jesse. The consequence of Whitman's fantasy was his conviction that the younger children were his children— "My Boys and Girls." In his fantasies Whitman not only usurped his father's place but also protected his mother and the younger children from a harsh, unloving, and unfair father and from a violently unstable older brother.

The most explicit poetic representation of Whitman's sense of his family is a passage from an early poem, "There Was a Child Went Forth." A child looks upward from the kitchen floor at his parents, witnessing with painful awe the blow and quick loud word his father seems to direct toward his gentle mother. Whitman was rarely so explicit in his poems, but in the fiction written between 1836 and 1845, a decade before the first *Leaves of Grass*, he was sometimes candid. The motifs that recur in crucial parts of his fiction suggest a great deal about the attitudes he carried through his greatly prolonged adolescence. His mothers are usually struggling widows who have outlived irresponsible or brutal or drunken husbands; children die (eighteen of them in the twenty-four extant works), often because of parental neglect or abuse. Drunkenness usually leads to insanity or violence. Fathers usually prefer their first-born sons to their more deserving younger children, so that the younger sons run away from home and come to bad ends. Seduction usually leads to the death of the girl and the ruin of the man (however common the moral in such plots during the forties, it was not common to show, as Whitman does eight times, the salvation of degenerate young men coming from idealized friendships with other young men). Gratuitous violence abounds in these tales. Whitman frequently shows a child's passive revenge on abusive adults, the moral being "They'll be sorry when I'm dead and gone." (The climax of "Death in the School-Room" comes when a child, mysteriously ill and wrongfully accused of theft, is beaten by a

29

sadistic schoolmaster; the child is dead before the beating begins.) The motif of dead children is important even in "My Boys and Girls." The last two children mentioned are dead, one a friend, the other the infant sister who died when Whitman was six. The motif, in "My Boys and Girls" and elsewhere, means that children generally need better fathers than they have.

"As I Ebb'd with the Ocean of Life" (1859) also ends with a symbolic image of a dead infant. It is the poet, who imagines himself stillborn, destroyed not only by a rejecting father but also by a querulous, seductive mother. Whitman's attitudes toward fathers are strikingly more complex in this poem than in his fiction. "As I Ebb'd" shows the poet demanding love, intimacy, paternity from his symbolized father; his demand is ignored. Whitman's plea for paternal advice and a kiss in "As I Ebb'd" compels us to weigh anew the claims made against fathers in the fiction. "Wild Frank's Return" ends with an auctorial assault against Frank's mother, rather than his father, whose injustice caused the boy to leave home. Whitman's conscious moral—a father's unfairness causes family strife—is at odds with the relish with which the gory ending is served up to the mother. Although the stories are much less complicated than the poems, evidence of Whitman's unresolved Oedipal conflicts appears long before the first *Leaves of Grass.*

Like the rest of us, Whitman could confront some aspects of himself more easily than others because some of his feelings and attitudes suited his idealized image of himself better than others. He could readily acknowledge and express anger toward his father, but he could release negative feelings toward his mother only indirectly. In *Leaves of Grass,* mothers, as such, are invariably idealized; but the maternal sea is usually presented as seductive, nagging, quarrelsome, and destructive. Fathers, as such, are usually represented as harsh or brutal; but the paternal land is usually regarded as more sinned against than sinning, its worst inadequacy being its helplessness against the sea's erosions. Whitman's case against his father has as much to do with the old man's helplessness and withdrawal as it does with his brutality or drinking or injustice. That Whitman could express anger toward his father but not toward his mother implies that he was somehow less afraid of his father. Whitman's fiction often defines the kind of father he does not want to be to his boys and girls.

To the things we can infer from the early fiction we may now add a review of historical information about Whitman's relations with his family. I have suggested that Whitman organized his life around a fantasy of being father to his younger brothers and sisters and partner to his mother. Throughout his life Whitman repeatedly tried to recreate the conditions of his youth by adopting young semiliterate working-class men who resembled his brothers and who became his sons for a while; indeed, the Harry Straffords, Peter Doyles, and Herbert Gilchrists were the most nearly intimate friends the poet ever permitted himself. Among the numerous paradoxes in Whitman's character, perhaps none is more striking than the isolation he enforced upon himself while proclaiming that he was lover and spokesman for all mankind. Yet the paradox resolves itself when we understand that "lover and spokesman" were seen as attributes of the paternal role Whitman had adopted in his adolescent fantasies. He would love his sons as a father, but nevertheless remain distant enough to retain patriarchal authority. He would try to be the ideal father his brothers and sisters had not had; yet he would avoid becoming so close that his genial self-control was jeopardized.

We know little about the conditions that helped create the man who would "loafe" half his life, then between his thirty-sixth and forty-first years publish the most extraordinary poetry of his century; who was shy and remote in his private life, yet an unabashed controversialist and self-publicist. If there was artistic talent in the family, it has hidden itself utterly from a century of scholarship. We infer that Walter Whitman, senior, was a surly, taciturn man, who failed to maintain the prosperous family farm he in-

31

herited and did only slightly better when he moved his family from central Long Island into Brooklyn. In and around Brooklyn he made a fair living as a carpenter; later he built houses his family occupied until the houses could be sold. He may have been alcoholic (at least there is considerable concern in Whitman's early fiction about alcoholism, the tone of which seems too personal merely to be an echo of the temperance sentiment of the forties). For most of his life Mr. Whitman worked alone or with his sons, a fact that suggests that he did not get on easily with people. He died at sixty-one after a long and painful illness, the nature of which is unknown. Walt, his second son, who rarely mentions his father in surviving letters or journals, nevertheless kept throughout his life a "small oil painting" of him, which he bequeathed to his brother George. In all his poetry Whitman refers directly to his father only twice, but the older man's presence is nevertheless ubiquitous, symbolized by the land or the fish-shaped island, Paumanok.

Walter Whitman, senior, married Louisa Van Velsor when he was twenty-seven, six years older than his wife. To the second son (as the poet elegized in 1875) Louisa was "the most perfect and magnetic character, the rarest combination of practical, moral and spiritual, and the least selfish, of all and any I have ever known—and by me O so much the most deeply loved." But, as Edwin Miller observes (p. 55), her letters show that she was willful, nagging, complaining, penny-pinching, and self-centered. (Considering the problems of her family it would be surprising had she been otherwise.) Like many intelligent but uneducated people, Louisa was occasionally subject to evangelical religious enthusiasms—the only religious interest in the household. According to Katherine Molinoff, she may have had a physical or emotional breakdown about 1835, during and after her pregnancy with her last child, Edward.[8]

Until she died of a heart attack at nearly seventy-eight,

---

[8] *Some Notes on Whitman's Family* (Brooklyn, 1941), p. 11. This interesting pamphlet should be edited according to current scholarly standards and reprinted.

Louisa complained unceasingly about the inadequacies of her daughters-in-law and the neglect of her sons. That Mrs. Whitman was a difficult person and that Walt saw her as perfect does not indicate blind partiality in the poet so much as it means that he identified with her and understood the difficulties of her life. There were problems with her husband and anxieties about money; her first son died of syphilis in an insane asylum; the marital difficulties of her second daughter, a near-psychotic, demanded constant attention; her third son, an alcoholic, married a prostitute and died at thirty-six; her last son, an epileptic, was deformed and retarded.

In all, Louisa Whitman bore nine children:

Jesse Whitman (2 March 1818–21 March 1870). Difficult and unstable from childhood, prone to hysteria and jealousy. Never married but lived with prostitutes. Violent, especially when drinking. May have gone to sea as a youth; worked intermittently in Brooklyn ship-fitting yards. Committed to the Kings County Lunatic Asylum in December 1864, where he died of syphilis five years later; buried in Potter's field. According to a family legend, "he was considered to have the best mind of any of the children" (Molinoff, pp. 19-23).

Walter Whitman, Jr. (Walt) (31 May 1819–26 March 1892). Never married.

Mary Elizabeth Whitman (3 February 1821–6 August 1899). At eighteen married Ansel Van Nostrand, a successful shipbuilder, 2 January 1840; bore five children between 1841-1859 (Molinoff, pp. 3-4).

Hannah Louisa Whitman (28 November 1823–18 July 1908). Married Charles Louis Heyde, a landscape painter, 16 March 1852. According to her own statements Hannah eloped with Heyde from her boarding school at sixteen, thirteen years before their marriage (Molinoff, p. 25). Their relationship was a continual turmoil; both Hannah and Heyde were conspicuously and acutely unstable. Heyde was so subject to hallucinations that he was committed to a Waterbury, Vermont, insane asylum just before he died in 1892. Shortly after her husband's death Hannah suffered a paralytic stroke, but she lived on until her eighty-fifth year.

Infant girl, name unknown (2 March 1825–14 September 1825).

Andrew Jackson Whitman (7 April 1827–3 December 1863). Probably married one Nancy, an alcoholic prostitute with whom he had two children, the second born after Andrew's death. Like Jesse and his father, Andrew was probably alcoholic. He may have enlisted in the Union army near the beginning of the Civil War; if so, he was apparently mustered out almost immediately because of a tubercular condition in his throat. He died of this condition at the age of thirty-six.

George Washington Whitman (28 November 1829–20 December 1901). Married Louisa Orr Haslam, 14 April 1871, at the age of forty-two; they had one son, Walter Orr Whitman, who died in his second year. George was the most conventional and successful of the Whitmans. He enlisted in the Union army when war began, was soon commissioned, and when mustered out a major was awarded the permanent rank of captain at a time when nearly all permanent commissions went to West Pointers. After the war George returned to Brooklyn to begin a carpentry and contracting business (which eventually prospered, but not until George moved to Camden). George was named executor of Walt's estate.

Thomas Jefferson Whitman (18 July 1833–25 November 1890). Married Martha E. Mitchell ("Matty"), 23 February 1859, when he was twenty-five; Jeff and Matty had two daughters. Jeff was an engineer with the Brooklyn Water Works. In 1867 he moved his family to St. Louis to become Superintendent of Water Works. Matty died of lung cancer in 1873; Jeff died of typhoid fever at the age of fifty-six. Volatile, cheerful, somewhat selfish, Jeff was probably the most likable of the Whitman children. He was Walt's favorite brother.

Edward Whitman (9 August 1835–30 November 1892).

Edward was retarded and epileptic; he had a crippled left hand and a paralyzed leg. According to family legend, Edward's abnormalities resulted from a case of scarlet fever at the age of three. Another legend, however, says that Edward's birth led Mrs. Whitman to have a "breakdown" (Molinoff, p. 11), which may be evidence that Edward was visibly abnormal at birth. There is too little information to make much of a guess about the cause or exact nature of Edward's abnormality. Until her death Mrs. Whitman cared for Edward with help from George and Walt; afterwards, the responsibility for his care was shared by the brothers, who placed Edward in a succession of boarding situations on farms near Camden. Edward was reputed to have a fiery temper and to be unusually strong.

The characteristic pattern of relationships among the Whitmans was established by the parents: the father customarily withdrew or he withheld affection or attention; Mrs. Whitman demanded demonstrations of closeness and could not grant independence to any of her children. Although all the older children tried to leave home during their adolescence, only Mary made the break effectively. Jesse, Walt, and Andrew left from time to time but returned with their problems; Hannah apparently eloped with her future husband when she was sixteen but through a flood of letters from Vermont tried to live simultaneously with both of her families. (In spite of continual fights with her husband, Hannah could never carry out her frequent threats to leave him.) When George was nine he left Brooklyn for Huntington, Long Island, to share the apartment Walt inhabited over the presses of his newspaper and be nineteen-year-old Walt's office boy. When Walt gave up his paper after a year, George returned to his parents. Only Jeff was content to remain home, fighting happily with Jesse, Andrew, and Edward. After Jeff married, he and his wife lived for several years with Mrs. Whitman, then built their first home on the lot next door. The dilemma of the children is exemplified by George's situation after the war. The sober, responsible, capable mainstay of the family, George struggled for years to establish a building and contracting business in Brooklyn, frequently regretting he had not stayed in the army after the war. During his struggles, Mrs. Whitman continually complained of his parsimony. When George's business finally prospered and he married, Mrs. Whitman accused her new daughter-in-law of causing her son to neglect his mother, even while George supported her and Edward and provided them a home with his own family.

Whether Whitman was living at home or away, his characteristic role in the family drama was mediator during periodic crises. The crisis over Andrew's death in December 1863 is a fair example. It involved Jesse; Mrs. Whitman; Jeff, his wife, Matty, and their daughter; Andrew's wife, Nancy; and, at a distance, Walt. During Andrew's last twenty-four hours Nancy was so drunk Jeff could not bear her presence. After Andrew died Jesse came to call, but the sight of his brother's corpse so upset him that he threatened to whip Jeff's little girl for some misbehavior. When Matty defended her child, Jesse attacked Matty verbally and Jeff threatened to kill Jesse. In a letter to Walt, Jeff justified his rage:

"To think that the wretch [Jesse] should go off and live with an Irish whore, get in the condition he is in by her act [that is, Jesse had syphilis] and then come and be a source of shortening his mother's life by years I feel a constant fear for Mother—she says he has these kind of things quite often with her. Calls her everything—and even swears he will keel her over &c.—Ed I don't mind so much because he couldn't help being what he is—but Jess did to himself and made himself what he is—and I think is answerable for it." (Quoted by Allen, p. 307.)

Jeff decided that Jesse should be committed to an institution, but he met opposition. His mother, the very person Jeff ostensibly wished to protect from Jesse's rages, defended her oldest son, responding as she must have done decades before when, as a child, Jesse first began to be difficult. She wrote Walt on Christmas Day after Andrew's death:

"Jeffy must have wrote very strong about [Jesse] . . . well

36

Walt Jessy is a very great trouble to me to be sure and dont apprecete what i doo for him but he is no more deranged than he has been for the last 3 years i think it would be very bad for him to be put in the lunatic assilyim . . . he is very passionate almost to frenzy and always was but of course his brain is very weak but at the time of his last blow out we had everything to confuse and irritate . . . i think Walt what a poor unfortunate creature he has been what a life he has lived that as long as i can get any thing for him to eat i would rather work and take care of him that is as long as i see no danger of harm." (Quoted by Allen, p. 308.)

In 1863, when Andrew died, Whitman looked much older than his forty-four years, a patriarch indeed, it must have seemed natural for Jeff and his mother to call Walt as arbiter. But Whitman had always carried more than his share of family duties, and it was typical for him to have the unpleasant job of committing Jesse to the Kings County Lunatic Asylum, even though the poet was recuperating that winter of 1864-1865 from a serious "blow out" of his own.

The man whose mature character we can understand is clearly prefigured in what can be deduced about the child he had once been. Whitman's formal schooling ended when he was eleven; thereafter he worked at various jobs. Later he recalled the kindness of an early employer who bought him a library subscription so that he could read *The Arabian Nights* and the novels and poems of Scott. We do not know how much education Jesse or the other boys received, but we know that the family was able to send Hannah to a boarding school when she was sixteen. The Whitmans lived in several good houses in Brooklyn, built by Walt's father and either sold or lost when mortgage payments could not be met. Whitman's two earliest surviving personal letters, sent from New Orleans to his mother in 1848, instruct her to make an interest payment on the first of the month with money he enclosed.

To Hannah, Andrew, George, and Jeff, Whitman was the father. When they were young he disciplined them, taught them to read, taught them to play, took them places. This role must have been as satisfying to Whitman as it was necessary to the children, yet it was a satisfaction that had to end as the children grew. Only Jeff and Hannah would continue their adoration of their patriarchal brother into adult life. The emotional center of Whitman's early life was the paternal relationship he enjoyed with the younger children. Perhaps the experience of giving up these ties led to a famous passage in "Song of Myself":

> Sit awhile wayfarer,
> Here are biscuits to eat and here is milk to drink,
> But as soon as you sleep and renew yourself in
> sweet clothes I will certainly kiss you with my
> goodbye kiss and open the gate for your
> egress hence.

✿　✿　✿

> I am the teacher of athletes,
> He that by me spreads a wider breast than my own
> proves the width of my own,
> He most honors my style who learns under it to
> destroy the teacher.

In Whitman's life, the matter did not end with the young "athletes" striking out on their own, for as one set of students moved away, it was replaced by another. In *Specimen Days* Whitman described the Broadway tram drivers who were his friends during the early eighteen-fifties: "I should have trusted the general run of them, in their simple goodwill and honor, under all circumstances. Not only for comradeship, and sometimes affection—great studies I found them also. (I suppose the critics will laugh heartily, but the influence of those Broadway omnibus jaunts and drivers and declamations and escapades undoubtedly enter'd into the gestation of 'Leaves of Grass.')" (p. 19.)

It seems clear that these young men were taking places that had been or would be vacated by Whitman's growing brothers. Perhaps it was Whitman's discovery that his familial world might be extended indefinitely by the recruitment of new son-brothers that led to his *Leaves of Grass* ideal of universal brotherhood. His word "studies" is important: "great studies I found them." It seems to characterize Whitman's relations with the drivers; they were to be examined, analyzed, understood, given support and comradeship—his idea of fatherly love. This is how he approached the wounded and dying young men in Washington hospitals during the war, as well as his friends Peter Doyle, Harry Stafford, Herbert Gilchrist, and others. The chief satisfaction for Whitman in these relations was the proof they gave that he could replicate the self-aggrandizing world of his adolescence, a time when his privileged relation to his mother was clarified and simplified by his patriarchal influence over his brothers and sisters.

The great importance of the paternal role Whitman played from adolescence on is subtly evident in *Leaves of Grass*. The imaginary ideal reader Whitman wrote for was constructed on the model of his first "sons," and Whitman's personal role as speaker in the poems reflects his role in relation to his family. These early relations determine a considerable part of the tone and intention, conscious and unconscious, of *Leaves of Grass*, especially Whitman's ability to express or indeed experience strong feelings about people and things.

Along with Whitman's inability to make an early commitment to a profession or to relationships with persons outside his parents' home, a curious quality of affectlessness or anaesthesia seems to pervade his personal life, his early poetry and fiction, and the early portions of many *Leaves of Grass* poems (including "Song of Myself"). The false, melodramatic, or sentimental tone of nearly all the early fiction and poetry implies the presence of strong emotions not coherently related to the ostensible subjects of this early work. Whitman's own descriptions of his youthful self—drifting, lazing on beaches, idling his time with Broadway stage-drivers—suggest that his life lacked purpose because he was out of touch with his feelings and desires.

Although the violence we find in Whitman's early fiction

seems at odds with the calm serenity the poet insisted was his normal state, there are biographical hints that the poet had a temper. Gay Wilson Allen reports (p. 33) that at nineteen Whitman was arrested and charged with beating up a child who disturbed his fishing (the jury found his action justified, the foreman having been a fisherman himself; but according to George Whitman, the poet cared little for fishing). Whitman had such strong feelings against Charles Heyde, his brother-in-law, that his executors felt obliged to excise certain passages from the poet's letters and journals. Whitman's underlying aggressiveness seems to be revealed in a description of Franklin Evans (in the temperance novel Whitman wrote at twenty-three):

"My father had been a mechanic, a carpenter; and died when I was some three or four years old only. My poor mother struggled on for a time—what few relations we had being too poor to assist us—and at the age of eleven, she had me apprenticed to a farmer on Long Island, my uncle. It may be imagined with what agony I heard, hardly twenty months after I went to live with my uncle, that the remaining parent had sickened and died also. The cold indifference of the strangers among whom she lived, allowed her to pass even the grim portals of death before they informed me of her illness. She died without the fond pressure of her son's hand, or the soothing of a look from one she loved." (Brasher, p. 147.)

The fantasies here that kill off both parents seem clearly Oedipal assassinations. The father dies at the time of the boy's classical Oedipal crisis; the mother dies when the son is entering puberty—and when she has rejected her son by sending him off to live with an uncle. If Whitman was generally out of touch with his feelings, perhaps it was because those feelings in the context of his violent and chaotic family life threatened to lead to the most desperate consequences imaginable. Even fantasies of violence could not be tolerated by his consciousness unless they arose spontaneously in fictional displacements (where the subjective seems objective if presented in a fictive voice).

So it remains even into the time of Leaves of Grass. The

most curious aspect of many of the poetic catalogs is the emotional flatness of their presentation: no feelings, judgments, or evaluations are attached to the things enumerated. Whitman likes to say: I accept all, I tolerate the most grotesque. But one aspect of Whitman's tolerance and acceptance is the utter divorce of feelings from objects. And this tells us something important about how to read *Leaves of Grass*: very often there is a psychological movement in the poems, at least those written through 1860, in which initial anaesthesia is overcome and the poet learns increasingly to experience and express his emotions and to attach his feelings to external objects. This movement marks the course of individual poems just as it marked the course of Whitman's life through 1860.

In an 1855 poem the thirty-six-year-old Whitman sketched a portrait of an eighty-year-old patriarch, loved and loving, the center of his world. When we consider Whitman's youthful fantasy of being father to his brothers and sisters, his Civil War role as wound-dresser, and finally his enduring public image as the good gray poet, it becomes apparent that the patriarch described in "I Sing the Body Electric" is a version of an important ego ideal.

> This man was of wonderful vigor and calmness
>   and beauty of person;
> The shape of his head, the richness and breadth of
>   his manners, the pale yellow and white of his
>   hair and beard, the immeasurable meaning of
>   his black eyes,
> These I used to go and visit him to see. . . . He was
>   wise also,
> He was six feet tall . . . . he was over eighty years
>   old . . . . his sons were massive clean bearded
>   tanfaced and handsome,
> They and his daughters loved him . . . all who saw
>   him loved him . . . they did not love him by
>   allowance . . . they loved him with personal
>   love.

Versions of this patriarch appear in many subsequent poems, including Whitman's last good poem, "Prayer of Columbus" (1874):

> A batter'd, wreck'd old man,
> Thrown on this savage shore, far, far from home,
> Pent by the sea and dark rebellious brows,
>   twelve dreary months,
> Sore, stiff with many toils, sicken'd and nigh to death,
> I take my way along the island's edge,
> Venting a heavy heart.

The confidence with which Whitman portrays love and respect coming to the eighty-year-old patriarch not "by allowance" but "with personal love" has disappeared by 1874, partly because of external events (Whitman's paralyzing stroke and the death of his mother in 1873). But the loss of confidence had internal causes as well, which can be inferred when one considers the psychological relation of the patriarch to the god-like bard in "Song of Myself," who raises the dying "with resistless will" and whose genius can unify and liberate a nation of potential poets. These various fantasies seem to be adult analogues of a universal childhood phenomenon known to psychoanalysis as "infantile megalomania," in which an infant assumes that its wishes, impulses, and hallucinations control the external world.[9] The root of infantile megalomania lies partly in the child's primary processes and partly in his dependency on his mother, who exists, from the infant's point of view, to provide security and to love him unconditionally. When Whitman expressed his adult versions of these fantasies, he unavoidably risked exposing their infantile underpinnings to encounters with reality that they could not survive.

The version of the patriarchal figure given in "I Sing the Body Electric" carries a partial safeguard against the frustration of the wish to restore infantile omnipotence. The

[9] Otto Fenichel, *The Psychoanalytic Theory of Neurosis* (New York, 1945), p. 39.

42

old man earned the right to be loved unconditionally by surrounding himself with sons and daughters. But earlier, in "Lingave's Temptation," Whitman had portrayed a young man whose genius was ignored by an ignorant world, and later he was to show Columbus deprived of the recognition he had earned. Whitman's best safeguard against a whimsical and unpredictable external world was to create an internal world where external persons were indistinguishable from the phantasms of his imagined past. To the extent that Whitman could control his phantasms, he could be sure that the world would not whimsically or ignorantly or unjustly withhold "personal love" from its bard. Whitman had to build into his creative processes controls and safeguards analogous to those which marked the patterns of his personal relationships.

Previously I quoted a description of the creative process by Kris and Jacobson in which the ego is depicted uniting with and separating from the id, a description that helps us begin to understand Whitman's poetic processes. By means of linguistic symbolization Whitman moved between the internal and external worlds, each world informing and enriching the other; Whitman's ability to move back and forth afforded protection against the dangers of remaining too long in either world. The nature of these dangers is clear: to remain too long in the internal world is to risk madness; to avoid the interior altogether is to forgo any hope of integrating the two worlds and to be dependent on external whim and circumstance. When he began to write *Leaves of Grass*, Whitman adopted a device that enabled his ego to maintain sufficient flexibility to move back and forth between the internal and external worlds: he imagined himself writing for an ideal reader who would love and accept him unconditionally, acknowledge his genius and omnipotence, and affirm that the bard had reestablished, through poetry the psychologically archaic world of infantile security. As I will demonstrate later, Whitman's ideal imaginary reader was modeled on the introjected imago of his mother. The relationship Whitman fantasized with his ideal reader was analogous to the patriarchal relationship the poet enjoyed with his brothers and sisters.

By reestablishing through poetic symbolization the crucial element of youthful security, Whitman could confront to an unusual extent the partly unconscious conflicts that determined the subject, method, and form of his poetry. These conflicts, which emerged in the fiction, became increasingly prominent in the poetry of 1855-1860. The following are among the most important of Whitman's conflicts:

His impulse to express sexuality *versus* his fear of punishment for such expressions.

His fear of isolation *versus* his fear of intimacy with others.

His need to believe in immortality *versus* his rational doubts which opposed such belief.

His attraction to being cradled and nursed *versus* his fear of losing autonomy.

His belief that he was a genius *versus* his wish to be one of the "average unending procession" of mortals.

His need to feel a sense of identity *versus* his fear that having an identity reduced future options.

As I will demonstrate in the next chapter, one of Whitman's chief motives for writing poetry was his wish to resolve these and other conflicts. For Whitman the problem of identity was bound to his inability to make a strong vocational commitment. The work he did between 1855 and June 1857, which resulted in the first two editions of *Leaves of Grass*, constituted a substantial self-examination and enabled Whitman to commit himself to being a poet. Yet the commitment was not unequivocal, for Whitman soon found himself in a crisis that took about two years to resolve. Work on the third *Leaves of Grass*, which in June 1857 he thought nearly complete, was in fact not finished until the winter of 1859-1860.

Several scholars have hypothesized that an unhappy homosexual love affair caused the delay (though no one has ever found a shred of supportive historical evidence). It seems to me that this hypothesis is quite unnecessary, for, as I will show later, we have extensive psychological evidence indicating quite another cause: the self-examinations fundamental to Whitman's poetic processes did not lead to a resolution of psychological conflicts, but in many instances exacerbated neurotic anxieties to the point where Whitman was unable to continue making poems. As I noted at the beginning, regressions inherent in the creative process may lead to discoveries so intolerable to consciousness as to require that regressions cease. After 1860, Whitman's personal voice was withdrawn from most of his new poems. Five years after the third *Leaves of Grass*, the assassination of Lincoln called forth Whitman's personal voice to make a symbolic announcement that there would be no more confrontations with his unconscious self and that his conflicts would have to remain unresolved. The searching, doubting Whitman who had written the most remarkable poems of the nineteenth century gave way forever to the good gray poet.

An Approach to the Poems

THE PRECEDING biographical discussion explored some of the basic patterns of conflict in Whitman's psychological life. The intention of the present chapter is to demonstrate a method of reading his poetry based on an understanding of how his poems were responses to conflicts sharply felt but little understood. Occasionally Whitman achieved a limited degree of understanding of his unconscious conflicts, but the poet characteristically tried to avoid anxiety resulting from his conflicts by seeking psychological catharsis, an ecstatic feeling that gave him the illusion that conflicts had been resolved. At times he expressed not only ecstasy, but also, with remarkable directness and courage, the pain of his anxiety itself. Among other things, I will now try to show that the excellence of Whitman's poetic achievements does not depend on the mystical transcendence frequently attributed to his poems.[1] Rather, the excellence de-

[1] Almost all Whitman critics have assumed that the cathartic experiences that occur so often in the poems indicate the resolution of conflicts. As Stephen E. Whicher points out, an exception to this came in one of the first psychoanalytically informed studies of Whitman, Jean Catel's *Walt Whitman, la naissance du poète* (Paris, 1929). "The great upsurge of creative activity, Catel points out, which produced the 1855 *Leaves of Grass* partially resolved the conflicts that led to it, *but only partially* [my emphasis], 'for the work of art, even if a substitute for action, does not exhaust the forces that lie

pends on the fullness with which Whitman explored and confronted unconscious material discovered as a result of his poetic processes.

Scholars have generally agreed that Whitman's poetic intention was to seek a condition of elevated consciousness, a state they have variously compared to Emersonian transcendence and to several kinds of mysticism.[2] Whitman's procedures can also be compared to the cathartic method of psychological therapy that Freud's "talking cure" superseded. Catharsis is characterized by a climactic emotional explosion, often accompanied by tumultuous insight into the unconscious and by temporary relief from the pain of internal conflicts. No doubt Whitman frequently experienced catharsis, but I disagree with the widely held assumption that these experiences indicated that he had resolved the conflicts in which the poems originate.[3]

Let me carry a little further this analogy between the po-

---

in a dream-filled sleep within us' " (Whicher, "Whitman's Awakening to Death," in R. W. B. Lewis, ed., *The Presence of Walt Whitman*, New York, 1962, p. 10). The only recent critic I can find who challenges the view that the poems afford resolution is Richard Chase, " 'Out of the Cradle' as a Romance," also in *The Presence of Walt Whitman*, pp. 52-71. See E. Pierre Chanover, "Walt Whitman: A Psychological and Psychoanalytic Bibliography," *Psychoanalytic Review*, 59 (1972), 467-74, for the most comprehensive Whitman bibliography to date.

[2] See especially Howard J. Waskow, *Whitman: Explorations in Form* (Chicago, 1966); V. K. Chari, *Whitman in the Light of Vedantic Mysticism* (Lincoln, Neb., 1964); James E. Miller, Jr., *A Critical Guide to "Leaves of Grass"* (Chicago, 1957); and Gay Wilson Allen, *Walt Whitman Handbook* (New York, 1962), pp. 241-77.

[3] See Ernest Jones, *The Life and Work of Sigmund Freud* (New York, 1953), I. Although Allen (*Handbook*, pp. 241-77) describes Whitman's mystical experiences much as I have described catharsis, he makes no distinction between the experiences and Whitman's interpretations of them. If poetry is created by a process that is partly unconscious, we must find some way to understand more than the poet himself consciously understands. It should be clear that in a psychoanalytic context "catharsis" has a meaning nearly opposite to Aristotle's.

47

etic and psychoanalytic processes. Psychoanalysis began with Freud's realization that cathartic experiences, which he could induce by hypnosis, were short-lived, gave but temporary relief from symptoms of internal conflicts, and left the conflicts themselves unresolved. Freud sought a more gradual and controllable method for making unconscious material accessible, and he found it in a technique based on the principle of free association. In the "talking cure," catharsis became a means toward an end, rather than an end in itself; the objective was no longer the mere achievement of emotional discharge accompanying insight but the assimilation of insight into the conscious ego. In this process the psychiatrist aligned himself with the patient's consciousness in order to assist its integrative functions. For Whitman, writing a poem sometimes had an effect similar to talking to an analyst. Material that arose spontaneously from his unconscious to become part of a poem had to be organized into poetry. If we understand Whitman's cathartic experiences we may find a clue to the basis of organization of his poems. In "Song of Myself," for example, Whitman proceeded from one cathartic experience to another, joining those experiences by associative passages and stopping occasionally to assimilate some of the insights that free association and catharsis had enabled him to reach.

Whitman's ultimate intent seems to have been to strengthen and integrate an exceptionally uncertain sense of identity. Before we can approach the question of poetic identity, however, we must consider the relation between his cathartic experiences and the conflicts that led to the creation of poetry. Whitman usually discontinued his self-analysis when he reached catharsis, and many scholars have assumed that catharsis was itself his primary goal. That catharsis was only one of several psychological forces organized into poetic structures will become clear as we examine four poems: "Clef Poem," "As I Ebb'd with the Ocean of Life," "There Was a Child Went Forth," and "Out of the Cradle Endlessly Rocking."

I. *This Night I am Happy*

"Clef Poem" (1856) exemplifies the way initial poetic intentions tended to disappear in Whitman's late revisions. In this case the very roots and substance of the original poem evaporated. In the first version of eight stanzas (thirty-four lines), "Clef Poem" was essentially a cathartic outpouring in response to an implicit but unassimilated insight. When stanzas two through seven were deleted (from the 1867 *Leaves of Grass* and subsequently), the outward "unity" of the poem may have been improved, as Gay Wilson Allen asserts,[4] but the psychological substance of the poem faded. Here is the poem as it was first printed.

CLEF POEM

This night I am happy,
As I watch the stars shining, I think a thought of
 the clef of the universes, and of the future.

What can the future bring me more than I have?
Do you suppose I wish to enjoy life in other spheres?

I say distinctly I comprehend no better sphere
 than this earth,
I comprehend no better life than the life
 of my body.

I do not know what follows the death of my body,
But I know well that whatever it is, it is best for me,
And I know well that what is really Me shall live
 just as much as before.

I am not uneasy but I shall have good housing
 to myself,
But this is my first—how can I like the
 rest any better?
Here I grew up—the studs and rafters are grown
 parts of me.

---

[4] *Handbook*, pp. 180-81.

I am not uneasy but I am to be beloved by young
    and old men, and to love them the same,
I suppose the pink nipples of the breasts of women
    with whom I shall sleep will taste the same
    to my lips,
But this is the nipple of a breast of my mother,
    always near and always divine to me, her
    true child and son.

I suppose I am to be eligible to visit the stars,
    in my time,
I suppose I shall have myriads of new experiences—
    and that the experience of this earth will prove
    only one out of myriads;
But I believe my body and my soul already
    indicate those experiences,
And I believe I shall find nothing in the stars more
    majestic and beautiful than I have already
    found on the earth,
And I believe I have this night a clue
    through the universes,
And I believe I have this night thought a thought
    of the clef of eternity.

A vast similitude interlocks all,
All spheres, grown, ungrown, small, large, suns,
    moons, planets, comets, asteroids,
All the substances of the same, and all that is
    spiritual upon the same,
All distances of place, however wide,
All distances of time—all inanimate forms,
All souls—all living bodies, though they be in
    different worlds,
All gaseous, watery, vegetable, mineral processes,
    the fishes, the brutes,
All men and women—me also,
All nations, colors, barbarisms, civilizations,
    languages,

All identities that have existed or may exist on this
   globe or any globe,
All lives and deaths—all of past, present, future,
This vast similitude spans them, and always has
   spanned, and shall forever span them.

(Leaves of Grass, 1856, 249-51)

Like "As I Ebb'd" and "Out of the Cradle," this poem is
organized as a search for a "word," a "clew," a "hint"—the
"clef of the universe." And just as the organization of "Clef
Poem" is familiar, so the mood at the beginning is also common to Whitman, including the implication that there are
other nights when he is not happy.

In between the first and last stanzas the narrator moves
from a series of ambiguous questions to the development
of a metaphor that has no explicit relation to the rest of the
poem. Beginning in stanza five with the assertion that he
will "have good housing" after death, Whitman develops
the conceit according to his present housing. His free-
associating seems to have led him in a direction different
from the course he originally intended; nevertheless, the
meaning of the metaphor is discernible. In various Whitman poems, the house symbolizes the womb, where all
things are one; the foetus is identical with its mother and
need make no act of will to survive. At an unconscious level
Whitman equates the unified world of the womb with the
unified "vast similitude" of the transcendental vision.

If this seems to carry a subtlety too far, consider the next
stanza. The thought of the house apparently leads to
a thought of existence in which there is no conflict with old
or young men, and love is requited. Such fantasy in turn
leads to a thought of the "pink nipples of the breasts of
women with whom I shall sleep." By means of his fantasies
Whitman seeks to abolish time and return to infantile security. Whitman wishes to compensate for childhood deprivation and exclusion revealed in other poems. Yet there can
be no such compensation: time cannot actually be stopped,

51

the poet cannot resume infancy or reenter the womb. In the last two stanzas he can but assert a metaphor that extends the womb and cradle into the entire universe.

This metaphor (and the fantasy it speaks for) is almost certainly near the center of Whitman's narcissism,[5] but it characterizes only half his world view. If Whitman was part visionary, he was also skeptical. As often as his impulses led him to assert a vision of universal oneness, they led him to analyze the roots of his need for unity. Yet the visionary and analytic voices tend to be mutually exclusive; in this poem the visionary voice overwhelms, preventing the poet's rational mind from achieving order and coherence. Since Whitman's revisions of "Clef Poem" indicate that he did not understand or could not accept the connection I have shown between the infantile longings and the transcendental vision,[6] it is very doubtful that he consciously grasped

[5] Whitman described the protective nature of his narcissism in a letter to his friend, R. M. Bucke, the Canadian psychiatrist: "Nature has not only endowed me with immense emotionality but immense bufferism (so to call it) or placid resignation to what happens." Edwin Haviland Miller, ed., *The Correspondence of Walt Whitman* (New York, 1969), iv, 386.

[6] From evidence in *Walt Whitman's Blue Book*, ed. Arthur Golden (New York, 1968), the chronology of Whitman's revisions may be inferred. Whitman circled stanzas two and three, apparently to indicate that they were to be deleted. Short lines are drawn horizontally above stanzas seven and eight. Two wavy lines are drawn downward through stanzas four, five, and six on p. 229, beginning at the bottom of the line circling stanzas two and three (the points of origin being clearly visible) and implying that the circle was already drawn. On page 230 a long horizontal line appears above the first line of type on the page, parallel to the horizontal line above stanza eight, and wavy vertical lines, like those on p. 229, connect the two horizontal lines. Whitman seems first to have thought of excluding, successively, stanzas two and three, and then stanzas four, five, six, and seven; the short lines to the left above those stanzas were superseded by the wavy vertical lines. Finally he decided to omit all the middle stanzas. That he set about this revision in this sequence is ample evidence that only as he studied the poem did the "irrelevance" of the middle stanzas become apparent to him. From this evidence I infer that at the time of revision Whitman no longer had any under-

the implications I have drawn from this poem. Probably when he came to reexamine the poem after 1860 he deleted the middle stanzas because they made as little sense to him as they have made to most subsequent readers. Possibly he sensed that the catharsis in the last stanza was implicitly undermined by the presence in the poem of unassimilated material—the disunity that Allen speaks of.

I believe the disunity derives from Whitman's inability to bring together the psychic and poetic processes, or from his failure to coordinate the unconscious and conscious aspects of composition. In this poem he responded to internal conflicts in the way that is least effective for his art. Instead of seeking to express, poetically, the conflict or desire that impelled him to write, or seeking a more sustained insight into the motive, he seems to flee from awareness of his regressive impulses, to seek escape from the anxiety attending that insight by rushing into catharsis.

But there is reasonable doubt whether the transcendental vision, which allowed this escape, provided much comfort. As Stephen Whicher notes, the comings and goings of the vision are outside the visionary's control and the vision itself may bring either serenity or a nightmare.[7] Whitman had to survive the lapses of his vision and the sometimes nightmarish glimpses the vision afforded into a chaotic unconscious.

Recognition of the different voices in Whitman's poems leads to the observation that Whitman seems to have had

---

standing or conscious memory of the impulse that led him to compose the poem five to ten years before. This implies that the insight underlying stanzas five and six was not assimilated.

[7] "Whitman's Awakening to Death," p. 6: "The visionary gleam comes and goes by laws of its own, and each time it goes it leaves its votary face to face with the same spiritual emergency. It is not simply that the vision dies and is replaced by the unaltered facts it had denied. Vision itself is treacherous. A man may 'loafe and invite' his soul but he cannot predict or control what will accept the invitation. Vision may be demonic as well as transcendental, a nightmare confirmation of dread instead of a release of power and hope."

53

two modes of coping with experience—one prophetic, passive, and dominated by the unconscious, and the other analytic, active, and moving toward consciousness. The prophetic mode extends the womb or cradle throughout the world; it seeks to eliminate consciousness and the ego, thereby precluding conscious control over one's self or one's moods. Poetry thus becomes automatic writing with the poet seeking (as Whitman explicitly does in the "Calamus" poems) an intuitive, pre-verbal communion with his reader like that of an infant with its mother. The analytic mode rejects the transcendental promise of universal oneness and accepts the boundaries between the Me and Not Me. It demands that choices be consciously made and it seeks conscious control. From the analytic point of view poetry is the most powerful form of verbal communication, but poems do not communicate transcendentally, nor link readers to the Aeolian harp.[8]

Whitman could not commit himself altogether to either the analytic or the prophetic mode; he tended to alternate between them, hoping they could somehow become compatible. Whitman's struggle to believe in the "vast similitude" of a unified world womb brings to mind Hawthorne's famous description of Melville: "He can neither believe, nor be comfortable in his unbelief; and he is too honest and courageous not to try to do one or the other."

[8] The only modern psychoanalyst who has written about Whitman in detail, Gustav Bychowski, "Walt Whitman, A Study in Sublimation," *Psychoanalysis and the Social Sciences*, III (1951), 223-61, is but partly convincing in his argument that "by his poetic creation, Whitman did not only regain faith in himself, but also found gratification for his narcissism. Moreover, this fulfillment was of such a nature as to help him transcend the limitations of his own ego . . ." (251-52). The evidence for this "transcendence" consists of dubious readings of passages taken out of context from "When Lilacs Last in the Dooryard Bloom'd," "Song of Myself," and especially "Passage to India." In the introduction to *A Century of Whitman Criticism* (Bloomington, Ind., 1969), Edwin Miller qualifies his praise for Bychowski by noting that the latter is too insistent "upon smoothing out the stresses in Whitman's life" (pp. xxxvi-xxxvii).

II. *Elemental Drifts*

The habit of assuming that Whitman could resolve internal conflicts by means of catharsis has led scholars to put aside as "untypical" one of his finest poems, "As I Ebb'd with the Ocean of Life."[9] Yet Whitman thought it important enough to place it, in 1860, at the beginning of the "Leaves of

[9] See, for example, Harold W. Blodgett and Sculley Bradley, *Leaves of Grass: Comprehensive Reader's Edition* (New York, 1965), p. 253, note. Hereafter, references to this edition will be abbreviated *CRE*. In recent years a few extended readings of "As I Ebb'd" have been published, but I believe that its centrality to the whole of Whitman's work is not yet recognized. Waskow (see note 2, above) presents the most effective case for the widely held view that the poem ends on a note of mystical resolution. Schyberg, Asselineau, Chase, Whicher, and Edwin Miller take the opposite view, that (to state the matter in my terms) catharsis fails to overcome the poet's despair. In general I agree with Miller's three principal points of interpretation: that "As I Ebb'd" contains a recognition that many other poems are "unsatisfactory sublimations (or repressions) of the despair and isolation he endured from day to day"; that Whitman here realizes "his 'insolent poems' further estranged him from his family and from the common people he most admired"; and that the poem confirms that the " 'real I' [sic] is more passive than active, and the real subject matter is the restoration of infantile relationships" (*A Psychological Journey*, p. 46). However, Miller does not sufficiently examine the conflict of identity that I believe is at the center of the poem, nor does he analyze Whitman's ability to assimilate the insights contained in the poem. I propose that in this poem Whitman simultaneously expresses and explores the passivity that Miller and Whicher have mentioned.

Also see Fredson Bowers' study of this period of Whitman's life and work, *Whitman's Manuscripts*: Leaves of Grass (*1860*) (Chicago, 1955). Bowers speculates that the failure of a presumed homosexual affair sometime between 1856-1858 may have led to the "Calamus" poems. In another context Edwin Miller argues against the relevance of such speculation: "Attempts to find the origin of 'Out of the Cradle Endlessly Rocking' in a personal experience about 1858 or 1859 strike me as misguided and irrelevant, since the significance of an unsuccessful love affair (if one could be proved) would be not so much the event itself as the reactivation of the experience of loss, ultimately the loss of the beloved mother . . ." (*A Psychological Journey*, p. 175).

55

Grass" cluster, and in subsequent editions he put it next to "Out of the Cradle," where casual readers could not fail to discover it. In "As I Ebb'd" a pair of incompatible voices is again crucial. At the heart of the poem are competing ideas about the nature of identity: the idea that the self is immortal and infinite contends with the knowledge that the self exists in nature and is, according to all rational evidence, mortal and finite. At times Whitman characterizes his identity as "the eternal self of me," but at other times as "the real ME." He was probably not entirely conscious of the opposition implied between these two phrases; nevertheless these two ideas of self remain separate voices in the poem. When the "eternal self" speaks, it assumes the mystical cloud of unknowing; when the "real ME" speaks, it speaks of things that can be rationally known.[10]

The poem begins with the poet ebbing in a moment of despairing passivity, "wending the shores" he knows, "held by the eternal self of me that threatens to get the better of me, and stifle me." Seeking to suppress his despair beneath cathartic ecstasy, he permits his mind to associate freely. He produces in stanza three a catalog in which associative logic supplants sequential logic and in which he is incapable of predicting what nightmare the vision may yield. The dis-

[10] Whicher also notices the implicit opposition between the two voices of this poem: Whitman and "the 'Me myself' are opposed, not in union," pp. 13-14. Whicher argues that "As I Ebb'd" denies the victory over the unconscious that Whitman thought he had won in "Song of Myself." I would say that "As I Ebb'd" represents another stage in the process begun with "Song of Myself." Whicher claims that Whitman's "struggle" in "Song of Myself" "is a bit unconvincing since we cannot really believe in the possibility of his defeat" (p. 7); I would object that we cannot rationally believe in the possibility of his victory; at least there is no objective basis for the transcendental terms Whicher posits. In Whicher's context, victory would mean the actual attainment of immortality and the total assimilation of both unconscious and consciousness into some "reborn" self. Unless one has more constant faith in faith than I believe Whitman had, one can only regard these as hypothetical objectives and ask the same old question: Was Whitman's faith unswerving enough for an act of faith to resolve his doubts?

oriented "eternal self" leads the narrator to seek transcendental correspondences—"the old thought of likenesses"—and these lead him away from "the shores I know" to "the shores I know not" (in stanza 4). He has here entered his unconscious, but in the cathartic state he cannot understand what anything means: "the least thing that belongs to me, or that I see or touch, I know not." So lost is he in his unconscious that he doubts his very identity:

> O baffled, balked,
> Bent to the very earth, here preceding what follows,
> Oppressed with myself that I have dared to
>   open my mouth,
> Aware now, that, amid all the blab whose echoes
>   recoil upon me, I have not once had the least
>   idea who or what I am,
> But that before all my insolent poems the real ME
>   still stands untouched, untold,
>   altogether unreached.

Catharsis, which sometimes leads to ecstasy, here leads to a crisis. He cannot believe that his self is eternal when he finds such deep self-doubt. The appearance of this other sense of self, "the real ME," calls into doubt the honesty of his poems:

> *   *   * before all my insolent poems the real ME
>   still stands untouched, untold,
>   altogether unreached,
> Withdrawn far, mocking me with mock-
>   congratulatory signs and bows,
> With peals of distant ironical laughter at every
>   word I have written or shall write,
> Striking me with insults till I fall helpless
>   upon the sand.

This passage clearly reveals that one of the standards Whitman used to judge his poems was whether or not they enabled him to discover the truth about the hidden self. These lines tell of something false or inadequate found in previous poems—that his deepest self eludes his poetic search. The source of present conflict is in the past, and this source is what he searches for; to discover who and what he is, he must, through his poetic process, *touch* and *tell*— that is, take an accounting of—his private, unconscious world, where the past survives intact.

But his search begins indirectly with a series of disorganized insights: he sees that he understands nothing; that Nature darts and stings him because he has presumed to sing; that the ocean and land conspire with Nature to render him powerless. These perceptions attest above all to the confusion of his search: Why should he continue to write poems if "no man ever can" understand anything? (The confusion results from the transcendental view that the verbal communication possible through poetry is inferior to a "higher" intuitive form of knowing.) And Nature, which he identifies with the paternal land and the maternal ocean, may be not only external reality but also that which is innate—"the real ME." Apparently led by these confusions to seek some indisputable fact, he tries to fix on his relation to the "fish-shaped" island: "What is yours is mine, my father." From his father he seeks the intimate embrace denied him by the ocean and also "the secret of the wondrous murmuring" he envies. This secret is several things. The ebb and flow of the waves, corresponding to the ebb and flow of Whitman's despair and ecstasy, symbolize primal sexual knowledge, the sounds of parental lovers, as well as those immutable facts of nature the poet desperately wants to escape: conception and death. But while the reader may infer these insights, they remain too obscure for the poet to perceive; in fact, it seems that the poet does not want to understand. He gives up and the secret remains secret. Perhaps he has not yet the courage to acknowledge his passivity, his sexual confusion, or his refusal to accept his mortal identity. Whitman's poems repeatedly reveal the poet's unconscious association of identity with the continuity of time and the limitations of choice: that is, identity implies man's mortality, the ever-narrowing potential for his choices and the inexorable demands of his sexuality. To avoid these limitations Whitman revels in self-contradiction, shifting identities like Melville's confidence man and thus persuading himself that he has escaped definition and boundaries.

At this point in "As I Ebb'd," all Whitman can do is try to survive the ebb and wait for the flow to return. It is from this position that he frequently leaps to cartharsis, as he did in "Clef Poem," as if asserting his faith in immortality will make it a fact. But the self-doubt discovered in stanzas four and five makes this presently impossible and leaves him vulnerable to apparitions of chaos. He feels himself disintegrated by his awareness of another split-off self: in the last stanza his selves are now "little corpses," and he thinks of part of himself as having been stillborn. Incapable of integration through catharsis and unable consciously to accept disunity—that is, mortality—Whitman sees no way out of the dilemma. His ego warns of facts he cannot cope with. "The storm, the long calm, the darkness, the swell" lead not to life but to "Musing, pondering, a breath, a briny tear, a dab of liquid or soil." And until he becomes that final "dab of liquid or soil" he can only lament his mortality.

The pattern of conflicts in this poem prevents Whitman from obtaining the "secret of the wondrous murmuring" he "envies" and leads him to a sense of his passivity. The elemental conflict symbolically pits the poet against the sea and land, which symbolize his parents. The child he once was revives and again feels excluded by parental conflicts (lost, ebbing, stifled); he is one of the castaways the sea endlessly cries for. In poem after poem Whitman reverts to the past source of continuing conflict, lamenting the "yearning and swelling heart" with "cries of unsatisfied love." Since personal conflicts generated many of Whitman's poems, the repeated failure to get the secret, the clue, the word, makes the poems "insolent," mere "blab whose echoes recoil upon" him.

Unable in "As I Ebb'd" to get the secret, Whitman tries to explore the final horrific insight, leaving the reader to wonder why the secret eludes the poet. Whitman's superego characteristically seems overly zealous, the "little policeman" arresting by means of anxiety and fear. The conflict between instinctual drives and superego goes on unconsciously, while the ego, concerned only with survival, determines which unconscious impulses it can safely permit. When Whitman says "Creeds and schools in abeyance * * * I permit to speak, Nature, without check, with original energy," his ego is repudiating the superego's excessive zeal for law and order. But only in cathartic moments can Whitman permit Nature to speak with original energy; otherwise, Whitman witnesses and waits, unable to make judgments or let Nature speak. The secret of the murmuring eludes him because he fears that his ego may be weakened if he acknowledges the drives beneath the secret murmuring. It is no wonder that he was ambivalently attracted to Emersonian transcendentalism. "I am nothing," says Emerson; "the currents of the Universal Being circulate through me; I am part or parcel of God." Here was a ready-made justification for a condition which, to Whitman, must have appeared inescapable.

In "As I Ebb'd" the poet is divided between wanting to identify with the sea and being innately identical with the land; at the end of the poem the conflict is tacitly acknowledged, but remains unresolved. The opposed factions reflect the unconscious assumptions in which they originated: that his immortal self is bound to the powerful feminine sea; and that his mortal self languishes with the harried masculine island. These assumptions uncontrollably determine every aspect of Whitman's sense of identity. Unable to choose among loyalties, he wants all things for himself: masculine and feminine, mortal and immortal.

Whitman's typical response to such crises, as I have said, is to attempt a declaration of faith, to declare himself secure in his conviction of immortality. But such acts of faith bypass the problem, for while catharsis may bring temporary relief from the sense of ebbing, it ensures that the pain will return. In this poem Whitman rejects the easy way out and expresses as fully as he can the pain itself, seeking to understand his passive identification with Nature and with the elemental drifts:

> We, capricious, brought hither, we know not
>   whence, spread out before You, up there,
>   walking or sitting,
> Whoever you are—we too lie in drifts at your feet.

In the penultimate line he has personified "Nature," but he cancels the personification in the last line by the lower-case *you*.[11] The personification was a projection of Whitman's unconscious needs and wishes; its rejection seems to mark some recognition that Nature is not an external force but a force within. Finding neither release nor resolution in this poem Whitman must settle for the revelation of his own passivity. Nevertheless, the courage to confront weakness is a large courage. This is indeed a radical utterance out of the abysms of his soul.[12]

III. *A Child Went Forth*

Like many of Whitman's poems, "There Was a Child Went Forth" (1855) is organized as a search. The poet seeks to recover images from his childhood in the hope that his

[11] It appears that the typography of the "You" and "you" in these last lines was deliberate; despite meticulous correction of this poem in the *Blue Book* (p. 199) these words are unchanged and are so printed in subsequent editions until the passage was drastically changed in 1881.

With regard to the end of this poem, Waskow concedes that Whitman's "reconciliation" is unachieved but nevertheless claims that the final stanza, being mainly a "defense" and "apology" for poetry, is affirmative: Whitman "is no longer the debris itself but a gatherer of debris. . . . He is not really a drowned man at all, for just as the dead limbs in 'Song of Myself' give off 'sparkles,' his 'dead' lips exude an ooze with the 'prismatic colors' of life—the 'ooze' of poetry" (p. 209). While "As I Ebb'd" unquestionably carries important implications for Whitman's poetics, too much of the poem, including its tone, must be ignored to call it an apologia. Such a characterization ignores, among other things, the journey of discovery Whitman makes by means of his poetic processes.

[12] So Whitman described his poems in his 1876 preface (*CRE*, p. 751).

memories will tell him something about the core of his adult identity. In the first three stanzas the images recalled seem to be separated from the feelings that presumably attended their original perception. Consider what the child recalls: discovering a world beyond himself in his barnyard; "the old drunkard staggering home from the outhouse of the tavern whence he had lately risen"; staying at home while the schoolmistress and children passed him by. In stanza four there is a radical change of tone as Whitman imagines his own conception. The feelings attending this image lead to memories of his mother's mildness, his father's harshness, and his own "yearning and swelling heart." In stanza four the poet begins to react to long-dormant anxieties; his reactions prove so powerful that a period of general disorientation ensues. His doubt about "what is real" seems to indicate a temporary failure of his ego. At this point all he can do is retreat from the sources of confusion. The poem ends, with no obvious logic, in the poet's assertion that his memories will become part of his readers' memories.

The ending of the poem turns out to be understandable enough when we recall the psychological pattern of "Clef Poem." Whitman sought to allay possible doubts about his immortality by asserting imaginative control over the entire world—by converting the world into a cradle. The belief embodied in "As I Ebb'd" that poetry might be the medium of intuitive, non-verbal communication is merely another form of that conversion. It is this latter form that occurs in the ending of "There Was a Child" as Whitman again tries to allay his doubts and confusion by an act of transcendental faith. But the old opposition between the prophetic and analytic still exists. The poem begins with an analytic search for old images, but, as the images become threatening, the analysis must be abandoned. Yet shifting to the prophetic mode does not solve the problem. Doubts and confusions are not allayed by the poet's final assertion of faith, and he does not learn anything about his identity.

The question behind Whitman's search is: Who and what am I? In the first stanza the poet declares that he is a composite of all his experience; his identity is equal to his memory. He therefore searches for things forgotten, beginning (as Edwin Miller says) by "reenacting the Narcissus myth."[13] We know from psychoanalysis that narcissism characterizes a child's earliest relations with the external world, objects being "loved" as if they were part of the child himself. One of the ego's functions is to test reality, to distinguish between that which exists externally and that which is projected onto the environment from one's unconscious. As the ego develops, one becomes able to react emotionally to external phenomena, knowing that the objects are not part of one's self. But in this poem the objects that "became part of" the poet as a child are presented as he saw them before their introjection and until memory leads Whitman to images of his parents, there seems to be no emotional reaction whatever to the images recalled. The flowers, the infant animals, the fish, the drunkard, the schoolchildren are presented in the tone characteristic of Whitman's catalogs, without evaluation or feeling. Whitman's celebrated tolerance seems to stem from lingering infantile narcissism, which prevents his attaching emotional energy to many of the images which fill his memory.

The images of his conception in stanza four, however, are given with full emotional force, a force that testifies to the courage it must have taken Whitman to move so close to unconscious Oedipal conflicts:

> His own parents .. he that had propelled the
> fatherstuff at night, and fathered him .. and
> she that conceived him in her womb and
> birthed him .... they gave this child more of
> themselves than that,

[13] A *Psychological Journey*, p. 28. Miller continues (p. 31): "In the course of the journey—and the pattern established in 'There Was a Child Went Forth' is characteristic of most of his poems—the child-man in some mysterious way overcomes the paralysis of doubt and arrives at certainty." See also Waskow, pp. 129-35. There have been curiously few detailed analyses of this familiar and excellent poem.

> They gave him afterward every day .... they and
> of them became part of him.

We must recall two aspects of the Oedipal complex: first (in Charles Brenner's concise definition), "It is a twofold attitude toward both parents: on the one hand a wish to eliminate the jealously hated father and take his place in a sensual relationship with the mother, and on the other hand a wish to eliminate the jealously hated mother and take her place with the father"; second, the strength of lingering Oedipal conflicts stems not so much from the actual force of parental rejection as from the degree of intensity in the child's hostility toward his parents.[14] Taken together, these theories account for the progress of the poem in stanzas four and five.

Stanza five begins with a family portrait:

> The mother at home quietly placing the dishes
>   on the suppertable,
> The mother with mild words .... clean her cap and
>   gown .... a wholesome odor falling off her
>   person and clothes as she walks by:
> The father, strong, selfsufficient, manly, mean,
>   angered, unjust,

[14] *An Elementary Textbook of Psychoanalysis* (Garden City, N.Y., 1957), pp. 118, 131. Readers who fear that psychological descriptions which emphasize the Oedipal complex are inherently reductive may wish to consider the subtle studies of infant object relations by Jacobson (see note 7, Chapter 1) and by Anna Freud, *Normality and Pathology in Childhood* (New York, 1965). For a provocative discussion of the contribution of object relations theory to psychoanalysis, together with an application of this theory to a literary problem, see M. D. Faber, "Analytic Prolegomena to the Study of Western Tragedy," *Hartford Studies in Literature*, 5 (1973), 31-60. Early psychoanalysts studied the Oedipal constellation from the exclusive point of view of the infant; object relations theory seeks to examine the interaction between mother and child. The reader may note that many discussions of Oedipal matters in this book are concerned, to as large an extent as evidence permits, with the sort of family interaction that interests object relations theorists.

> The blow, the quick loud word, the tight bargain,
>   the crafty lure,
> The family usages, the language, the company, the
>   furniture . . . . the yearning and swelling heart.

The extreme simplification of these portraits indicates that a high degree of infantile narcissism still lingers in the adult Whitman's unconscious sense of his relation to his parents.[15] Whitman can only retreat from the anxiety created by these images. The thought of the "family usages" leads to the memory of his "yearning and swelling heart" and to the feeling of "affection that will not be gainsayed." This latter seems to refer to the urgency with which Oedipal feelings present themselves; willingly or not, Whitman blocks the whole matter by interposing a cloud of unknowing:

> * * * The sense of what is real . . . . the thought if
>   after all it should prove unreal,
> The doubts of daytime and the doubts of nighttime
>   . . . the curious whether and how,
> Whether that which appears so is so . . . . Or is it
>   all flashes and specks?

Whitman now retreats from the causes of his disorientation; the rest of the poem (until the final two lines) is presented from a point of view that moves steadily upward among the clouds and above the human landscape. Disembodiment and a blunting of emotional responsiveness are defenses against continuing Oedipal conflicts. At times like this, transcendentalism appeals to Whitman. But the assertion of faith at the end of this poem has a hollow ring,

---

[15] As mentioned in Chapter 2, Edwin Miller has noted evidence that Whitman's feelings about his mother were not as simple as the poet usually pretended: "In hundreds of letters to members of his family, not once is he critical of her obvious self-centeredness and wilfullness. . . . Yet his ambivalence . . . is evident in his failure during the years when he was a government employee to act upon her repeated suggestions that she come to Washington and establish a home for him" (A *Psychological Journey,* p. 55).

promising neither resolution nor lasting serenity. Transcendentalism seems merely another name for regressive narcissism, a world womb to which the poet secretly knows he can never return.

IV. *A Word from the Sea*

Most interpretations of "Out of the Cradle Endlessly Rocking" argue that the poem is evidence of the "emotional equilibrium" Whitman had reached by 1859.[16] Such arguments either state or imply that the poet has allayed the fears of mortality and the sexual conflicts apparent in earlier poems. From the psychoanalytic point of view the silencing of these conflicts could occur only if Whitman had been able to incorporate the conflicts into his consciousness or if he had somehow become able to repress them utterly. It seems to me that some of each occurred: that Whitman did reach a limited amount of conscious insight (which was nevertheless far from enough to afford resolution), and that Whitman's apparently greater tranquility after, say, 1860, was due to his increased ability to keep repressed the roots of the problems that had been manifest for perhaps as long as ten years. I believe that we should approach "Out of the Cradle" with the following questions in mind: How did Whitman deal consciously with the facts of death and sex? Is there resolution in his poetry of the conflict between eros and death?[17] Death and sex seem to receive only very limited acknowledgment. In "Out of the Cradle" Whitman seems to substitute a preoccupation with death for its unconscious equivalent—a confrontation with his own sexuality—and to use this preoccupation as a screen to conceal his deeper concerns, thus limiting rather than enlarging his consciousness.

[16] Among the best such readings is Gay Wilson Allen's in *The Solitary Singer*, pp. 231-36.

[17] These questions are suggested by Edwin Miller's conclusions (*A Psychological Journey*, p. 185). Although I disagree with Miller's conclusions, I find his reading the most effective of those yet published.

At the beginning of "Out of the Cradle" is a "Pre-Verse," which establishes the setting for the narrative to come and which defines the narrator and his search. In the middle is the "Reminiscence" (stanzas one to twenty-seven in the 1860 text), a narrative about the boy and the birds into which is woven the boy's "translation" of the he-bird's songs. At the end are the narrator's responses to the Reminiscence: a limited cathartic experience in stanza twenty-eight is followed by an attempt to analyze the Reminiscence and by the perception of the "word out of the sea"—"death" —that the narrator tries to fuse with the bird's songs and his own songs.

The Pre-Verse announces the search for origins, that recurring motive for Whitman's poetic journeys. The narrator acknowledges the *role* he plays as an adult but seeks to discover the little boy inside him (ultimately discovered by "these tears"). The tone of the Pre-Verse is essentially similar to that of "There Was a Child," in which the narrator passively attributes his existence to his original experiences: the "rocked cradle," the "mother's womb" and breasts. To the previous questions another must be added: Does the poetic creation of the Reminiscence imply, as Whitman hoped, a triumph over passivity? Is "activity" the same as victory over chaos and disorder?

Still another problem is implicit in the Pre-Verse. In naming his world Whitman mentions earth, air, and water, but omits fire. As noted before, earth takes the form of the paternal fish-shaped island, water the maternal sea, and air symbolizes poetic utterances. The omission of fire, which in stanza thirty will signify the poet's awakened sexuality, indicates an imbalance. Certainly part of what the poet searches for is his sexual identity, but in the Pre-Verse all he knows is that he looks for a "word stronger and more delicious than any."

The private self Whitman seeks emerges in the Reminiscence when the child within the poet begins to speak. At the beginning the child's understanding of the birds corresponds to some sense he already has acquired of the way things are or ought to be. Envying the birds, the poet wants transcendental intimacy with his "lovers"; like the birds, he measures his well-being by the rapport he feels with the sun, the winds, the waters, and the earth. But the serenity of the birds is as fragile as the poet's: neither bird nor poet can control sources of happiness.

In the Reminiscence the boy's identity merges with that of the he-bird, enabling the boy to express indirectly his fear of abandonment and loss. In the second aria the bird's former rapport has disintegrated; fire (the sun) is not mentioned, and the he-bird blames air, earth, and water in turn for the loss of his mate. The boy weeps for the birds and for himself as he shares the he-bird's sense of loss. The boy, like the bird, has been turned out "of the ninth month midnight," abandoned in a world he doesn't understand. As the world of the birds "*together*" was once all one and all home, womblike, so the world of the he-bird alone has become hostile and uncontrollable. Love, in Whitman's fantasies, once meant "*two together*"; now it means loss and abandonment, and the word discovered in the arias is not "love" but "*loved.*" In the last seven stanzas of the second aria the he-bird's grievances are reiterated, but there is no hint of reconciliation, nor any acknowledgment of the paradox that he must subjectively accept his own mortality in order to survive. The he-bird's grief comes not from the loss but from his inability to accept its finality.

Yet the boy reacts to this song with ecstasy—"The love in the heart pent, now loose, now at last tumultuously bursting." This cathartic reaction apparently comes from the boy's discovery in the Reminiscence of his present world's origins, though he does not yet understand the relation between these origins and specific assumptions he now unconsciously holds.

> The aria sinking,
> All else continuing—the stars shining,

The winds blowing—the notes of the
    wondrous bird echoing,
With angry moans the fierce old mother yet,
    as ever, incessantly moaning,
On the sands of Paumanok's shore gray
    and rustling,
The yellow half-moon, enlarged, sagging down,
    drooping, the face of the sea almost touching,
The boy extatic—with his bare feet the waves, with
    his hair the atmosphere dallying,
The love in the heart pent, now loose, now at last
    tumultuously bursting,
The aria's meaning, the ears, the Soul,
    swiftly depositing,
The strange tears down the cheeks coursing,
The colloquy there—the trio—each uttering,
The undertone—the savage old mother,
    incessantly crying,
To the boy's Soul's questions sullenly timing—
    some drowned secret hissing,
To the outsetting bard of love.

At this point the reader may understand not only why the
poet is ecstatic but also why the ecstasy fades so rapidly.
Along with the pleasure of having his suspicions confirmed
(regarding his abandonment by the female in the re-
created eternal triangle of child and parents), the poet
learns how terrible the confirmation is. There is little ultimate comfort in the incessant moaning and crying of the old
mother, and little hope for the passive boy in the example
of "Paumanok's shore gray and rustling." The sea may seem
to hold answers to the "boy's Soul's questions," but the questions are incomprehensible and seem to mock the outsetting
bard. Recalling the mockery of the poet's words in "As I
Ebb'd," that it is the "real ME" who mocks the poet, we may
ask if it is the poet's projections in the "translation" of the
arias that mock him here also. If this is so, then the poet will

understand answers to his questions only if he approaches
the whole matter more analytically—and this he tries to do.

> Bird! (then said the boy's Soul,)
> Is it indeed toward your mate you sing? or is it
>   mostly to me?
> For I that was a child, my tongue's use sleeping,
> Now that I have heard you,
> Now in a moment I know what I am for—I awake,
> And already a thousand singers—a thousand songs,
>   clearer, louder, more sorrowful than yours,
> A thousand warbling echoes have started to
>   life within me,
> Never to die.

Here is the narrator's first conceptualization of his previous relation to the bird's song. He understands that the
song has awakened him by touching important analogs in
his memory, and that having grasped little consciousness,
he can never return to what had previously seemed like innocence. Similarly, he learns how dangerous a little consciousness can be. But he does not realize, and he will not
in this poem, that the source of the song is himself, and that
the translation was a projection of his own wishes and assumptions. No matter what else he may learn, meanings will
remain incomplete until he accepts responsibility for the
world he has made.

What he does know, however, is that since he cannot retreat to "innocence," he must seize as much consciousness
as he can reach.

> O throes!
> O you demon, singing by yourself—projecting me,
> O solitary me, listening—never more shall I cease
>   imitating, perpetuating you,
> Never more shall I escape,
> Never more shall the reverberations,
> Never more the cries of unsatisfied love be
>   absent from me,

Never again leave me to be the peaceful child I was
    before what there, in the night,
By the sea, under the yellow and sagging moon,
The dusky demon aroused—the fire, the sweet
    hell within,
The unknown want, the destiny of me.

The reader can see (as Whitman cannot) that the "demon" and "the fire, the sweet hell within" are names for another kind of "real ME"—the masculine equivalents of the archaic feminine identity discovered in "As I Ebb'd." The "cries of unsatisfied love" seem clearly to imply not only the wish Whitman so often expressed for a pre-rational intimacy with others, but also the awakening within himself of sexual longings—fire and sweet hell. When he was a child these longings were submerged beneath narcissistic wishes for a transcendent world womb; now he knows he can never again be "the peaceful child I was before." Expressing all this still leaves the "want, the destiny," unknown. The achievement of consciousness and understanding still eludes him.

The ambivalence of Whitman's wish partly to see, partly not to see, is made clear in the next stanza (truncated in later editions):

O give me some clew!
O if I am to have so much, let me have more!
O a word! O what is my destination?
O I fear it is henceforth chaos!
O how joys, dreads, convolutions, human shapes,
    and all shapes, spring as from graves
    around me!
O phantoms! you cover all the land, and all the sea!
O I cannot see in the dimness whether you smile
    or frown upon me;
O vapor, a look, a word! O well-beloved!
O you dear women's and men's phantoms!

The first four lines tell of the chaos Whitman discovered on this journey, but the rest of the stanza tries to smother reality beneath the same transcendental prophecy that has repeatedly failed to comfort him. A little glimpse of the chaos within is enough to send him looking for correspondences and for sources outside himself by which to account for the chaos he fears. Although Whitman wants to understand these phantoms and shapes, his symbolic mode of perception obscures as much as it clarifies. At best he will be able to see only part of the reality within. In stanza thirty-two he becomes dimly aware that he has always known the answer to the question this poem asks. And in stanza thirty-three he becomes conscious of part of that "answer":

> Answering, the sea,
> Delaying not, hurrying not,
> Whispered me through the night, and very
>   plainly before daybreak,
> Lisped to me constantly the low and delicious
>   word DEATH,
> And again Death—ever Death, Death, Death,
> Hissing melodious, neither like the bird, nor like
>   my aroused child's heart,
> But edging near, as privately for me, rustling
>   at my feet,
> And creeping thence steadily up to my ears,
> Death, Death, Death, Death, Death.

The word "Death," like the previous word "*loved*," comes not from the sea but from the poet himself, and the attribution of the word to the sea confuses the very issue the poet seeks to clarify. Not only is the attribution of the word confused, the word itself is confused with the fact it signifies. With reiteration the word "Death" takes on some of the quality of what psychoanalysis calls "magic words," words that give their speaker a sense of omnipotence and the illusion that he controls the thing named.[18] The illusion of control is evident in Whitman's assertion that the fact of death can be allocated to the sea: he places it and therefore has it to place. In the middle portion of "Out of the Cradle"

---

[18] Otto Fenichel, *The Psychoanalytic Theory of Neurosis*, p. 296.

death is seen as existing externally and is the cause of grief over loss and abandonment; in the end the poet tries to master his opponent by controlling it magically. In the final stanza Whitman seeks to extend the magic by incorporating words and songs into a comprehensive synthetic prophecy:

> Which I do not forget,
> But fuse the song of two together,
> That was sung to me in the moonlight on
>   Paumanok's gray beach,
> With the thousand responsive songs, at random,
> My own songs, awaked from that hour,
> And with them the key, the word up
>   from the waves,
> The word of the sweetest song, and all songs,
> That strong and delicious word which,
>   creeping to my feet,
> The sea whispered me.

The very need to "fuse" his own songs with the song of the bird and the word from the waves indicates that Whitman still fails to recognize that all these words had the same origin—in himself—and that they indicate more about his unconscious than about external reality. Whitman's feeling that the fearful "chaos" he momentarily apprehended in stanza thirty-one is made orderly by the subsequent discovery of the word "Death," and his later feeling that the word not only provides order but is sweet and delicious, seem to indicate more than what Stephen Whicher calls the discovery of reality, or what Edwin Miller calls the acknowledgment of death. What Whitman seems to do in stanza thirty-one and thereafter is to substitute the word "death" for the word "sex." The discovery of "the fire, the sweet hell within" in stanza thirty led to a question: "O what is my destination?" The answer seemed to be that the acceptance of sexual identity implies the acceptance of mortality.

Instead, Whitman substitutes a preoccupation with death for the acknowledgment of sex and thereby tries to elude the demands of the "unknown want." At first this interpreta-

73

tion seems to justify Richard Chase's objection to the "melo-drama" of this poem's ending: Whitman's embracing death with "tender eroticism, not to mention gustatory delight." When the sea represents his mother, the poet can explore unresolved Oedipal impulses within a symbolic context in which the actual nature of the impulse is disguised. Characteristically, Whitman's poems *stop* (rather than *conclude*) when the poet's insights can carry him no further. Yet this tendency indicates neither insincerity nor coward-ice, but the limitations of Whitman's ability to make fully conscious the unconscious meanings of his fantasies. But when we fully accept the impermeability of the repression barrier, we may challenge Chase's devaluation of the melo-drama in "Out of the Cradle." Our sense of the greatness of "Out of the Cradle" does not depend on the brilliance of Whitman's rhetoric, nor even on his fulfillment of his psy-chological goal. Rather it depends on our identification with his exploration of unconscious territory, an exploration at which we can expect to succeed no more than he. If Whit-man's fusion of *"loved"* and "Death" does not resolve un-conscious conflicts, it nevertheless affords the partial satis-faction of dreams and fantasies, as well as the immense gratification of having written an exquisite poem.[19]

[19] Chase, " 'Out of the Cradle' As a Romance," pp. 67, 69-71. Here and in *Walt Whitman* (Minneapolis, 1961), pp. 27-32, Chase nearly reverses the view he expressed in *Walt Whitman Reconsidered* (New York, 1955), pp. 120-24. Most readings of "Out of the Cradle" sup-port Allen's conclusions (quoted in my text). (In addition to those mentioned elsewhere, see Paul Fussell, Jr., "Whitman's Curious Warble," in Lewis, *The Presence of Walt Whitman*, pp. 28-51, and Leo Spitzer, *"Explication de Texte* Applied to . . . 'Out of the Cradle Endlessly Rocking,' " in Edwin Miller, *A Century of Whitman Criticism*, pp. 273-84.)
The answer to Chase proposed in my text resembles the position taken by Norman Holland, *The Dynamics of Literary Response* (New York, 1968), *passim*, that readers respond affirmatively when a poet gives them defenses by which to manage anxiety provoked by a poem's unconscious roots and analogs. As mentioned in Chapter 1, notes 4 and 5, I accept Professor Holland's position with many reservations. It is appropriate here to propose a somewhat more open-

As mentioned in Chapter 2 Whitman paused while writing the preface to the 1876 *Leaves of Grass* to mourn his mother, who had died two years before. The protraction of his grief implicitly nullified the wish Whitman had expressed just before: " * * * with cheerful face estimating Death, not at all as the cessation, but as somehow what I feel it must be, the entrance upon by far the greatest part of existence, and something that Life is at least as much for, as it is for itself."[20] The unacknowledged aspect to that old fusion of "*loved*," "Death," and the sea had been the fear of death that threatened to attend any sexual expression. The

---

ended alternative to Professor Holland's view. This alternative derives from the theoretical considerations I stated in Chapter 1.

First, a poem requires its readers to experience a world different from the reader's own and to recognize that a difference exists. Holland claims that the reader accepts those of the poet's psychological habits which correspond to the reader's own, rejecting the rest. In contrast, I suggest that as in other human relationships, a reader may suspend his narcissism and engage the poem in an object relation. Second, a reader who permits himself an object relation with a poem may undergo "creative regression" parallel to the poet's, with similar adaptive-maladaptive potential (as described at the beginning under "Some Theoretical Considerations"). And, third, just as the need met by making a poem may be a need for complex object relations, so may readers read poems to fulfill parallel needs.

The reader reads Whitman and his unresolved poems because he seeks a complex object relation which may satisfy an instinctual-like need. As in his object relations with people, a reader experiences the poem within aesthetic and formal boundaries that include periodic "conclusions," "culminations," and "reconciliations," none of which necessarily end or resolve psychological tensions. The reader of "Out of the Cradle" experiences the differentness of Whitman's world as well as the regressions required to enter that world. Having shared Whitman's regressions, the reader may or may not be uneasy (as Chase and I are) about the way in which the period of regression ends. But the fact that the reader survives regression appears to be more important than the fact that the ending is reached by means of an unsatisfactory defense. We must add that "service to the ego" may include the service rendered by engaging in complex object relations if we are to agree that Kris' dictum, "regression in the service of the ego," describes both the creative and recreative processes.

[20] *CRE*, p. 746.

effect of the fusion was to enhance the poet's repression of that part of the Oedipal complex which he could least acknowledge: the wish "to eliminate the jealously hated mother and take her place with the father." The death of Louisa Whitman must have reawakened feelings of guilt and fear of retribution that were as strong as they had been fifty years before. No doubt these feelings were the source of all those phrases which described the maternal sea as "fierce" and "savage."

Consider again the last line of "Out of the Cradle": "The sea whispered me." Does Whitman mean merely that the sea whispered the word "Death" to him? Does he also mean that the sea uttered him—gave birth to him? If the latter, then Whitman must mean that the sea caused him to be mortal, and in this way death actually comes from the sea. Because of what "Out of the Cradle" reveals of Whitman's lingering Oedipal anxieties, it is difficult to believe that the final stanza resolves the poem's psychological tensions. Nor did the poet enhance the sense of resolution by later adding an ambiguous penultimate line, "(Or like some old crone rocking the cradle, swathed in sweet garments, bending aside)."

The final ambiguity of "Out of the Cradle" leaves the reader wondering what order exists in Whitman's world. In the first three editions of *Leaves of Grass*, the poet develops a vision of order oriented to three matters, two of which I will discuss in subsequent chapters (Whitman's a-contextual perceptions of persons and objects in the external world and the various myths about the external world accepted by people as folklore, religion, science, etc.). The third component of Whitman's vision—his largely unconscious identification of elements in the natural world with particular aspects of his private experience—may be described in a way that summarizes much of what this chapter has suggested about reading a Whitman poem:

Fire: usually signifies the poet's sexual drives ("The fire, the sweet hell within"), but it can also be the fire that destroys a ship or forest or home. The implication of the second meaning is that Whitman fears that destruction will result from expressions of sexuality. His usual response to his fears is autoerotic fantasy.

Earth: the "fish-shaped island," the father with whom Whitman finds himself inescapably and uncomfortably identified by virtue of his physical masculinity. The poet's castration anxiety, implied in many poems, may originate in a wish not to resemble the father.

Water: mother, total immersion in which threatens castration—the quenching of the fire—or death by drowning. On the other hand, permitting himself to be "caressed" by the sea in a contact less total than immersion is one of the poet's sources of ecstasy. Best of all is being carried *upon* the sea but safely protected from possible immersion (as in "Crossing Brooklyn Ferry").

Air: the poems Whitman sings, by which his finite dimensions are extended through time and space, implying immortality. Later it will be seen that the poems enable Whitman to enter into "economic" exchanges with the external world, trading poems for actual gratification of needs.

In order for Whitman to make successful poetry, all three components of his myth must function: he must perceive both the internal and external world in order to avoid anaesthesia or incoherence. He knew that he must always be ready to destroy his myth and build it anew; his poetic method must operate according to laws of motion and process. Despite this, he wanted to believe that his myth would ultimately reach a perfected form. We cannot fault his hope eventually to be free from the agony that accompanied explorations of his unconscious. But neither the internal nor the external world could stop changing, as Whitman himself knew all too well. Constant change requires either that explorations be constant also, or that defenses be found against the anxieties change may bring. In the rest of this book we will see how Whitman confronted this dilemma.

2

Leaves of Grass, 1855, 1856

FOUR

A Biography of an Imagination:
II

HAVING examined some of the basic patterns of Whitman's psychological life, and having proposed some techniques for reading Whitman's work, I now turn to the poems with which Whitman began his poetic career.

My first consideration will be the development of Whitman's poetic vocation. Nothing in the first half of Whitman's life foretells that he would ever be regarded as one of the major poets of his century. Quite the reverse, for nothing distinguishes Whitman's early life from the lives of countless other competent nineteenth-century New York journalists. We should recall that Whitman's commitment to journalism was tentative and that the fiction he wrote in late adolescence sometimes betrayed its author's fantasy of his genius, a fantasy that probably inhibited his achievement. All that history tells us about the five years preceding the first *Leaves of Grass* (1850-1855) is that Whitman apparently abandoned journalism about 1851 to work as a carpenter, presumably with his father and brothers.[1] If we seek to know more, we must turn to the poems for information.

---

[1] Allen, *The Solitary Singer*, pp. 134-48, summarizes nearly all that is known about this period in Whitman's life.

Whitman probably did not begin to write poetry in the style of *Leaves of Grass* until a few months before the first edition was printed (July 1855).[2] When we approach the poems of 1855-1856 we may expect to find continued evidence of the fantasy of genius, as well as some clue to the accommodation Whitman made with the fantasy that permitted him to become the bard he had long fancied himself. The bare facts of Whitman's poetic activity between 1855 and 1857 are startling. By early July 1855 Whitman had written at least ten poems, including "Song of Myself." Fourteen months later, by September 1856, he had written at least twenty more poems, including "Crossing Brooklyn Ferry," "Song of the Broad-Axe," and "By Blue Ontario's Shore." By June 1857, eight months later, he had written at least sixty-eight more poems that would eventually be published in the third *Leaves of Grass*. The facts tell us that when Whitman finally found his poetic style the purposelessness that inhibited his early work ended.

The abruptness of Whitman's commitment to so demanding a vocation poses an interesting and important question: what caused the change? Our chief source of information, the poems of 1855-1856, says little about that question, but much about two related issues. These poems enable us to define the main line of Whitman's poetic development and to understand the ideal reader to whom the poems were addressed. If we understand these related issues, we should understand a good deal about Whitman's poetic intentions;

[2] I base this inference (common to many scholars) on a comparison of the style of "A Boston Ballad," known to have been written after June 1854, with the style of the ten new poems of 1855. "A Boston Ballad" is a strong, effectively organized political poem, lacking entirely the regressive, dithyrambic quality of, say, "Song of Myself." The style of "A Boston Ballad" is not repeated in Whitman's later poetry. It therefore appears reasonable to assume that it was sometime after the composition of "A Boston Ballad" that Whitman began in earnest the regressive journeys of discovery that became fundamental to the poetic process of *Leaves of Grass*.

in turn, we should then be able to reconstruct the development that led to his commitment to being a poet.

Whitman's psychological and poetic development follows a line that extends from "Song of Myself" (1855), through "As I Ebb'd" and "Out of the Cradle" (1860), to "When Lilacs Last in the Dooryard Bloom'd" (1865). By the act of writing "Song of Myself" Whitman developed an effective poetic process that enabled him to begin to fulfill the ego ideals evident in his adolescent fiction ("My Boys and Girls," "Lingave's Temptation," and the story of Archie Dean). The act of writing "Lilacs" a decade later ended the process begun in "Song of Myself." In "Lilacs" Whitman conceded that he could not resolve his most important psychological conflicts and would cease trying to confront them. As I have said, Whitman's major poems do not describe psychological events; they *are* the events.

For Whitman, the psychological importance of having written "Song of Myself" is inestimable. It was probably his first, and certainly his most complete, attempt to establish a process by which unconscious material could become available to poetic craftsmanship. Whitman's is an artistic process that does not often lead to an aesthetic resolution of poetic material because his process binds poetic subjects to problematic unconscious material. The psychological conflicts in "Song of Myself" are not resolved, but the artistic process by which Whitman presents the conflicts leads to an extraordinary degree of psychological integrity. The historical truth is that the conflicts underlying "Song of Myself" were never effectively resolved, and the poem's irresolute ending reflects the historical truth. One can even surmise that Whitman's enormous poetic power results from the reader's identification with the unresolved tensions on which the poems rest.

Behind much of "Song of Myself" is a wish to justify lingering infantile desires, especially a fantasy of omnipotence: Whitman imagines becoming God, the "loving bedfellow" who raises the dead and covers continents with the palms of his hands. As we have seen, the interference in infancy with fantasies of omnipotence (by his father, his brothers and sisters, by his mother, by sheer time and growth) is Whitman's unconscious subject in "As I Ebb'd" and "Out of the Cradle." In "As I Ebb'd" the unresponsive paternal island and the fiercely seductive maternal sea overwhelm the poet. When he tries to grasp the meaning of the "wondrous murmuring" that echoes in his mind, he finds a terrifying image symbolizing himself stillborn. The same search for meaning continues in "Out of the Cradle" as Whitman determinedly seeks to understand his sexuality, "the fire, the sweet hell within." When his explorations lead to apparitions of chaos, he tries to fuse the words of the he-bird and the she-ocean, *loved* and *death*, evading rather than resolving the basic conflict. In "Song of Myself," as in "Out of the Cradle" and "As I Ebb'd," Whitman's poetic and psychological explorations lead to the expression of a continuing crisis, rather than to the resolution of a conflict.

Whitman's efforts to deal poetically with his personal conflicts culminate in "Lilacs." In the five years between the fall of 1859 (when "Out of the Cradle" was written) and the spring of 1865, Whitman's private voice disappears from the poems. The poems written just before and during the Civil War make no further attempt to confront the secret of the wondrous murmuring, or the words *loved* and *death*. "Lilacs" symbolically announces the poet's resignation from the battle of the preceding decade, conceding indirectly that his sexual identity will remain forever submerged. He will no longer challenge the unconscious forces he once hoped to tame. In the elegy to Lincoln, Whitman accepts the mantle of good gray poet laureate.

These four great poems delineate the mainstream of Whitman's major work. The rest of the poems arrange themselves in relation to the mainstream according to how much or how little new exploration Whitman can undertake in a given poem. When we approach the poems of 1855-1856, we seek development of psychological patterns present in "Song of Myself." We learn how "To Think of

Time" and "The Sleepers" further explore Whitman's fantasies about death and sexuality, and what "Song of the Broad-Axe" and "By Blue Ontario's Shore" reveal about the development of Whitman's poetic vocation.

But locating the mainstream solves only part of the problem of how to read Whitman's poetry. Between 1855 and 1860 Whitman's inclination to conceive his poetic identity in relation to an ideal imaginary reader facilitated his search for a poetic process. In his personal life and through his poetry, he was trying to recreate the family of his childhood at the time he first thought of himself as father to his brothers and sisters and partner to his mother. His unconscious assumptions about maternal and paternal qualities determined the nature of the ideal reader the poet imagined. He began to define this reader in the preface to the first *Leaves of Grass*:

"The greatest poet has less a marked style and is more the channel of thoughts and things without increase or diminution, and is the free channel of himself. He swears to his art, I will not be meddlesome, I will not have in my writing any elegance or effect or originality to hang in the way between me and the rest like curtains. * * * What I tell I tell for precisely what it is. Let who may exalt or startle or fascinate or sooth[e] I will have purposes as health or heat or snow has and be as regardless of observation. What I experience or portray shall go from my composition without a shred of my composition. You shall stand by my side and look in the mirror with me." (*LG*, 1855, vii.)

The metaphor at the end of this passage betrays the narcissism fundamental to Whitman's poetic intentions. If his subject appears in a mirror, it must be Whitman himself, and the least distorted perception of what the mirror reveals can come only through his eyes. In short, the reader must become identical with the poet in order for the poetry to satisfy the psychological motive behind its creation.

Whitman continually refined his implicit definition of his ideal reader through the writing of the poems of 1855-1856. By the summer of 1859 (in what was to be the third

"Calamus" poem of 1860) he could define his ideal reader more explicitly:

> Who is he that would become my follower?
> Who would sign himself a candidate for my
>   affections? Are you he?
>
> The way is suspicious—the result slow, uncertain,
>   may-be destructive;
> You would have to give up all else—I alone would
>   expect to be your God, sole and exclusive,
> Your novitiate would even then be long
>   and exhausting,
> The whole past theory of your life, and all
>   conformity to the lives around you, would
>   have to be abandoned;
> Therefore release me now, before troubling
>   yourself any further—Let go your hand
>   from my shoulder,
> Put me down, and depart on your way.

✿   ✿   ✿

> Or, if you will, thrusting me beneath your clothing,
> Where I may feel the throbs of your heart, or
>   rest upon your hip,
> Carry me when you go forth over land or sea;
> For thus, merely touching you, is enough—is best,
> And thus, touching you, would I silently sleep
>   and be carried eternally.

I will return to this passage later in my discussion of "Calamus." For the time being I will limit myself to describing the deeply narcissistic element suffusing Whitman's idealized world, the "vast similitude" of "Clef Poem." By the creation of an imaginary ideal reader, Whitman tries to relieve the loneliness inherent in the narcissistic world. In "Calamus," loneliness was to become Whitman's explicit subject, a loneliness unrelieved by ordinary human company. In an analogous context Erik Erikson describes the demand made by patients of their psychotherapist, who must be "as immediate and as close, as exclusive and as circumspect, as generous and as self-denying, a counterplayer as only a mother of an infant child can be."[3] What Whitman sought from his ideal reader was something very like the psychotherapist Erikson describes or, rather, the lost idealized mother mourned by both Erikson's patients and by Whitman.

In Chapter 3 I demonstrated that to Whitman the poetic process had some of the same goals as the psychotherapeutic process, since the poet seeks more effective defenses against anxiety, a clearer and fuller sense of reality, an increased unity between his conscious and unconscious lives. In the major poems of 1855 and 1856 Whitman reaches for these goals, and it is to these poems that we now turn.

[3] *Young Man Luther* (New York, 1958), p. 103.

FIVE

"Song of Myself"

LENGTH, stylistic and psychological complexity, and lack of apparent logical structure combine to make "Song of Myself" exceptionally difficult to read. In the interest of clarity I have divided the discussion that follows into three parts, each of which is focused on one of the poem's principal motifs: the identifications Whitman makes with people and things he perceives, the several cathartic episodes, and the role Whitman defines for the democratic bard—that is, himself. By emphasizing the poem's psychological patterns I intend to link "Song of Myself" to the inferences made about Whitman's life in this study and to persuade my reader that attempts by most preceding critics to interpret the poem by comparing it to philosophical systems miss the mark.[1] As Edwin Miller has said, "Song of Myself" is indeed

[1] Among numerous readings of "Song of Myself," see the following: Roy Harvey Pearce, *The Continuity of American Poetry* (Princeton, 1961), pp. 69-83; Waskow, *Whitman, Explorations in Form*, pp. 156-89; Chari, *Whitman in the Light of Vedantic Mysticism*, pp. 121-27; Carl F. Strauch, "The Structure of Walt Whitman's 'Song of Myself,'" *English Journal*, 27 (1938), 597-607; Chase, *Walt Whitman Reconsidered*, pp. 58-98; Allen, *The Solitary Singer*, pp. 157-64; James E. Miller, Jr., *A Critical Guide to "Leaves of Grass,"* pp. 6-35, and *Walt Whitman* (New York, 1962), pp. 92-97. Of these, Waskow, Chari, Allen, and James Miller seek to interpret "Song of Myself" by means of philosophical or spiritual analogy, while Pearce

88

a coherent poem.[2] Yet its coherence rests in psycho-logic, rather than intellectual logic. "Song of Myself" evolves not around concepts and philosophical ideas, but around the poet's shifting and ambivalent attitudes toward ideas and concepts, and toward his relation to external objects and internal imagoes. Since Whitman's attitudes are partly unconscious, we must regard the process of the poem as a journey of discovery, taking the bald assertions that occur throughout as veiled questions asked by Whitman of himself.[3] After beginning in a mood of celebration, he soon

---

and Chase tend to equate Whitman's poetic intention with his myth of democracy. My disagreement with the assumptions or procedures of these scholars does not blind me to the excellence of many of their perceptions, especially those of Chase, Pearce, and Waskow.

[2] Only Miller, *A Psychological Journey*, pp. 85-114, and, to a lesser extent, Chase, recognize the ultimate irresolution of "Song of Myself."

[3] What I believe to have been Whitman's mental state in the period when "Song of Myself" was composed has been described, in a similar context, by Erikson in *Young Man Luther*, pp. 99-103. Erikson says that many persons who delay making vocational commitments experience a period of "moratorium," the characteristics of which include "identity diffusion," a "tortuous self-consciousness," an inability to work coherently or consistently, and a rejection of society's requirement to "adjust":

"It is as if the young person were waiting for some event, or some person, to sweep him out of this state by promising him, instead of the reassuring routine and practice of most men's time, a vast utopian view that would make the very disposition of time worthwhile. . . .

"Most of all, this kind of person must shy away from intimacy. Any physical closeness, with either sex, arouses at the same time both an impulse to merge with the other person and a fear of losing autonomy and individuation. In fact, there is a sense of bisexual diffusion which makes such a young person unsure about how to touch another person sexually or affectionately. The contrast between the exalted sexual fusion of his autoerotic dreams and the complete sense of isolation in the presence of the other sex is catastrophic."

In *Leaves of Grass* Whitman evinces many of the characteristics Erikson lists. Whitman seeks a "vast utopian view" (for example the "vast similitude" of "Clef Poem"); his identity is diffused; and his self-consciousness tortures him. As I demonstrated in Part One, threats of intimacy conflict with a catastrophic sense of isolation, leading to "bisexual diffusion." For Whitman, the poetic process discovers every imaginable self-doubt; he ends with an utterly ambiguous image of himself stopping "somewhere" to wait for his reader. The development of "Song of Myself" occurs in the changes of attitude toward recurring issues and ideas. The changes mark Whitman's growth. We may be misled (as I believe Chase and Pearce are) if we assume that Whitman's ultimate intention was to fix for himself an unchanging sense of order, because his poetic method taught him to value the process of poetic exploration as much as any vision of order yielded by the exploratory journeys. By writing "Song of Myself" Whitman learned that psychological fluidity may be more viable than any particular set of defenses.

I. *Identity and Identifications*

One of the fundamental problems for readers of "Song of Myself" is the poet's predilection for identifying himself with persons and things in the world around him.[4] I believe that these identifications lead us to the basic dilemma of the poem, the poet's ambivalent attitudes toward conflicting views of his world. Whitman may commit himself either to a mystical act of faith or else to a rational, psychological, and personal exploration of both the external world and his fantasy world. The impulse to make identifications derives from the poet' reluctance to confront this choice.

Whitman's tendency toward identification dominates the latter portions of section thirty-three and continues through section thirty-seven. The first clear identification is a good example:

---

became a means by which "severe regression to a play with nothingness" could be systematized and "experimental, an adventure in reaching rock bottom to find something firm to stand on" (Erikson, p. 104).

[4] In a different form, my discussion of the identifications in "Song of Myself" was presented orally to the meeting of the Learned Societies of Canda, June 1968, Calgary; that paper was subsequently printed in *Walt Whitman Review*, 15 (December, 1969), 223-30.

I am a free companion . . . . I bivouac by
    invading watchfires.

I turn the bridegroom out of bed and stay with
    the bride myself,
And tighten her all night to my thighs and lips.

The reader does not accept this report as objective truth
any more than he believes, in the subsequent lines, that the
poet's voice is also the wife's voice or that it is really the
poet's body that is fetched up "dripping and drowned."
These things occur in a context of fantasy as Whitman projects himself into the perceptions and emotions of other
people.

The passage just quoted indicates a radical change from
Whitman's earlier attempts to perceive and understand
other people. Previously he stood apart, witnessed and
waited, peered from above at the infant in its cradle, at the
lovers walking up the hill, or at the suicide sprawled on the
floor (section eight). But later in the poem he lowers the
barrier between himself and others. Apparently reversing
himself, he tries to become the person he sees.

His reversal raises two crucial questions: What do the
identifications imply about the poet's attitude toward the
people with whom he identifies? What relation exists between the poet's identity and the identifications he makes?
I will approach these questions indirectly.

In section thirty-three, a few lines beyond the passage
quoted above, the poet identifies with a slave:

I am the hounded slave . . . . I wince at the bite
    of the dogs,
Hell and despair are upon me . . . . crack and again
    crack the marksmen,
I clutch the rails of the fence . . . . my gore dribs
    thinned with the ooze of my skin,
I fall on the weeds and stones,
The riders spur their unwilling horses
    and haul close,

> They taunt my dizzy ears . . . . they beat me
> violently over the head with their whip-stocks.

The episode fantasized here seems to be another version of an encounter first described in section ten, but Whitman's attitude toward the slave changes from section ten to section thirty-three. In the earlier episode the poet maintained a cautious distance between himself and the "runaway slave":

> The runaway slave came to my house and
> stopped outside,
> I heard his motions crackling the twigs
> of the woodpile,
> Through the swung half-door of the kitchen I saw
> him limpsey and weak,
> And went where he sat on a log, and led him in
> and assured him,
> And brought water and filled a tub for his sweated
> body and bruised feet,
> And gave him a room that entered from my own,
> and gave him some coarse clean clothes,
> And remember perfectly well his revolving eyes
> and his awkwardness,
> And remember putting plasters on the galls of his
> neck and ankles;
> He staid with me a week before he was recuperated
> and passed north,
> I had him sit next me at table . . . . my firelock
> leaned in the corner.

The juxtaposition of the poet's declaration of tolerant acceptance with the portrait of a rolling-eyed, gawky minstrel unwittingly implies that Whitman accepts this man only categorically, as a slave.

The attitude here is generally typical of Whitman's tenuous relations with the people mentioned in the first half of "Song of Myself." The identification in section thirty-three, therefore, seems to indicate a general reversal of attitude. Whitman rejects the isolation in which he has held himself and substitutes for isolation a total, if momentary, merging of his own sensibility with the sensibilities of others whom he has previously kept at great distance. In section thirty-three he becomes as fully empathic as he has previously been distant. But a major question remains: Does identification with someone necessarily imply an uncategorical acceptance of another human being? For in section thirty-three no less than in section ten the poet is more preoccupied with his own sympathies than with the slave. In section thirty-three the slave still exists only as an idea by which the poet measures his humanity.

If "Song of Myself" is intended to represent a love affair between the poet and the world, the quality of the love must be examined. We may wonder whether Whitman can love anyone else when his feelings about himself are in doubt. At the beginning of "Song of Myself" he boasts,

> I celebrate myself,
> And what I assume you shall assume,
> For every atom belonging to me as
> good belongs to you.

Whitman's unconscious ambivalence toward himself is manifest in the ambiguity of the third line. If the atoms that belong "as good" to others as to himself comprise his body, it is fair to ask who is the *me* to whom the atoms belong? The *me* must be separate from the body, but if the *me* is the soul, the soul must dominate the body. If Whitman intends a mystical assertion of faith, he must soon run afoul of his own conviction that body and soul are equally important. What begins as a celebration of the self becomes a troublesome question: who and what *am* I?

In response to this question the poet sets himself "apart from the pulling and hauling." By so doing, he apparently hopes to discover whatever uniqueness may define the "me myself." Although separation may engender valuable introspection, it can finally lead only to further isolation that inhibits (among many things) communication through poetry. Whitman's attraction to isolation inhibits the love he wants between himself and others. One might predict that Whitman's ambivalence will show itself in dramatic reversals, "Tiresian" detachment giving way to identifications.

The process of identification enables Whitman to express his feelings directly and with power. In early parts of the poem, Whitman wanders among the debris that clutters his memory, temporarily abandoning the categories by which people ordinarily give order to such data. He perceives, in relative isolation, things that are separated from the feelings normally attached to them. Apart from a few striking passages, the tone of the first twenty-five sections remains curiously flat, as if the poet could not connect his feelings to things recalled. All this changes, however, in section twenty-six, where Whitman deliberately tries to merge his ego with his unconscious (intimations of which previously came to him accidentally and symbolically as day- or night-dreams, or during immersion in the sea). By this time the poet has developed, through preliminary introspection, enough courage to confront his previously unconscious feelings, and in the orgasmic sections twenty-six to twenty-nine he expresses such feelings. Nevertheless, whatever skill for expression Whitman may have developed remains tentative. Such skill depends on his ideal of uniting his conscious and unconscious worlds. By section thirty-three he has only begun to assimilate into consciousness and to relate to his feelings the images discovered within the isolation of his unconscious.

In a rare moment of explicit synthesis, Whitman bridges three episodes that have not previously seemed related:

> Swift wind! Space! My Soul! Now I know it
>   is true what I guessed at;
> What I guessed when I loafed on the grass,
> What I guessed while I lay alone in my bed . . . .
>   and again as I walked the beach under
>   the paling stars of the morning.

For the first time, the poet learns that the orgasmic moment recorded in section five ("when I loafed on the grass") parallels the visitation of the loving bedfellow in section three ("While I lay alone in my bed"), as well as the experience of sections twenty-one and twenty-two, when he resigned himself to the sea. To account for these cathartic experiences the poet asserts his faith in his own apotheosis:

> My ties and ballasts leave me . . . . I travel I
>   sail . . . . my elbows rest in the sea-gaps,
> I skirt the sierras . . . . my palms cover continents,
> I am afoot with my vision.

His act of faith leads Whitman to the identifications of section thirty-three and to a series of misunderstandings he must later reject. The orgasmic moments seem at first to be mystical communions with something like Emerson's Oversoul, which prove the poet's relatedness to all other persons and his transcendence over space and time, death and mortality. But the mystical act of faith requires the permanent obliteration of all doubt and confusion. Identifications bring Whitman new doubts that prove even more threatening than his previous isolation.

When the poet merges with someone else, he can momentarily escape the mortal limitations of time and space. But, as Howard J. Waskow has also noticed, the identification carries with it the burden of the other man's suffering and pain.[5] Since every threat to anyone else is a powerful symbolic threat to the poet, it seems to him no exaggeration to say "No doubt I have died myself ten thousand times before." With every death he has witnessed, he has suffered the terror and helplessness of the dying person. Where the identifications begin almost as boasts of the poet's largeness of sensibility, they soon become descriptions of intolerable terror. After insisting that "Agonies are one of my changes of garments," and after suffering with the mashed fireman, Whitman discovers that the resuscitated "Distant and dead

[5] Pp. 178-79.

95

* * * / show as the dial or move as the hands of me . . . . and I am the clock myself." The clock symbolizes Whitman's painful awareness of his mortality. His life's movement through time delimits his faith. In further efforts to escape time, Whitman projects himself back into history, becoming the "old artillerist," then fantastically describing the battle of Goliad and the "oldfashioned frigate-fight." But he cannot long deceive himself by such blatant evasions, and in section thirty-seven he resumes the more subtle tactic of identifying with prisoners in a jail:

> For me the keepers of convicts shoulder their
> carbines and keep watch,
> It is I let out in the morning and barred at night.

He suffers with patients in a hospital:

> Not a cholera patient lies at the last gasp, but I also
> lie at the last gasp,
> My face is ash-colored, my sinews gnarl . . . . away
> from me people retreat.

And he begs in the street:

> Askers embody themselves in me, and I am
> embodied in them.

In this series of identifications, the threats attending the process balance the illusion of closeness to others. At last the poet has had enough and brings this phase of the poem to a close:

> Somehow I have been stunned. Stand back!
> Give me a little time beyond my cuffed head and
> slumbers and dreams and gaping,
> I discover myself on a verge of the usual mistake.

The "usual mistake" is not only to engage in the process of identification, but to do so in an effort to escape mortality. It has brought him the cathartic feeling that he can rise "extatic through all, and sweep with the true gravitation, / The whirling and whirling is elemental within me." But his efforts have also led him to suffer the cuffed head (while identifying with the slave), as threatening a situation as the half-aliveness of his previous isolation ("slumbers, dreams, gaping"). As Whitman discovers the inadequacies of both these defenses (a "usual mistake"), he reaches a new understanding: that his sense of identity depends on his acceptance of mortality's limitations. He cannot begin to live until he has accepted the fact that he will die.

With awe he discovers more and more implications of his usual mistake:

> That I could forget the mockers and insults!
> That I could forget the trickling tears and the blows
> of the bludgeons and hammers!
> That I could look with a separate look on my own
> crucifixion and bloody crowning!

Isolation and identifications both deny the self Whitman wants to celebrate. To identify with Christ requires a separation within his self between experiences, his feelings about experience, and the expression of feelings. He witnessed his "own crucifixion and bloody crowning" with a "separate look," the observing part failing to recognize the implications of either the action or the separation. He uses the language of the Christian resurrection to assert a personal and psychological resurrection.[6] He rejects his forgetfulness, the disunity in himself which led to his previous identification with Christ:

> I remember . . . . I resume the overstaid fraction,
> The grave of rock multiplies what has been confided
> to it . . . . or to any graves,
> The corpses rise . . . . the gashes heal . . . . the
> fastenings roll away.

To forget was to reject awareness, a rejection he justified as Christlike forgiveness: forgive and forget. But the pretense to Christlikeness is abandoned when the poet chooses

---

[6] Waskow, p. 180, comes closer to perceiving this passage as I do than any other previous critic.

97

the more precise word, *forget*. By "remember[ing]" he repudiates his former rejection of awareness, bending now to assimilate what he has learned through isolation and identifications. He calls together the "overstaid fraction," the long-standing division within himself. He recognizes that to identify with Christ is to share Christ's grave, which "multiplies what has been confided to it." That is, because Christ died for all men (and because the poet identifies with all the dying), every grave symbolically threatens death. But the narrator's growing awareness of his own mortality suggests a way to avoid the newly discovered peril. By conceding that he is not Christ he escapes morbidity. When the threats no longer terrify him, corpses rise, gashes heal, fastenings roll away. The example of Christ's metaphysical resurrection gives way to desire for psychological liberation.

The wish for liberation reverses the ancient Christian paradox in which one becomes free by enthrallment to God (as in Donne's fourteenth sonnet). Whitman's new paradox says that to attempt to escape mortality is imprisoning and to accept finiteness may open the prison. Compare the next to last stanza of section thirty-eight to an analogous passage at the beginning of section thirty-three. The earlier passage follows an attempt to leap out of time and space.

> My ties and ballasts leave me . . . . I travel I
>   sail . . . . my elbows rest in the sea-gaps,
> I skirt the sierras . . . . my palms cover continents,
> I am afoot with my vision.

At first Whitman did not distinguish between his "vision" and his physical self. The physical became metaphysical after the denial of mortality. Later, the poet returns to the objective:

> I troop forth replenished with supreme power, one
>   of an average unending procession,
> We walk the roads * * *
> Inland and by seacoast and boundary lines . . . . and
>   we pass the boundary lines.

Our swift ordinances are on their way over the
　　whole earth,
The blossoms we wear in our hats are the growth
　　of two thousand years.

Having rejected identification with God, with Christ, or
with other men, Whitman settles for joining the "average
unending procession" of mortals, subject to the bio-organic
cycle of death and chemical regeneration. These finite be-
ings fill the earth, not with a single gigantic form, but with
their individual dying bodies.

Yet if Whitman seems to acknowledge his mortality in
section thirty-eight, the impulses beneath his previous
denials linger on. Since the insight of section thirty-eight
has taught him that neither separation from others nor
identification with them can solve existential problems, he
changes the form of his search. At the beginning he sought
identity negatively: these things he is not. In the middle, he
tried to identify with specific others, or rather with his
images of specific others. After section thirty-eight Whitman seeks to create imaginatively an identity for himself
that derives partly from the grab-bag of myths and ideas
that constituted his higher education: some noble savage,
some *Übermensch*, some Emerson, some Orientalisms, some
evolutionary biology, some Yankee pragmatism. The chief
importance of these ideas and archetypes lies in what they
contribute psychologically to the poetic identity emerging
at the end of "Song of Myself."[7]

[7] In later years, when Whitman thought of himself as "America's
bard" and was trying to educate himself about philosophy and the
arts, he wrote a great many biographical notes about famous bards
and philosophers (printed in *The Complete Writings*, IX, New York,
1902, *passim*). Whitman appears to have abstracted encyclopedia
articles about Shakespeare, Spenser, Kant, Hegel, and others. The
notes on philosophical subjects so assiduously avoid subtleties that
they reveal practically no substantive interest in philosophical thought.
Whitman was more interested to learn that Fichte "was a fervid and
telling speaker" than what his ideas were or how they differed from
Kant's. The quality of these notes appears to have been overlooked
by many of the scholars who seek philosophical analogies.

As I have said, Whitman's turn from identifications does not signal an end to the old needs and conflicts. He still wants to define himself in ways that will gratify his tendencies toward narcissism and megalomania. The idea of the *Übermensch* justifies precisely these tendencies. To Whitman, Emerson and the Orienda proclaim a narcissistic world without end. But something in Whitman will not be wholly satisfied by a mystical assertion. The possessiveness implicit in narcissistic relations is rejected when Whitman finds himself a "teacher of athletes." The mind that does not despise priests nor reject science tries to create a world in which oppositions—all oppositions—may remain suspended. Although such a world exists in the unconscious, conflicts arise when the ego perceives the object world. The mere acknowledgment in section forty-eight of irreconcilable oppositions seems to lead Whitman to greater tranquility than he has previously known in "Song of Myself." The last five sections summarize contradictory appeals and tendencies in a tone that suggests that by one means or another the poet hopes to survive, the former ideal of apotheosis having been moved aside to accommodate his enlarged sense of mortality.

II. *Catharsis*

To grasp the psychological integrity of "Song of Myself," the reader must be attentive to the way the catalogs in the poem change between the beginning and the end. At the beginning Whitman organizes his catalogs according to the logic of free association, mingling popular myths, his objective perceptions, and his unconscious sense of himself and his place in the object world. In the last phase of the poem (sections thirty-nine to fifty-two) Whitman reorganizes the material from the earlier catalogs to gain a more coherent and orderly sense of experience. Yet, as I have said, Whitman's impulse to seek life's grand design is balanced against a willingness to let disorder prevail. From this balance of forces comes the poet's recognition that the exploratory fluidity of the poetic process may itself be as viable an axis

for life as any particular idea of order. The cathartic episodes in "Song of Myself" have as much to do with
the change in Whitman's intentions as the identifications
previously examined.

The first cathartic episode occurs in section two, when
the poet's intuition of his physical relation to the natural
world leads to a brief fantasy of autoerotic sensuality.

> My respiration and inspiration . . . . the beating of
>   my heart . . . . the passing of blood and air
>   through my lungs,
> The sniff of green leaves and dry leaves, and of the
>   shore and darkcolored searocks, and of hay in
>   the barn,
> The sound of the belched words of my voice . . . .
>   words loosed to the eddies of the wind,
> A few light kisses . . . . a few embraces . . . . a
>   reaching around of arms * * *

Before the fantasy can reach a genital stage it becomes
diffuse:

> The play of shine and shade on the trees as the
>   supple boughs wag,
> The delight alone or in the rush of the streets, or
>   along the fields and hillsides,
> The feeling of health . . . . the full-noon trill . . . . the
>   song of me rising from bed and meeting the sun.

The sensual terms in which Whitman expresses this experience reveal his conscious and unconscious attitudes toward the experience. The poet assumes a role which is profoundly passive. Cathartic sensuality is basically regressive,
resembling an infant's earliest experiences of being held,
petted, kissed by his mother. The regressive impulse underlying Whitman's cathartic experiences parallels a conscious
poetic theme: the attempt to return to his origins and find
a new way to understand himself.

But another aspect of Whitman's "mystical" fantasy is
less conscious. Fantasy tends to grant a sense of partial sat-

isfaction to the wishes that first led to the fantasy. In fantasy Whitman sees himself attuned to nature; as his corporeal boundaries extend outward by means of the air he breathes, nature caresses his whole body. Once more he has found a way to imagine himself cradled by the universe, marked with that special sense of grace which defines infantile symbiosis. Fantasies give momentary reassurance against the doubts and dissatisfactions that elsewhere trouble him. We cannot doubt the sincerity with which he feels his moment of security, but we may doubt the durability of this defense against anxiety.

The next cathartic experience occurs late in section three, preceded by an assertion of happiness:

> I am satisfied . . . . I see, dance, laugh, sing;
> As God comes a loving bedfellow and sleeps at my
> side all night and close on the peep of the day,
> And leaves for me baskets covered with white towels
> bulging the house with their plenty * * *

The narrator's passivity transforms itself into femininity when the poet specifies his lover. Instead of nature, generalized, it is God who "comes," leaving the poet pregnant and "satisfied."[8] Cathartic experiences give but a fleeting

---

[8] Edwin Miller, *A Psychological Journey*, p. 90, has also noticed this image of pregnancy, that is, that the house symbolizes a body which is "bulging" after the loving bedfellow's visitation. In his discussion of Whitman's sexual imagery, James Miller notes several analogies between Whitman's images and sexual symbols described by Freud (*Walt Whitman*, pp. 173-74). Miller does not mention that throughout *The Interpretation of Dreams* Freud adduces evidence supporting his interpretation that houses in dreams often symbolize the dreamer's body. Freud does not mention "baskets," but he does say that "Boxes, cases, chests, cupboards and ovens represent the uterus" (*Standard Edition*, v, p. 354). As early as Shakespeare's time, "come" is used to mean sexual emission (*Much Ado*, 5:2, 23-29). If, as I believe, Whitman recorded an actual dream in section three of "Song of Myself," Freud's remarks on dream symbolism tend to confirm the interpretations by Edwin Miller and by me.

sense of satisfaction. Whitman must decide whether to accept the burden of his pregnancy or to abort:

> Shall I postpone my acceptation and realization and
>   scream at my eyes,
> That they turn from gazing after and down the road,
> And forthwith cipher and show me to a cent,
> Exactly the contents of one, and exactly the contents
>   of two, and which is ahead?

Pregnancy apparently symbolizes an opportunity to turn away from everyday business to something else, the journey "down the road" that represents an explorative venture into the unconscious. That Whitman sees himself as having a choice suggests a recognition that he may discipline and exploit his constitutional tendency toward auto-hypnosis, and that by evoking and then examining such experiences he may approach the goals he set forth at the beginning of the poem. What is required is nothing less than a general change in the mode of his life. He must abandon the world of ciphering, "pulling and hauling," and give himself over to loafing at his ease.

Whitman pledges to "witness and wait" and makes another declaration of faith:

> I believe in you my soul . . . . the other I am must
>   not abase itself to you,
> And you must not be abased to the other.

As before, the declaration seems to precipitate an influx of sensuality:

> I mind how we lay in June, such a transparent
>   summer morning;
> You settled your head athwart my hips and gently
>   turned over upon me,
> And parted the shirt from my bosom-bone, and
>   plunged your tongue to my barestript heart,
> And reached till you felt my beard, and reached
>   till you held my feet.

103

The fantasy of oral sexuality recalls to the reader not only the coming of God, the "loving bedfellow," but also the cradling experience of section two. The experience of section five is "oral" rather than "genital"[9] and therefore more regressive than the fantasy in section three (in accord with the poet's new intention to let himself go backward in order to recapture his origins). As before, the sense of ecstasy evaporates, leaving section five to trail off into partial incoherence.

Apparently Whitman begins to realize that cathartic experiences, by themselves, will not resolve his conflicts nor answer his questions. At any rate, the tone shifts after section five; the tone of the child's questions and the poet's associative answers is slightly more analytical. This mode of questions and answers continues through section seven, but in sections eight, nine, and ten the poet turns his attention outward, recalling things he has seen and experiences he has had. He makes little effort to interpret or evaluate his memories until he recalls the episode of the runaway slave, which he develops more fully than preceding memories. We may only guess at the origin of the events Whitman recalls. Had he been in the "far West" he might have seen the trapper marry the red girl; had a slave come to his home he would have dressed the wounds.

The imaginary nature of these "memories" accounts for the otherwise inexplicable movement from the tale of the runaway slave to the celebrated rape of the twenty-eight young men by the promiscuous and "richly drest" lady "aft the blinds of the window." In sections eight to ten Whitman seems to develop a technique for exploring fantasies, the first result of which is the "poem" of the twenty-eight young men. Because Whitman begins to value the processes of his art as much as the ends he hopes to achieve, he can make

[9] In the psychoanalytic theory of personal evolution, the "oral" stage is the first phase of libidinal and ego development; "genital" refers to an ideal of conflict-free maturity. I use "genital" loosely in this sentence of my text to refer to adult, rather than infant, sexuality. For an epigenetic model of psychosexual development, see Erik Erikson, *Childhood and Society* (New York, 1963), pp. 48-108.

this splendid poem. Section eleven is a superbly realized psychological penetration into sexual frustration and fantasy: it is a fantasy about fantasy. Like the poet himself, the lady confines her sexual experience to her imagination, her fantasy giving her the satisfaction implied by the last lines:

> The young men float on their backs, their white
>   bellies swell to the sun . . . . they do not ask who
>   seizes fast to them,
> They do not know who puffs and declines with
>   pendant and bending arch,
> They do not think whom they souse with spray.

The lady seems to be a manifestation of the imago that came to Whitman in the night, lay with him on the grass, and nursed the wounds of the slave (that is, she symbolizes a combination of instinctual drives and superego controls). The projection of the cathartic experience onto the lady indicates a new mode that will later be central: catharsis prepares the way for the identifications that will dominate sections thirty-three through thirty-eight. Section eleven seems anomalous in its context chiefly because it occurs before Whitman can consciously understand its relation to other internal processes. In his early cathartic moments he feels both ecstasy and terror at finding a void inside himself. He accidentally discovers the void when the child asks him about the grass, for his answers fill nothingness with meanings. The catalogs of things and experiences that follow section six are further attempts to find meaning and structure. He must overcome the doubts of daytime and nighttime before he can proceed on his journey to explore the insights afforded by catharsis.

In sections twenty to twenty-one Whitman makes a series of abstract statements intended to define the role he wants to create for himself: "I know I am deathless * * * I know I am august * * * I am the poet of the body, / And I am the poet of the soul * * * I am the poet of the woman the same as the man * * * I am he that walks with the tender and growing night;/ I call to the earth and sea half-held by the night." The role he wants to play must not only enhance his ego ideals and renew his declaration of metaphysical faith, it must also lead him to catharsis. In sections twenty-one to twenty-two Whitman projects himself into a symbolic love affair with the maternal sea, an unmistakable though disguised Oedipal fantasy. In this respect the episode differs from earlier cathartic experiences in its metaphorical form and in the extent to which the poet initiates catharsis. Previously he has believed himself wholly passive, but now he declares that he and the sea "must have a turn together . . . . I undress." Similarly, in earlier fantasies when he called the lover "God" or "soul," the sensuality of the experience symbolized mystical intimacy. Now he can explore sensuality with less emphasis on making it stand for something else. Finally, the previously disguised threats of death related to Oedipal fantasy are now explicit as he perceives the "Sea of unshovelled and always-ready graves." Whitman had presumed death to be an extension of life, but after section six the presumption no longer comes easily. Through all these changes it is apparent that catharsis increasingly provides a release of sensuality. As Whitman becomes more active, he begins to relate his poetic vocation to sensual impulses long denied or disguised.

In section twenty-four Whitman begins to define for himself a new role as medium for "long dumb voices":

> Through me forbidden voices,
> Voices of sexes and lusts . . . . voices veiled, and I
>   remove the veil,
> Voices indecent by me clarified and transfigured.

Here is a paradox central to transcendentalism. The poet plays a role Emerson called *active*: he makes himself a vehicle for the expression of universal or archetypal thoughts. It is an *active* choice to be passive. Ahab may choose to run unswerving on "grooved" rails, but Whitman must be free at any moment to jump the tracks and ramble wherever his fancy leads. Whitman's new conception of the poet's role will prove unsatisfactory when he perceives the threat to his identity implied by merging. The conflict between speaking for others and speaking for himself becomes apparent in the late portions of section twenty-five when Whitman begins to argue with himself:

> My voice goes after what my eyes cannot reach * * *
>
> Speech is the twin of my vision . . . . it is unequal
> to measure itself.
>
> It provokes me forever,
> It says sarcastically, Walt, you understand enough
> . . . . why don't you let it out then? * * *
>
> My final merit I refuse you . . . . I refuse putting
> from me the best I am.
>
>   *   *   *
>
> Encompass worlds but never try to encompass me,
> I crowd your noisiest talk by looking toward you.

Since speech threatens self-betrayal, silence may be the best course. Section twenty-six, which begins the most powerful and complex cathartic experience in the poem, opens with a promise to be silent and only perceive:

> I think I will do nothing for a long time but listen,
> And accrue what I hear into myself . . . . and let
> sounds contribute toward me.

In its immediate context, such a decision requires courage. The previous fantasies, the carefully distant relations with other people, and the intense exploration of an inner world betoken a general withdrawal from the world, one motive for which is to protect the poet against his fear of intimacy. He declares he will abandon his defenses (more or less specifically described in subsequent lines) and let himself feel.

The orgasmic experience developed in the next sixty-one lines has an extraordinary coenesthetic power. Whitman feels himself overwhelmed the moment his defenses relax:

The sentries desert every other part of me,
They have left me helpless to a red marauder,
They all come to the headland to witness and assist
    against me.

I am given up by traitors;
I talk wildly . . . . I have lost my wits . . . . I and
    nobody else am the greatest traitor,
I went myself first to the headland . . . . my own
    hands carried me there.

The last phrase describes an autoerotic orgasm to which the music—with the help of his hands—has led him. In his allegorical description, his senses focus exclusively on his genitals ("the headland"); his blood (a "red marauder") conspires with his senses to lead to an erection and orgasm. He need not go far to reach the object of his love:

Blind loving wrestling touch! Sheathed hooded
    sharptoothed touch!
Did it make you ache so leaving me?

Parting tracked by arriving . . . . perpetual payment
    of the perpetual loan,
Rich showering rain, and recompense richer
    afterward.

Sprouts take and accumulate . . . . stand by the curb
    prolific and vital,
Landscapes projected masculine full-sized
    and golden.

It is his own sense of touch he loves, as clear an example of narcissistic autoerotism as we may hope to find. Having sought to engage the external world and having accordingly relaxed his "sentries," the poet is overwhelmed by sensations and flooded by all the anxieties that originally led him to repress his sexuality. At the moment of panic he short-circuits the original process, and by abruptly transforming the metaphor of his "blind loving wrestling touch" into a less threatening landscape, he wards off the threat of actual sexual relations and reverts to masturbation.

This is the most powerful cathartic experience in "Song of Myself." When catharsis occurs in later portions of the poem, it always comes in a more highly organized and integrated context (as when he feels himself able to raise the dead or buoy up the drowning). Eventually, in "Song of Myself," at least, a more placid sense of well-being will replace the need for ecstasy. Perhaps Whitman dared go no closer to loss of control. At such moments in the rest of "Song of Myself" he convenes defenses that enable him to emerge from his unconscious when engulfment so total threatens him. The sexuality of such experiences would later be embedded in metaphors that did not oblige him to confront the roots of conflict. Like the process of identification, catharsis contributes to the ambivalence that determines the ending of "Song of Myself."

III. *The Bardic Role*

The conflicting impulses toward passivity and activity underlying the transcendental idea of the poetic process correspond to Whitman's experience of catharsis. A similar correspondence exists with the psychoanalytic theory of the artistic process described at the beginning of Chapter 1. The artist's ego becomes "passive," relaxing its defenses to merge with the id; yet the ego may retain enough integrity to survive its engulfment in the unconscious either with its old defenses intact, or with new defenses formed, to reengage the object world. Whitman's ego survived its engulfment with most of its former defenses neither weakened nor enhanced, with the exception that the experience of engulfment now threatens him less. If on one level the composition of "Song of Myself" does not result in the resolution of unconscious conflicts, on another level it yields the poetic process by which *Leaves of Grass* was to be made. From Whitman's subjective viewpoint, "Song of Myself" ends with a mixed sense of triumph that its author has proved

109

himself a poet and of failure because existential facts continue to evoke neurotic anxieties.

In section thirty-eight Whitman confronts and seems to reject his ideal of apotheosis. Yet the seeming acceptance of mortality is belied almost immediately. In section thirty-nine he recalls his promise in section twenty-four to be "a kosmos" and decides to be the "friendly and flowing savage": "Is he waiting for civilization or past it and mastering it? * * * Wherever he goes men and women accept and desire him." His behaviour is "lawless as snow-flakes . . . . words simple as grass . . . . uncombed head and laughter and naivete":

> Slowstepping feet and the common features, and
>   the common modes and emanations,
> They descend in new forms from the tips of
>   his fingers,
> They are wafted with the odor of his body or breath
>   . . . . they fly out of the glance of his eyes.

In another reversal, Whitman tries again to escape mortality and justify existence. Attuned to nature's laws if not to man's, untroubled by internal conflicts, the savage may create new means to express a new life.

In section forty, Whitman the "savage" feels the old exaltation of infant megalomania; he condescends to the sun (which cannot penetrate beneath surfaces) and to the inarticulate earth (which cannot ask its question). Yet even in exaltation the poet himself cannot articulate how he likes "Man or woman," what is in him or in them, what "pinings" he has and "the pulse of my nights and days." The compulsion to justify existence returns again, stronger than ever. Although he has rejected Christ's martyrdom, he still wants to raise the dead "with resistless will," to fill with his breath the impotent and "loose in the knees," to start "bigger and nimbler babes" on "women fit for conception": "This day I am jetting the stuff of far more arrogant republics." To all those dying:

> I dilate you with tremendous breath . . . . I buoy
> you up;
> Every room of the house do I fill with an armed
> force . . . . lovers of me, bafflers of graves:
> Sleep! I and they keep guard all night;
> Not doubt, not decease shall dare to lay finger
> upon you,
> I have embraced you, and henceforth possess you
> to myself,
> And when you rise in the morning you will find
> what I tell you is so.

It is as if he has now become the "loving bedfellow" that impregnated him in section three and started him off on this journey. Who the people are that he will save, "that is not important to me,/ You can do nothing and be nothing but what I will infold you." As bard he need not accept a different reality from his own because the narcissistic world remains as closed as ever.

In section forty-one Whitman shifts slightly away from the role of superman. The help he promises the "sick" and "upright" is more human than that of section forty. Whitman tries to define himself historically, asking how the role of bard fits what he has heard of the universe, of the "several thousand years." The mythology he sketches unifies all creeds and sects around the working-class men to whom he feels a paternal attachment. The catalog of religions filling section forty-one shows an intellectual eclecticism that parallels Whitman's previous willingness (in sections twenty-six to twenty-nine) to let his senses be stimulated. It differs from earlier catalogs in the degree of intellectual synthesis by which it is organized. Whitman's increased ego control corresponds to an increased willingness to confront mortality and ambivalence. Section forty-one ends:

> The supernatural of no account . . . . myself waiting
> my time to be one of the supremes,
> The day getting ready for me when I shall do as

> much good as the best, and be as prodigious,
> Guessing when I am it will not tickle me much to
>   receive puffs out of pulpit or print;
> By my life-lumps! becoming already a creator!
> Putting myself here and now to the ambushed womb
>   of the shadows!

The theme of creativity links the poetic process to procreation and gives Whitman an inkling of how it might feel,
should he succeed in his intent. Increasing confidence in his
poetic craftsmanship enables him to imagine creating by his
"life-lumps" as well as by his pen. With greater confidence
he no longer requires himself to raise the dead nor demand
that the world accord him "puffs out of pulpit or print."[10]
The hint of success brings Whitman, in section forty-two,
to greater awareness of himself as an artist and as a mortal.
He can recognize the "call in the midst of the crowd" as his
own voice, and he thinks of himself as the nervous fledgling
performer. "Come my boys and girls," he says to the crowd
around him, before realizing "they are no household of
mine." With evident ambivalence Whitman tries to relin-
quish his lifelong fantasy of patriarchy. He explains his relation to citizens of the city in terms other than "love" or
identification:

> This is the city . . . . and I am one of the
>   citizens;
>
>   ❊   ❊   ❊
>
> I acknowledge the duplicates of myself under
>   all the scrape-lipped and pipe-legged
>   concealments.

Still he equivocates:

> The weakest and shallowest is deathless with me,
> What I do and say the same waits for them,

[10] The confidence Whitman expresses here was not to endure.
Within a year he would take Emerson's complimentary letter out of
pulpit and put it into print; he would write his own reviews all his
life; and he would find it difficult to converse about any subject
removed from himself.

Every thought that flounders in me the same
    flounders in them.

Whitman cannot acknowledge the average unending
procession without including individual mortal identity.
The acknowledgment thus transforms itself into a veiled
question about the poet's relation to his reader:

I know perfectly well my own egotism,
And know my omnivorous words, and cannot say
    any less,
And would fetch you whoever you are flush with
    myself.

What Whitman means by "egotism" I have called narcissism. Those he calls his "duplicates" and would fetch flush
with himself he creates in fantasy; they are the ideal readers he needs to work poetic miracles. If "we" exist in his fantasy he must exist as creator: being a bard is a way to be
immortal.

Yet reality forces itself on his attention in section forty-
three. The consolations of the priests cannot prevent his
"Ranting and frothing in my insane crisis—waiting dead-
like till my spirit arouses me." Others, like himself, feel
"down-hearted," "dull and excluded":

Frivolous sullen moping angry affected disheartened
    atheistical,
I know every one of you, and know the unspoken
    interrogatories,
By experience I know them.

In the face of despair so cosmic—and of existence so
precarious—he can do nothing except try to allay the "insane crisis" by an act of faith:

I do not know what is untried and afterward,
But I know it is sure and alive and sufficient.

              *   *   *

It cannot fail the young man who died
    and was buried,

113

Nor the young woman * * *
Nor the little child * * *
Nor the old man * * *
Nor the present, nor the least wisp that is known.

What it is that "cannot fail" remains unspecified. Section forty-four tries to "explain" the basis for his faith through the consolations of biology:

Before I was born out of my mother generations
    guided me,
My embryo has never been torpid . . . . nothing
    could overlay it;
For it the nebula cohered to an orb . . . . the long
    slow strata piled to rest it on . . . . vast
    vegetables gave it sustenance,
Monstrous sauroids transported it in their mouths
    and deposited it with care.

All forces have been steadily employed to complete
    and delight me,
Now I stand on this spot with my soul.

Apparently Whitman wants to believe that biological evolution implies the survival of consciousness beyond death; logically nothing in this proposition indicates anything except that somehow life continues although we live on the leavings of death. Whitman's assertion of confidence is undercut by its context:

Were mankind murderous or jealous upon you my
    brother or my sister?
I am sorry for you . . . . they are not murderous or
    jealous upon me;
All has been gentle with me . . . . . . I keep no account
    with lamentation;
What have I to do with lamentation?

In fact Whitman has quite a lot to do with lamentation. For the moment he blocks the memories of his recently passed despair, finding in natural law an analogy to justify his existence. This dubious logic suggests that Whitman's questions have led him to a quandary answerable only by flight to catharsis. He resumes an old defense, which is supported by an evolving myth and by his growing confidence in his poetic vocation. If anything could make him happy to stand on this spot with his soul, it is the sense that he has a name and a role to play: Walt Whitman, a Kosmos, an American bard.

In section forty-five a mild catharsis enables the poet to develop in a poetic context his longstanding fantasy of being father and teacher to a "wayfarer" (who, in later versions of "Song of Myself," becomes "dear son"). The old impulse to justify existence seems partly answered by the fantasy; Whitman's myth takes a step forward in its evolution. When Whitman sends his disciple leaping out in the midst of the sea and letting go of Father Walt's plank, he makes that disciple do what the teacher cannot, submit to immersion in the maternal sea. The fantasized disciple will therefore do what grants the master vicarious gratification (while it simultaneously justifies the poet, whose pupil outswims the teacher).

The meditation that begins section forty-seven confirms the preceding interpretation:

> I am the teacher of athletes,
>
>   ❖   ❖   ❖
>
> He most honors my style who learns
> under it to destroy the teacher.

The slight disingenuousness of this famous passage suggests that even if Whitman wants to end the possessiveness that has marked all relationships in "Song of Myself," he does not want to be responsible if his imaginary disciple should drown. The fantasized disciple is a part of Whitman himself, split away from the central Oedipal constellation in order to permit some gratification of instinctual urges through fantasy. The ambivalence remains in full force, unmitigated by the fantasy:

115

> I teach straying from me, yet who can stray from me?
> I follow you whoever you are from the present hour;
> My words itch at your ears till you understand them.

Unable to distinguish between himself and others, Whitman continues to see himself the messiah of a new natural religion that would make all men one. In the vein to be developed in "Calamus," Whitman refuses to speak his poetry indoors; it can be understood only on "heights or watershore." The anticipated accomplishments of his poetry relate more immediately to the poet than to the disciples. When Whitman claims that none will ever again feel aloneness or despair, the reader may suspect that the author himself seeks to be consoled and immortalized.

Section forty-eight begins a summation that does not indicate conflicts resolved but reiterates the old ambivalences and hints at a manner of coping with their continued existence. Whitman's insistence,

> I have said that the soul is not more than the body,
> And I have said that the body is not more than the
> soul,

requires a new scrutiny in the light of everything we have learned since he first made the statement in section five. The assertion resembles a basic tenet of post-eighteenth-century romanticism and post-fourteenth-century Anglo-European mysticism, but it must also be understood according to what we have learned of the psychological processes at work in "Song of Myself." In this poem the assertion indicates a conflict that the poet determines to keep in suspension, a conflict between the superego (soul) and the instinctual drives (body). His concept of equality between body and soul tacitly concedes the inability of human will to master the unconscious, reminding us that William James discovered "the real core of the religious problem" in a cry, "Help! Help!"

Whitman can believe, for the moment at least, that the "bitter hug of mortality" no longer alarms him, and he finds reassurance in contemplating the biological cycle:

To his work without flinching the accoucheur comes,
I see the elderhand pressing receiving supporting,
I recline by the sills of the exquisite flexible doors
    . . . . and mark the outlet, and mark the relief
and escape.

In these tranquil lines the poet seems to accept somewhat the impossibility of restoring infantile security and the inevitability of remaining outside the exquisite flexible doors until his corpse becomes good manure to nourish the growing roses and the polished breasts of melons. Whatever change has occurred in Whitman comes from his new belief that he is ready to become a full partner in the economy of the object world, repaying with poetry the breast he sucks. As he sees it, his poetry makes "offspring great or small" emerge, bringing the beginnings of new lives to his readers.

Section fifty reiterates his former understanding of the world: that which is "in me" is identical with what is out there. "It is not chaos or death . . . . it is form and union and plan . . . . it is eternal life . . . . it is happiness." Yet saying that the only reality is the world of the mythic vision leads him to recognize his ambivalence:

Do I contradict myself?
Very well then . . . . I contradict myself;
I am large . . . . I contain multitudes.

The compulsion to resolve the unresolvable seems momentarily suspended in favor of a determination to survive, to cope with the things remaining beyond the control of his imagination. Whitman's growing confidence in his poetic process seems to quiet the urgency of his determination to wrench everything in himself and outside into a unified and coherent wholeness. The process of making the myth becomes more important than the myth itself.

In the last section both the peaceful tone and the ambivalences continue—it could be no other way. At first Whitman conceives his departure as a physical diffusion with the elements. He envisions himself merging with the air, the sun,

117

the water, and the earth. Yet he knows he will return to the earth, and his final words locate his ambivalence terrestrially. When he dies his body will be atomically transformed into the grass, which will be "good health" to us, filtering and fibering our blood. As for his soul, that too will wait for his reader—"some where." But whether he "waits" metaphysically or through his poetic leaves of grass he does not and cannot say. The passionate intensity of earlier acts of faith gives way to reasonably cheerful willingness to live with a more limited conviction. By writing "Song of Myself" Whitman developed a process for making further explorations.

The Psychological Structure of the
First *Leaves of Grass*

IF THE structure of "Song of Myself" cannot be effectively defined in ideological terms, its psychological movement is nevertheless clear. Whitman creates a narcissistic world that he partly rejects as he becomes increasingly committed to his emerging vocation. His growing confidence in his poetic craftsmanship enables him to begin to discover his identity, a discovery that leads to tangible if limited relations with the external world. My qualifying words—"*partly* rejects," "*emerging* vocation," "*growing* confidence," "*begin* to discover," "*limited* relations"—indicate areas of conflict that require further defensive maneuvers on the part of Whitman's ego. Except for "Europe" and "A Boston Ballad,"[1] the poems of the first *Leaves of Grass* are addressed to sources of personal anxiety. Three of the poems—"A Song for Occupations," "Who Learns My Lesson Com-

---

[1] An earlier version of "Europe" (entitled "Resurgemus") was published by the New York *Daily Tribune*, 21 June 1850. "A Boston Ballad" was apparently written in response to the arrest of a fugitive slave, Anthony Burns, in Boston, June 1854. See Stephen D. Malin, "'A Boston Ballad' and the Boston Riot," *Walt Whitman Review*, 9 (1963), 51-57. Although "Europe" was revised for the first *Leaves of Grass*, neither poem resembles in style the other ten poems printed in the first edition.

plete," and "Great Are the Myths"—repeat without further exploration affirmations made in "Song of Myself." The remaining six poems are more complex. Of these, "To Think of Time" and "The Sleepers" have the most to tell us about the psychological patterns fundamental to Whitman's growing vocation and to the growth of *Leaves of Grass*.

I. *"To Think of Time"*

One of the most undeservedly neglected poems in *Leaves of Grass*, "To Think of Time," is a virtual anatomy of Whitman's morbidity and his wish to escape mortality. It is hard to imagine a more personally conceived, or more agonized, response to the "wounds" to humanity's "narcissism" that Freud once attributed to the revelations of Copernican cosmology, Darwinian biology, and psychoanalysis.[2] Although the last of these blows had not been struck in 1855, Whitman nevertheless sensed its most desperate implications— that we cannot escape our personal past, nor separate our conscious lives from unconscious, instinctual drives, and that consciousness can do little to mitigate the facts of existential mortality. "To Think of Time" begins with the poet's subjective apprehension of mortality, implied by time; the poem continues with the poet's attempts to escape dying. When he fails, the poet protests that death does not mean annihilation, but as the poem ends, intimations of mortality emerge like weeds in a garden.

At the start the poet recognizes that because "retrospection" depends on time and memory, time and memory imply mortality:

> To think of time .... to think through the
>   retrospection,
> To think of today .. and the ages continued
>   henceforward.
>
> Have you guessed you yourself would not continue?
> Have you dreaded those earth-beetles?

[2] "A Difficulty in the Path of Psycho-Analysis," *Standard Edition*, xvii, 135-44.

> Have you feared the future would be nothing
>   to you?

The shift in line three from the impersonal infinitive (implying that the poet himself has these fears) to the second person suggests that mortal terror may be dissipated by asserting its universality. Simultaneously, Whitman seeks to diffuse his sense of self among everything he perceives, adding that unless we accept the future as *something*, the past and present are *nothing*. Whitman's dubious logic seems to mean that although he does not wish to accept mortality, he can find little basis for denying it. The defensive position he takes is probably as old as mankind: existence (*now, was*) points to future continuity, preparing man for eternity.

As if for the first time, Whitman imagines a past that did not include his consciousness, and at the same time he recognizes his current location within the present. Lines seven to nine suggest a cosmos in which individual lives seem intolerably unimportant.

> To think that the sun rose in the east . . . . that men
>   and women were flexible and real and alive . . . .
>   that every thing was real and alive;
> To think that you and I did not see feel think nor
>   bear our part,
> To think that we are now here and bear our part.

So long as the apprehension of death remains abstract, the terror Whitman feels remains inexpressible. Although this is what he seems to want, he can neither let the subject drop nor continue to abstract it. His fantasy turns to a particular death:

> When the dull nights are over, and the dull
>   days also,
> When the soreness of lying so much in bed is over,
> When the physician, after long putting off, gives
>   the silent and terrible look for an answer,

121

> When the children come hurried and weeping, and
>   the brothers and sisters have been sent for,
> When medicines stand unused on the shelf, and the
>   camphor-smell has pervaded the rooms,
> When the faithful hand of the living does not desert
>   the hand of the dying,
> When the twitching lips press lightly on the forehead
>   of the dying,
> When the breath ceases and the pulse of the heart
>   ceases,
> Then the corpse-limbs stretch on the bed, and the
>   living look upon them,
> They are palpable as the living are palpable.

The first lines of this passage take us back to the lines immediately preceding. The "dull" nights and days seem similar to bearing "our part," the period between "accouchement" and death. From the beginning of the episode the poet identifies with the dying man. Whitman unconsciously compares the tedium of bearing his part with the high drama on which the dying man embarks, a moment when one's specialness and identity are indisputable. Then, as at no other time since infancy, one is unmistakably in the center of his world and is the deserving recipient of all attention. Doctor and relatives alike must stand back and proclaim: Here is a phenomenon beyond understanding, control, or sharing. But the poet's identification takes an odd turn at the end of the scene:

> The living look upon the corpse with their eyesight,
> But without eyesight lingers a different living and
>   looks curiously on the corpse.

If Whitman intended to affirm that the soul of the recently dead hovers above its former body and looks on curiously, another implication exists, one in which the poet identifies with the dying man up to the moment of death, then becomes the disembodied, detached, and "curious" witness. As in "Song of Myself," loss of identity results from continuing too long in identification. Whitman's characteristic ambivalence continues: without identity he is a voyeur of life, incapable of relationships with other people and things; yet he prefers lingering in painful ambivalence to commitment one way or the other.

The man's death leads Whitman to imagine life going on without him. He reflects on the futility of "building the house" that serves "seventy or eighty years at most" and of building the coffin that serves "longer than that." He abandons this meditation and returns to the stagedriver's funeral, during which he compulsively contemplates that which he can neither escape nor accept. The funeral is presented with great power and economy, but the presentation leaves an overwhelming question: in the face of death's certainty: Does anything else matter? Why bother with farms, crops, wages, goodness or sin? And yet, what else can one do?

Perhaps one can renew the infantile "oceanic" feeling:

> [Sensual pleasures] flow onward to others . . . . you
> and I flow onward;
> But in due time you and I shall take less interest
> in them.

✿ ✿ ✿

> The sky continues beautiful . . . . the pleasure of
> men with women shall never be sated . . nor the
> pleasure of women with men . . . nor the
> pleasure from poems;

In yet another twist of the fantasy, Whitman seems to verge upon diagnosis of his own crisis:

> You are not thrown to the winds . . you gather
> certainly and safely around yourself,
> Yourself! Yourself! Yourself! forever and ever!
>
> It is not to diffuse you that you were born of your
> mother and father—it is to identify you,
> It is not that you should be undecided, but that
> you should be decided;

123

> Something long preparing and formless is arrived
>   and formed in you,
> You are thenceforth secure, whatever comes or
>   goes.

Whitman wanted "identity" to mean the mark of uniqueness he saw conferred by the living on the dying man, but
the concept gets out of hand. Mortality is inseparable from
identity; and mother, father, and birth are to blame for
mortality. He recalls the vague alternative that came in a
dream: "there is no life without satisfaction." But he moves
in a circle, for only immortality can grant this satisfaction:
"We cannot be stopped at a given point . . . . that is no satisfaction." The inadequacy of the dream is all too apparent:

> If otherwise, all these things came but to ashes
>   of dung;
> If maggots and rats ended us, then suspicion and
>   treachery and death.
>
> Do you suspect death? If I were to suspect death
>   I should die now,
> Do you think I could walk pleasantly and well-suited
>   toward annihilation?

But dreaming of immortality no more makes him immortal than contemplating the "beautiful and perfect" animals
makes him invulnerable to the pains of introspection. The
more emphatically Whitman "swears" his faith, the more
desperate is his uncertainty:

> I swear I see now that every thing has an eternal
>   soul!
>
> ❋   ❋   ❋
>
> I swear I think there is nothing but immortality!
> That the exquisite scheme is for it, and the nebulous
>   float is for it, and the cohering is for it,
> And all preparation is for it . . and identity is for
>   it . . and life and death are for it.

The psychoanalytic theory that defense mechanisms are motivated by the inexpressibility of instinctual drives supports my contention that Whitman's affirmation of immortality, like his morbidity, is itself a defense against something else. In my earlier discussion of "Out of the Cradle" I showed that Whitman preoccupies himself with death in order to escape "the fire, the sweet hell within,/ The unknown want, the destiny of me." That is, preoccupation with mortality defends against accepting latent sexual identity. "To Think of Time" indicates that this defense existed as early as 1855.[3]

II. *"The Sleepers"*

Deeply buried in "To Think of Time" are Whitman's longings to share with the dying man a central place in the world's attention and to win recognition for his uniqueness and importance. The longings emerge as prominent themes in "The Sleepers," one of Whitman's most widely admired and analyzed poems.[4] In "The Sleepers" the poet seems to accept from the start certain difficult facts he tried to avoid in "Song of Myself." Twin threats inhibit his achieving a secure sense of identity: loss of autonomy from merging with others if he should permit object relationships, and the actuality of mortal and sexual limitations that imply an end to infantile desires and fantasies. Although the anxiety created by Whitman's ambivalence energizes "The Sleepers," the poet makes little progress toward resolving his

[3] The description of the dying man near the beginning of "To Think of Time" seems related to the death of Whitman's father on 11 July 1855 (the first *Leaves of Grass* was published a few days earlier). Louisa Whitman wrote her daughter Hannah about the death: "jeffy . . . and walter came they felt very much to blame themselves for not being home but they had no idea of any change your father had been [ill] so long and so many bad spells" (quoted in Allen, *The Solitary Singer*, p. 151). Whitman probably envisioned the ending long before it became a fact.

[4] Among the many recent readings of "The Sleepers," see especially Edwin Miller, *A Psychological Journey*, pp. 72-84.

dilemma. Finally, when he seeks to evade the confrontation by an act of transcendental faith, the act fails and the former doubt and ambivalence return. In the end he yields to the authority of his vision and retreats into the maternal night, with whom he seeks passive unity.

Whitman announces the problem of "The Sleepers" immediately: separated in his vision from those who sleep, he wanders, watching with "open eyes over the shut eyes of the sleepers." What follows suggests the tension and alienation of the watcher:

> Wandering and confused . . . . lost to myself . . . . ill-
> assorted . . . . contradictory,
> Pausing and gazing and bending and stopping.

Everyone can sleep but the poet, who emphasizes his isolation by naming the others. Though he may well have something in common with each of those he names (the "ennuyees," the drunkard, the onanist, the married couple), the something in difference is presently more important. These others seem more capable of letting go in sleep, of risking temporary "death," than he. That fear of death is fundamental to Whitman's sense of loss and confusion is suggested by the profusion of morbid things pervading the first six stanzas (not to mention the four narratives in the middle). The poet's visionary associations relentlessly lead to the puzzle of mortality early in the poem. Whitman responds by creating a mythical role that lets him merge with the sleepers and the elements:

> I go from bedside to bedside . . . . I sleep close with
> the other sleepers, each in turn;
> I dream in my dream all the dreams of the other
> dreamers,
> And I become the other dreamers.

Thus the poet deals with his fear of mortality by identifying with the sleepers. The evasion is temporarily successful enough for him to feel a moment of ecstasy:

I am a dance . . . . Play up there! the fit is whirling
  me fast.

I am the everlaughing . . . . it is new moon and
  twilight,
I see the hiding of douceurs . . . . I see nimble ghosts
  whichever way I look,
Cache and cache again deep in the ground and sea,
  and where it is neither ground or sea.

The expression of ecstasy reveals the infantile sexual fantasies at the core of the poem. In fantasy the poet becomes
the infant tyrant identifying with those who in reality might
tyrannize him. By regressing, Whitman momentarily resolves through wishful dreaming a problem of adult mortality. Physical sexual delights no longer carry the threats
that forbid their expression in reality. The infant tyrant
leads his "gang" of adult "journeymen":

Well do they do their jobs, those journeymen
  divine,
Only from me can they hide nothing and would not
  if they could;
I reckon I am their boss, and they make me a pet
  besides,
And surround me, and lead me and run ahead
  when I walk,
And lift their cunning covers and signify me with
  stretched arms, and resume the way;
Onward we move, a gay gang of blackguards with
  mirthshouting music and wildflapping pennants
  of joy.

This is one of those occasions when Whitman finds sudden release from his customary anaesthesia. The sensual
pleasure now available to him replicates the polymorphous
sexuality of infancy, as characterized by his relation to
"those journeymen divine," the "nimble ghosts" who have
hidden "douceurs" from him. Whitman flees, fearing that
abandonment or rejection will result from heterosexual in-

timacy. He seeks not homosexual love (which involves another objective person), but masturbation, the ecstatic climax of which floods him with an infantile sense of oneness. The stanzas that follow develop various aspects of the poet's uncertainty about his identity, including permutations of Oedipal conflicts. After identifying with various public roles (the "actor, the actress"), the poet becomes a woman who has a confusing autoerotic fantasy.

The woman is alone, acting out her desire in masturbation. Even in fantasy Whitman can convincingly express sexuality only in autoerotic terms. The wish for vicarious homosexual fulfillment in this passage is thwarted by the imperfection of the identification, for the poet does not identify with the woman but with the role he thinks she plays. He attributes a form to her fantasies that originates in himself and that is psychologically determined by his inability to differentiate between the feminine and the maternal. As with the first intimations of sensual gratification (the "journeymen divine"), the fantasies become regressive and finally self-destructive. In stanza twenty-two the poet feels himself falling back toward the first discovery of phallic sexuality:

> Pier that I saw dimly last night when I looked from
>   the windows,
> Pier out from the main, let me catch myself with
>   you and stay . . . . I will not chafe you;
> I feel ashamed to go naked about the world,
> And am curious to know where my feet stand . . . .
>   and what is this flooding me, childhood or
>   manhood . . . . and the hunger that crosses the
>   bridge between.

As in "Out of the Cradle" (and as Edwin Miller has said) it is this bridge that Whitman cannot cross.[5] Whitman often substitutes death for sex, unconsciously hoping that morbidity will drive the "unknown want, the destiny of me"

[5] *A Psychological Journey*, p. 77.

128

from consciousness. In "The Sleepers" he moves from the moment of troubling discovery to the earlier period of infantile polymorphous sexuality when he confused breast with penis and the mouth with the genitals.

> The cloth laps a first sweet eating and drinking,
> Laps life-swelling yolks . . . . laps ear of rose-corn,
>   milky and just ripened:
> The white teeth stay, and the boss-tooth advances
>   in darkness,
> And liquor is spilled on lips and bosoms by touching
>   glasses, and the best liquor afterward.

The regressive impulse apparently led back to the first physical gratification: nursing. Nevertheless, the poet identified less with his former infantile self than with the woman whose naked shame he discovered in stanzas twenty-one, and whose breast spilled "liquor" on "lips and bosoms." By now he is so deeply committed to his fantasy that he cannot easily withdraw. His identification with the woman continues as she is suddenly transformed into decrepitude:

> I descend my western course . . . . my sinews are
>   flacid,
> Perfume and youth course through me, and I am
>   their wake.
>
> It is my face yellow and wrinkled instead of the old
>   woman's,
> I sit low in a strawbottom chair and carefully darn
>   my grandson's stockings.
>
> It is I too . . . . the sleepless widow looking out on
>   the winter midnight,
> I see the sparkles of starshine on the icy and pallid
>   earth.
>
> A shroud I see—and I am the shroud . . . . I wrap a
>   body and lie in the coffin;

It is dark here underground . . . . it is not evil or
pain here . . . . it is blank here, for reasons.

It seems to me that everything in the light and air
ought to be happy;
Whoever is not in his coffin and the dark grave, let
him know he has enough.

As usual, Whitman's fantasies of sexual gratification bring
to the surface the morbidity that always waits just beneath.
At the last moment the identification shifts from the woman
to the shroud—that which envelops her in blankness. Blankness—meaninglessness—characterizes the poet's visionary
state and reveals his own lack of identity, his inability to
make order, to give meaning, or even to perceive. To the
extent that he identifies with the woman, he escapes blankness, for her narrative has order and meaning. But the identification brings nothing resembling resolution. The poet's
morbidity does not end; nor does he escape the sense of isolation that prompted this journey among the sleepers. As he
complains in the last of these stanzas, he is still nothing; nor
has he, at this moment, any faith in immortality. A brief
symbolic glance at deadness is altogether enough.

In an effort to fill the blankness of his vision, Whitman
resorts to mythmaking, the imposition of structure on certain items he discovers in his chaotic memory. Four stories
of commitment, battle, destruction, and ritual sacrifice
exemplify the apparent impossibility of one person's con-
necting with others. These myths lead at last to what he will
call "the myth of heaven," which he fervently hopes will
afford beautiful peace. The telling and thus the ordering of
each story gives the poet a momentary insight into himself
and his relation to the situation he describes, but neither
catharsis nor assimilation occurs. Instead, the very activity
of mythmaking objectifies the insight and enforces the
poet's tendency toward stasis. Once something is perceived
by means of the myth, whatever was formerly dynamic in
the material becomes fixed. Although, having told the story,

the poet may better understand his mother's attraction to the Indian woman, the process of mythmaking turns the living into frozen figures, as on the Grecian urn. The mythic insight becomes irrelevant as soon as it is formed; its continued existence repudiates the process by which it was made.

Telling of the "beautiful gigantic swimmer swimming naked through the eddies of the sea," the poet imparts Promethean qualities to the swimmer and simultaneously evokes the usual elemental conflict. Similarly, Whitman emphasizes his own detachment in the very act of identification. Having learned (when the woman aged and died) the penalty for too close an identification with someone else, the poet is now careful to keep his distance, to remain on the shore. The swimmer is an example to the poet, and the story is a cautionary tale: there but for sexual immobility goes Whitman's own Oedipal body. For Whitman what is horrible in the story is that the swimmer must die merely because of his impulse to swim. Should Whitman fail to identify with this man, he would fail blatantly in courage. Perhaps by mythmaking and through identification he can be both swimmer and watcher. But he cannot escape the story's grim ending, for the sea bears out of sight the "brave corpse." Morbidity as a defense against sexuality has created more problems than it has solved and now requires new defenses against itself.

The poet tells his stories from inside the confusion that dominates most of "The Sleepers": "I turn but do not extricate myself;/ Confused . . . . a pastreading . . . . another, but with darkness yet." In the visionary ambience, the story of the swimmer is obscure and can be seen "but with darkness yet." In fact, the mythic qualities attributed to the swimmer assure that the poet will never perceive the story clearly. Whitman tries to become more intimate, telling of a shipwreck he witnessed and the impotence of rescuers to combat the sea's icy destructiveness. All the poet can do about the death of the swimmer is to give the protagonist epic proportions. The poet's function in the story of the shipwreck is to "help pick up the dead and lay them in rows in a barn." He witnesses both disasters, sensing man's powerlessness. But the unconsciousness of Whitman's assumptions about earth, air, fire, and water cause the stories of the swimmer and the shipwreck to remain incomprehensible. The morbidity that leads him to become a voyeur of death precludes acceptance of his own mortality. Whitman places myths and rituals between nature and his vulnerable, protesting self, as if by stereotyping his reactions he can ensure that his world will no longer be lonely and separate.

Whitman's defense against morbidity directs the poet to evade the subjective. In the next two stories, he removes himself from the action. Both stories are passed to the reader as received myth; as such they are beyond scrutiny or revision. The narrative of Washington's defeat at Brooklyn comes to us as the remotest and most objectified of battles; all its actions are ritualized, none is particularized. The battle, the defeat, the deaths are given the same emotional weight as the tears on the general's face. Similarly, the story of the red squaw and Louisa Whitman is presented as if Whitman intends to distill his own feelings out of the poetic atmosphere, leaving us and himself not the distillation, but the mash: "the distillation would intoxicate me also, but I shall not let it."

Whitman's most important literary problem is to learn to permit the distillation to "intoxicate" him into regression, where he can express the discoveries of his poetic journeys and especially the feelings awakened by those discoveries. By regression unattached emotions can be integrated into a poetic structure. On the other hand, when Whitman seems least coherent, it is usually because he cannot relate his feelings to his poetic material. The outburst against Lucifer that follows seems unrelated to anything else in "The Sleepers"; the anger expressed has existed from the beginning of the poem—so we may infer—but its cause is by no means clear:

> Now Lucifer was not dead . . . . or if he was I am his
> sorrowful terrible heir;

I have been wronged . . . . I am oppressed . . . . I hate
   him that oppresses me,
I will either destroy him, or he shall release me.

Various tensions generated by the fantasy underlying
"The Sleepers" cause this outburst, in which catharsis takes
the form of rage rather than ecstasy. Here catharsis carries
a confused latent insight. Although Lucifer, the archetypal
rebel, unconsciously symbolizes the poet's aggressive id-
drives, Whitman attacks what he thinks symbolizes hated
qualities in his father. The "father" is both Whitman's interpretation of his real father and the poet's unconscious
superego; if Whitman could destroy an uncontrollable object he might be less troubled by the uncontrollable inner
self. With his declaration that he will either "destroy" or be
released by his oppressor, Whitman's attention begins to
wander:

Damn him! how he does defile me,
How he informs against my brother and sister and
   takes pay for their blood,
How he laughs when I look down the bend after
   the steamboat that carries away my woman.

Now the vast dusk bulk that is the whale's bulk . . . .
   it seems mine,
Warily, sportsman! though I lie so sleepy and
   sluggish, my tap is death.

The fantasy of identification with a slave (lines 2 and 3
above) comes from one who feels too weak to compete for
a woman he cannot win; to retaliate the poet becomes
Moby Dick. But the narcissistic fantasy of omnipotence inhibits coping with either external or internal reality. The
fantasy ensures that the poet will never have to test his actual strength against objects.

And yet, for all his fears, Whitman genuinely wants to
confront the external world—a fact we learn from the four
narratives. All four deal with freedom, confinement, and
identity. When the swimmer lets go in his battle with the

sea, he is destroyed. The shipwreck victims lose their identities as they are laid out in rows. Washington's soldiers alternate between civilian and military restraints, conventions
and morality. The poet's adolescent mother falls suddenly
and possessively in love with the unpossessive freedom represented by the red girl. The idea of freedom pervades the
questions that cloud the problem of identity. Because freedom implies the chaos and meaninglessness of the visionary
world, it may lead to paralysis: when nothing can be known
for certain, no choice is better than any other. But to want
freedom implies a desire for strength and autonomy. The
idea of freedom leads the poet away from orderly narrative
back to wandering in his vision. The shift in poetic mode
from meditation to narration and back brings the poet's
half-understood desires to feel ecstatically free and to
imagine himself in harmony with the elements. By asserting
physical and metaphysical order Whitman intends to allay
the sense of chaos previously felt:

> A show of the summer softness . . . . a contact of
>   something unseen . . . . an amour of the light
>   and air;
> I am jealous and overwhelmed with friendliness,
> And will go gallivant with the light and the
>   air myself,
> And have an unseen something to be in contact with
>   them also.
>
> O love and summer! you are in the dreams and
>   in me,
> Autumn and winter are in the dreams . . . . the
>   farmer goes with his thrift,
> The droves and crops increase . . . . the barns are
>   wellfilled.
>
> Elements merge in the night . . . . ships make tacks
>   in the dreams . . . . the sailor sails . . . . the
>   exile returns home * * *

Since the poet previously identified the light and air with life, he now feels he can live and be free. Narrative logic abandoned, the poetry becomes meditative and associative. In the next stanzas, as the poet revisits the sleepers he witnessed at the start, he tidies up their lives with fantasies of unity and integrity. All of the sleepers become whole and even "beautiful," as the "myth of heaven" allocates to the ugliest a place in the orderly universe. Yet the images of chaos, ugliness, and disorder overwhelm the poet's assertions of peace and order.

The peace found through the "myth of heaven" encompasses the miraculous healing of injuries and deformities, the closing of gulfs between people and castes, the cessation of desire. The beauty of the sleepers is the beauty of the dead—the dead swimmer, the dead shipwreck victims, the dead soldiers, the dead woman in her grave, the mother's dead desire to be free. Only in death can there be such unity and order. Yet because death is imagined to be merely analogous to creative passivity it seems to offer escape from subsequent discoveries.

> The swelled and convulsed and congested awake to
>   themselves in condition,
> They pass the invigoration of the night and the
>   chemistry of the night and awake.

The "myth of heaven" leads to immortality and the cessation of fear and desire. If the objective world of slavery, insanity, prisons, consumption, and paralysis may be left behind, perhaps the poet may also escape his personal terrors. He asserts that his former fears of sleep and the night are gone, that he will sleep as peacefully as the other sleepers:

> I too pass from the night;
> I stay awhile away O night, but I return to you
>   again and love you;
> Why should I be afraid to trust myself to you?
> I am not afraid . . . . I have been well brought
>   forward by you;

135

I love the rich running day, but I do not desert her
in whom I lay so long:
I know not how I came of you, and I know not where
I go with you . . . . but I know I came well and
shall go well.

I will stop only a time with the night . . . . and rise
betimes.

I will duly pass the day O my mother and duly return
to you;
Not you will yield forth the dawn again more surely
than you will yield forth me again,
Not the womb yields the babe in its time more surely
than I shall be yielded from you in my time.

The assertions that end "The Sleepers" are set in terms
that raise more questions than they answer. When Whitman
asks, "Why should I be afraid to trust myself to you?" he
makes explicit a fear the reader has previously been able
only to infer. If the reader can accept at face value the
poet's assertion of having overcome former fears and
doubts, he can accept the poem in the terms Whitman
clearly intends, as proving rebirth in a narcissistic world
where nature takes the place of the lost mother. But the associations that link the night to maternity—"her in whom
I lay so long," "I will duly pass the day O my mother and
duly return to you," "Not the womb yields the babe in its
time more surely than I shall be yielded from you in my
time"—reveal that beneath the idea of transcendence lies
the impossible wish to return to primary symbiosis.

The last two lines of "The Sleepers" (deleted after 1855)
show the poet as passive as ever, as incapable of touching
the other sleepers as before. Whitman's passivity indicates
an openness to regressive impulses that the creative process
requires, yet it also indicates one of Whitman's "usual mistakes," which is that the poet could not always be satisfied
if regression yielded a poem instead of restoring the infantile security he sought. The assertion of universal order that
ends "The Sleepers" lets the poet momentarily believe that

he can be again the child he once was. Ideas of transcendental order support regressive impulses by promising that the "exquisite flexible doors" of the uterus permit both outward and inward passage; "immortality" means life before birth.

But, as we know, Whitman's scheme of order failed to provide the psychological comfort required to cope with the ebbing of visionary faith. If the sea and night become angry again, Whitman will be as devastated as he was in the past. As the poems of 1856 and 1860 show, the unconscious conflicting attitudes toward the maternal continue at full force.

III. *The Psychological Structure of the First* Leaves of Grass

The first *Leaves of Grass* evolved according to a definable psychological movement rather than according to philosophical ideas or logic. In "Song of Myself" Whitman sought to accommodate regressive impulses to his need to find a vocation to which he could commit himself. Whitman's search required the establishment of new psychological defenses against unresolved neurotic conflicts, defenses that were sometimes successful. His most important psychological needs and defenses (evident in "Song of Myself," "To Think of Time," and "The Sleepers") may be expressed as follows:

NEEDS	DEFENSES
Sexual expression	Autoerotic fantasies; masturbation; morbidity
Restoration of infantile security; justification of existence	Assertion of immortality; creation of ideal, sexually diffused reader
Justification of infantile feelings of megalomania	Creation of narcissistic fantasy world
Oral gratification	Exchange of poetry for breath and breast

137

Apparently Whitman's inability to satisfy his needs through ordinary "adult" relations with external objects led to intolerable anxiety, from which he sought relief by creating a narcissistic fantasy world. When, as was inevitable, regression to narcissism failed to give adequate satisfaction, Whitman looked for surrogate identities by identifying with others, hoping to avoid isolation by participating vicariously in the others' experiences. The second line of defense also failed because it jeopardized autonomy and exacerbated fears about mortality: identification led merely to another form of secondary narcissism. When the second line of defense failed, Whitman began to explore a third, which arose from his growing confidence in his poetic processes. Because regression is an inherent part of the creative process, Whitman's commitment to poetry did not conflict with the wish to restore primary symbiosis. Whitman sought to identify himself as a bard whose poems might be exchanged with external objects in return for gratification of basic needs.

The movement through these lines of defense is reflected in the placement of poems in the first *Leaves of Grass*. I suggest the following relationships and transitions between the poems.

From "Song of Myself" to "A Song for Occupations." Whitman needed to affirm the existence of his ideal reader, to justify his "occupation" as the bard.

From "Occupations" to "To Think of Time." The least secure defense achieved in "Song of Myself" is that against fears of mortality. Whitman's poetic method, depending on memory and a sense of time, constantly and inevitably led the poet to thoughts of death.[6]

From "Time" to "The Sleepers." Fear of mortality almost

---

[6] "A Song for Occupations" and the last two 1855 poems, "Who Learns My Lesson Complete" and "Great Are the Myths," repeat without further exploration or development affirmations expressed in "Song of Myself." Whitman clearly intended the poems of 1855 to affirm transcendence and immortality, but the weakness of the three affirming poems vitiates his intent.

138

always reminded Whitman of his lack of sexual identity; the two sources of anxiety were interwoven in the poet's Oedipal neurosis, the unconscious foundation of "The Sleepers."

From "The Sleepers" to "I Sing the Body Electric." From adolescence on, Whitman escaped Oedipal anxieties by imagining himself a family patriarch, as loved and honored as the eighty-year-old farmer in "Body Electric." Whitman's unconvincing attempt to imagine himself in heterosexual intercourse testifies to a reaction formation against fear of sexual intimacy.[7]

From "Body Electric" to "Faces." "Faces" further ex-

[7] Despite explicit descriptions of sexual intercourse with "the female form," the effect of "I Sing the Body Electric" is autoerotic. It is Whitman's own physiology and reactions that preoccupy him. Because the woman to whom he feels a "fierce undeniable attraction" remains fictively unobjectified, this episode might be described as a "rapist's" fantasy. The aggression this phrase suggests is implicit when the woman is urged, "Be not ashamed" (for being sexual? for evoking the poet's desires?). Next she is offered the justification of being "the gates of the body" and "the gates of the soul." The poet asserts that the "female contains all qualities and tempers them . . . she is in her place . . . she moves with perfect balance" apparently to reassure himself rather than the "female." The metaphysical justification offered for the poet's imaginary act and for the woman's imaginary cooperation ("I see the bearer of the great fruit which is immortality . . . the good thereof is not tasted by roues, and never can be") is both condescending and crudely self-deceptive. The point is not merely that Whitman is sexually guilt-ridden and therefore hostile to women. We have here a clearer glimpse than ever before of the roots of Whitman's sexual anxieties. His saying that "she moves with perfect balance" and that she is "the gates" of the body and soul indicates that Whitman assumes women have an innate place in the universe not granted to men. The "female form," that mindless but powerful body, seems free from the guilt that accompanies the poet's introspection. To Whitman, women seem free from paralyzing internal conflicts, invulnerable to the ambivalences and lack of identity that plague him. Whitman's sexual dilemma, as noted before, leads to identification with the patriarchal farmer, a version of the ego ideal expressed as early as the adolescent story "My Boys and Girls."

plores the poet's fear of sexuality, especially his feeling of guilt for horrible things being as they are.[8]

From "Faces" to "Song of the Answerer." "Answerer" attempts to justify being a bard in a world pervaded by injustice, sickness, deformity—the world of "Faces."

From "Answerer" to "Europe." One "answer" is that the bard must explain the external world and reorganize it according to his poetic vision.

From "Europe" to "A Boston Ballad." These two poems contrast the failing ideals of American democracy with revolutionary European movements toward democratic ideals.

From "Boston" to "There Was a Child Went Forth." The doubts about America expressed in "Boston" parallel the "doubts of daytime and the doubts of nighttime" Whitman meets in "There Was a Child." Whitman's uncharacteristically direct expression of childhood unhappiness constitutes

[8] As Whitman told Horace Traubel (*With Walt Whitman in Camden*, New York, 1908, II 56-57), the poet's brother Edward had "inspired 'Faces,'" but there are also hints that Whitman had other brothers in mind, especially Jesse and perhaps Andrew. The ambivalence of Whitman's feelings toward these brothers-sons-readers reveals that it was to them he felt he must justify being a poet (the explicit theme of the next 1855 poem, "Song of the Answerer"). Whitman says that the sick and deformed he perceives in "Faces" are fundamentally healthy; this act of faith leads him by association to the episode in which a "limber-hip'd" man is seduced by a woman who is transformed into "the justified mother." Construed simply as a dream, "Faces" ends with an implicit, unanswered question: who is responsible for the sick and deformed who (by the logic of association) issue from the union of the man and the justified mother? Whitman seems to say that the woman is responsible for the seduction and transmission of the "albescent honey." If the reader infers that the man is an unconscious representation of Whitman himself and the woman his mother, it follows that the poet seeks to evade a considerable sense of guilt not necessarily sexual. As explained in Chapter 2, during his adolescence Whitman shared responsibility for raising his parents' troubled or defective children— Hannah, Andrew, and Edward. It is not unreasonable to infer that such responsibility created profound confusions, ambivalences, and guilts; nor is it unlikely that Whitman may unconsciously have blamed his mother for placing these burdens on him.

a moment of profound doubt in the midst of a clear and strongly willed movement, throughout the book, toward affirmation.

From "There Was a Child" to "Who Learns My Lesson Complete." "Who Learns" denies the doubts expressed in the preceding poems and affirms the poet's recently attained bardic identity by affirming Whitman's belief in the existence of an ideal reader.

From "Who Learns" to "Great Are the Myths." "Great Are the Myths" clearly, if unconvincingly, asserts that although there is little reason to believe in immortality, he must try to believe.[9]

The first *Leaves of Grass* attests to the growth of Whitman's courage to explore his unconscious and to his increasing skill to speak from the deepest abysms of his soul.

[9] See Pearce's introduction to *"Leaves of Grass," Facsimile Edition of the 1860 Text* (Ithaca, 1961), pp. 1-li.

SEVEN

The Growth of Whitman's Vocation and the Second *Leaves of Grass*

IN ADDITION to demonstrating how Whitman's poetic processes served as a means for psychological exploration, I have sought to show that a quality of psychological fluidity in Whitman's best poetry enables him to move freely among the components of his poetic world. The most important of the components are, first, Whitman's unconscious worldview, heavily influenced by various neurotic conflicts; second, his a-contextual recollections of external objects linked by preconcious associations; and, third, conventional myths that give order to the external world (folkore, religion, science, etc.). In the first *Leaves of Grass* Whitman developed the poetic method in which he juxtaposed his private responses to the external world beside popular ideas of order and meaning and beside the conscious and unconscious processes by which he perceived the world and its myths. The key to the success or failure of Whitman's method is its fluidity. The process by which he recognizes and expresses his vision of himself and his world becomes more important than the vision itself. The vision must remain responsive to changes in the poet and his perceptions.

The surge of creativity responsible for at least a hundred poems (early 1855 to June 1857) ended the search that occupied the first half of Whitman's life. The poems of 1855 reveal that the inhibitions which long made Whitman's vocational search fruitless were rooted in psychological conflicts that the poems explored and tried to resolve.

Whitman's commitment to being a poet, which came halfway through his life, was very strong, yet deeply ambivalent.[1] Since his ambivalence about being a poet was not resolved until all the major poems had been written, it appears that Whitman's vocational ambivalence was itself a necessary part of his creative processes. The ambivalence is especially clear in two of the longest and least studied poems of the second *Leaves of Grass*, "Broad-Axe Poem" and "Poem of Many In One" (better known as "Song of the Broad-Axe" and "By Blue Ontario's Shore"). It is with the latter that I begin my discussion of the poems of 1856.

I. *"By Blue Ontario's Shore"*

The apt but awkward title "Poem of Many In One" introduces one of the strongest and most direct of Whitman's poems about his poetic processes.[2] The vast amount of revision this poem was to receive over the years suggests that Whitman intuitively understood more about what he was up to than he could consciously say, and that his sense of his poetic processes changed over the years. By his revisions Whitman tried to keep up with the changes in himself.

Although "Poem of Many In One" reiterates some ideas and several passages written for the 1855 preface, the force of the poetic statement is very different from that of the earlier declaration of American poetic independence. The 1855 preface is an advertisement after the fact, a letter of introduction written by Whitman the publicist to his ideal reader. The preface lacks the processive quality by which

---

[1] When he embossed on the cover of the second *Leaves of Grass* a phrase from Emerson's famous congratulatory letter, "I greet you at the beginning of a great career," Whitman gave public testimony to his new commitment. By using the word "career" so boldly, Whitman declared, as much to himself as to the world, that his work as a poet was to be the work of his life.

[2] Neither "By Blue Ontario's Shore" nor "Song of the Broad-Axe" has evoked substantial critical response.

the best poems seem almost alive. Developing the myth that began evolving in "Song of Myself," "Poem of Many In One" begins by declaiming the organic relation the poet feels with his "America":

> A Nation announcing itself,
> I myself make the only growth by which I can be
>   appreciated,
> I reject none, accept all, reproduce all in my own
>   forms.

Whitman carries his myth farther than ever before: the entire nation is Whitman and he is the nation. He can reject nothing without rejecting some part of himself. The former personal conflicts are projected outward:

> Nothing is sinful to us outside of ourselves,
> Whatever appears, whatever does not appear, we
>   are beautiful or sinful in ourselves.

The projection neither minimizes nor obliterates the sense of conflict. If our internal judgments (our sense of "sinfulness") make us "sick," the cure is to believe ourselves "Supremes": "All comes by the body—only health puts you rapport with the universe [sic]."
But "Poem of Many In One" prescribes more than positive thinking, as the poem's subsequent development shows.

> How dare a sick man, or an obedient man, write
>   poems?
> Which is the theory or book that is not diseased?

> Piety and conformity to them that like!
> Peace, obesity, allegiance, to them that like!
> I am he who tauntingly compels men, women,
>   nations, to leap from their seats and contend
>   for their lives!

I am he who goes through the streets with a barbed
tongue, questioning every one I meet—
questioning you up there now,
Who are you, that wanted only to be told what you
knew before?
Who are you, that wanted only a book to join you
in your nonsense?

Perhaps we should enroll Whitman in the Devil's party,
or in Kingsley Widmer's society of literary rebels, for his
taunts about peaceful obesity and allegiance occur in a social and political context. Whitman's disobedience and
"questioning" include an attack on public values, morality,
and tastes:

Fear grace! Fear delicatesse!
Fear the mellow sweet, the sucking of honey-juice!
Beware the advancing mortal ripening of nature!
Beware what precedes the decay of the ruggedness
of states and men!

Ages, precedents, poems, have long been
accumulating undirected materials,
America brings builders, and brings its own styles.

Mighty bards have done their work, and passed to
other spheres,
One work forever remains, the work of surpassing
all they have done.

But if Whitman merely advocates *civil* disobedience, how
shall we understand the echoes of "To Think of Time" in the
warning to beware nature's ripening: "If otherwise, all
these things came but to ashes of dung;/ If maggots and
rats ended us, then suspicion and treachery and death"?
And what of the immensity of the task Whitman defines for
himself, to surpass the work of the past's mightiest bards?
The disobedience Whitman advocates is to one's superego,
a disobedience broader and deeper than his version of political radicalism. The bard must disturb his own and his

145

reader's customary balance, leaving reader and poet never again to be the peaceful children they once were. The difference between these two kinds of radicalism can be expressed easily: one involves regression in service to the ego; the other, regression in service to the superego. We may alter our sense of social and political values by introjecting different (perhaps opposite) values that become part of the superego. But Whitman's psychological revolution involves far more than merely finding new values by which to judge external conditions. Whitman pursues a new mode of perception continually responsive to changes in the external world and in himself. We indeed do right to fear nature's mortal ripening, for external growth—time itself—demands corresponding growth and change within. Because the poetic self must continually reflect psychological evolution, Whitman's task is to assure that coordination. Poems like "Europe," "A Boston Ballad," and "To A Foiled European Revolutionaire" (the twenty-first 1856 poem) may do nothing more than point to failures in public policies or achievements, but most of Whitman's "democratic chants" have the larger ambition of reconstructing our reality testing habits along evolutionary lines. The success or failure Whitman experienced in such intentions depends on the extent to which, at a given moment, he could escape neurotic inhibitions.

Whitman identifies the "America" he conceives in "Poem of Many In One" with his ideal reader, the fantasized object, both paternal and maternal, into which he plunges his "semitic muscle," the source to which he attributes all his qualities:

> To him the hereditary countenance bequeathed,
>   both mother's and father's,
> His first parts substances, earth, water, animals,
>   trees,
> Built of the common stock, having room for far and
>   near,
> Used to dispense with other lands, incarnating this
>   land,

146

> Attracting it body and soul to himself, hanging on
> its neck with incomparable love.

The merest hint of mortality and the possibility that love
may be withdrawn require Whitman to search for visionary
escape. He organizes the long catalog that follows upon the
hope first expressed in "Song of Myself" of escaping "ties
and ballasts," and of creating the nation by his song: "By
great bards only can series of peoples and States be fused
into the compact organism of one nation." Whitman's list of
the ideal poet's attributes centers around attunement between the poet and the elements of his world: "He judges
not as the judge judges, but as the sun falling around a
helpless thing." The values of the superego are supplanted
by sheer perception of natural facts. When such attunement
exists, the poet and his reader escape the dread of
mortality.

When Whitman comes to ask whether he is the bard he
wants to be, he can answer only with guesses about how
that bard will be recognized:

> If [America's] poets appear, it will advance to meet
> them, there is no fear of mistake,
> The proof of a poet shall be sternly deferred till his
> country absorbs him as affectionately as he has
> absorbed it.

Whitman boasts that he himself is the bard whose work
will supersede the work formerly left to priests, and he
demands recognition (the "affectionate" absorption) testi-
fying to his bardic stature:

> Give me the pay I have served for!
> Give me to speak beautiful words! take all the rest;
> I have loved the earth, sun, animals—I have
> despised riches,
> I have given alms to every one that asked, stood up
> for the stupid and crazy, devoted my income
> and labor to others,
> I have hated tyrants, argued not concerning God,

had patience and indulgence toward the
people, taken off my hat to nothing known or
unknown,

❁ ❁ ❁

I have studied my land, its idioms and men,
I am willing to wait to be understood by the growth
of the taste of myself,
I reject none, I permit all,
Whom I have staid with once I have found longing
for me ever afterwards.

The context and diction seem to offer a clue about how
to interpret the demand. The clue comes when we ask
whom the poet addresses and what, exactly, he asks for.
Who can "give [him] to speak beautiful words"? If the pay
he demands is the ability to speak beautiful words instead
of the "affectionate" absorption, then he would seem to address what an earlier poet might have called his muse. The
terms by which he justifies his demand suggest that he has
felt himself serving a novitiate that has consisted of the
arduous study of his craft. In later versions of this poem,
Whitman's "muse" was to be the "phantom" appearing on
Ontario's shore, to whom he would attribute the requirements and judgments first attributed to "America." In either
version the reader infers that Whitman's ideal reader is an
aspect of the poet's superego.

With this in mind, consider that Whitman's boast consists
of revealing the fantasy that sustains his continued commitment to his vocation, now the mainstay of his life itself. By
revealing the fantasy, Whitman risks having it judged fool-
ish and himself judged an arrogant clown. No doubt such
a fantasy exists in almost every beginning artist (Whitman
himself expressed it years before in "Lingave's Temptation"). To some extent the fantasy is at odds with the dedi-
cation to craft required to win recognition: because fantasy
partially gratifies psychological need, the incentive to create
art is somewhat diminished, replaced by the illusion that
recognition has already come. An important question of

goals arises: is it enough if he convinces himself that he has in his soul poetry that surpasses the poems of all previous bards, or must he commit that poetry to public words and syntax and submit it to the world's judgment? Whitman plainly requires external confirmation that corresponds to the terms of praise established in his superego. This need accounts for his habit of writing unsigned reviews of his own work and for the friendships he sought, in later life, with those whose judgment he could trust to confirm his own. The balance between his wish for immediate recognition and the need for external confirmation of his judgment would always be precarious. But if Whitman were to write poems at all, he would have to allay his fears of being judged inadequate either by a direct confrontation with his anxiety or by a more devious defense able to ward off the sense of threat. Most of the time Whitman looked, without much success, for an effective defense.

In "Poem of Many In One" he eventually confronts the issue squarely. He "swears" belief in his safety, in friendship, in his soul, in "the similitude that interlocks me with all identities." This declaration leads to a pledge:

> I swear I will not be outfaced by irrational things!
> I will penetrate what it is in them that is sarcastic
>   upon me!
> I will make cities and civilizations defer to me!
> I will confront these shows of the day and night!
> I will know if I am to be less than they!
> I will see if I am not as majestic as they!
> I will see if I am not as subtle and real as they!
> I will see if I am to be less generous than they!
> I will see if I have no meaning, and the houses and
>   ships have meaning!
> I will see if the fishes and birds are to be enough
>   for themselves, and I am not to be enough for
>   myself!
>
> I match my spirit against yours, you orbs, growths,
>   mountains, brutes,

I will learn why the earth is gross, tantalizing,
   wicked,
I take you to be mine, you beautiful, terrible, rude
   forms.

It is hard to imagine what further commitment Whitman might make in response to the invitation first presented by the "loving bedfellow" in "Song of Myself." The poet's willingness to perceive "beautiful, terrible, rude forms" in himself and outside, to measure himself against others with every possibility of discovering himself wanting, sets the terms within which we must understand and evaluate his achievements. Since every object perceived in the world challenges his sense of adequacy, the challenges must be faced. It seems to me that no poem of Whitman's ends with a more solid or specific acknowledgment of external reality's most imposing qualities than "Poem of Many In One." In Kafka's *Trial* Joseph K. insists, "It is only a trial if I recognize it as such." Since the loving bedfellow appeared, Whitman has indeed acknowledged that he was on trial and that within himself dwelt his own highest judge. He must transform the inner judge from one who judges "as the judge judges" into one who judges like the "sun falling round a helpless thing." The force of this last image comes not from the helplessness of the "thing" but from the existential fact of its being in the sun's path. The sun warms it, illuminates its obscurest aspects, gives it life, but does it judge? Judgment comes with the illumination, an exposure equivalent to Whitman's exposure of his fantasy world. However much Whitman wants to suspend creeds and schools, he cannot easily avoid the inner judge who condemns outright the rude, terrible, beautiful forms and sends them back into the unconscious invisibility of the "shows of the day and night." When can "the fire, the sweet hell within" become the sun, illuminating the world with its procreant urge and urge and urge? Only when the rudeness and terribleness he attributes to the fire's form is confronted, when the fire forges the broad-axe.

II. *"Song of the Broad-Axe"*

The opening of "Broad-Axe Poem" is as brilliantly crafted as anything Whitman ever wrote:

> Broad-axe, shapely, naked, wan!
> Head from the mother's bowels drawn!
> Wooded flesh and metal bone! limb only
>   one and lip only one!
> Gray-blue leaf by red-heat grown! helve
>   produced from a little seed sown!
> Resting the grass amid and upon,
> To be leaned, and to lean on.
>
> Strong shapes, and attributes of strong
>   shapes, masculine trades, sights and
>   sounds,
> Long varied train of an emblem, dabs
>   of music,
> Fingers of the organist skipping staccato
>   over the keys of the great organ.

The tetrameter couplets of the first stanza describe the formed and identified axe; the dithyrambs of the second stanza correspond to the evolving "shapes" the axe will create and destroy. The axe's creative and destructive potential symbolizes the poem's conscious theme, the civilization of a wilderness and the destruction of a decadent culture. The axe's potential also symbolizes an unconscious theme, the conversion of sexual energy into poetic creativity. The axe destroys as well as creates the poetic vision itself, adapting what has previously been perceived and incorporating changes into the evolving myth. The axe is at once born out of the mother's bowels and withdrawn after disembowelling her in imaginary rape. Most of all it exists, has uses, and is used; it makes the forms, the "strong shapes, masculine trades, sights and sounds" of the organ to be discovered in the ensuing poetic journey.

The journey first leads to the discovery and "welcome" of the land's natural resources made useful to man by the axe. In section three the poet fixes his attention on a particular settlement and moves from there to a chronology of America's growth from the first colonists to the contemporary industrial and urban culture. As the chronology evolves into the scene of a fire, where axes smash through floors, the poet's associations lead to the forge where an axe is being made. Behind the forge's flames the poet detects "the shadowy processions of the portraits of the past users also," the ancient "users" who sack an old city:

> The bursting in of mercenaries and bigots
> tumultuously and disorderly,
> Roar, flames, blood, drunkenness, madness.

We see rape, looting, war, prostitution, thievery, and finally the agent responsible for all this, "The power of personality, just or unjust." Whitman's myth takes the popular idea that America grew out of the past's mistakes and combines it with elements of the poet's fantasy world and with the identity he is forging as a poet. "Personality, just or unjust," defines the function of the poet in this mythic history. The poet makes order according to his powers and limitations, justifying the ugliest as well as the most beautiful. As Whitman tries to attune himself to both the external and internal realms, he seeks a position of supreme power in relation to these worlds. As poet he must surpass the work of the greatest bards by exerting ego-like control over the "shapes" arising during the poetic journey.

In section four Whitman leaps from his mythical history to a celebration of "muscle and pluck forever," qualities he construes as assuring personal immortality: "nothing endures but personal qualities":

> Do you think the greatest city endures?

> ❈   ❈   ❈

> Away! These are not to be cherished for themselves,
> They fill their hour, the dancers dance, the musicians
> play for them,

> The show passes, all does well enough of course,
> All does very well till one flash of defiance.

> The greatest city is that which has the greatest
>   man or woman,
> If it be a few ragged huts, it is still the greatest
>   city in the whole world.

Apparently the greatest man or woman will be known by the "one flash of defiance" that will end the celebration of cities and redirect it toward that great individual. The "flash of defiance" takes us back to the angry creator of "Poem of Many In One," who "tauntingly compels men, women, nations, to leap from their seats and contend for their lives!" The poetic task remains the same, but the broad-axe is now the compelling instrument.

But can the great man or woman endure? Evidently the great one endures because, being poet-like, he or she speaks beyond words and particularities to ages yet to come: the great one becomes "electric"—immortal—in perfection. Section five projects an ideal civilization, an entire *America* of poets, in which "no monuments exist to heroes but in the common words and deeds":

> Where the slave ceases and the master of slaves
>   ceases,
> Where the populace rise at once against the audacity
>   of elected persons,
> Where fierce men and women pour forth as the sea
>   to the whistle of death pours its sweeping and
>   unript waves,
> Where outside authority enters always after the
>   precedence of inside authority.

Even more important than the ideal nation Whitman projects is the ideally organized personality. Free from enslaving compulsions, free from the judgments of an overweening superego, anger and action unite in the ideal personality to master the environment and force from it gratification of unconscious desires. The result is the "greatest city" that can be known by the "healthiest fathers" and the "best-bodied mothers" who inhabit it. In the face of such ideals, "How beggarly appear poems, arguments, orations." Whitman faces his familiar problem of how to value poetry in relation to "electric deeds," the only answer being to regard poetry as able to generate as much electricity (transcendence, immortality) as great human acts. The poet must believe that his readers will find, through poetry, new senses of themselves and their immortality parallel to that Whitman seeks for himself.

Only the broad-axe can plough the ground Whitman works, "A sterile landscape" that covers the ore. The axe served the phallic poet whom Whitman believes to be the principal artificer of ancient, medieval, and modern times. But if the axe serves the poet, it also serves the "European headsman," the executioner who "stands masked, clothed in red, with huge legs, and strong naked arms." The fusion of sexual and aggressive acts into this overwhelming phallicism leads Whitman to define the poet's task as washing the blood "entirely away from the axe" by creating a new culture where men shall no longer have to die "for the good cause." The poet who is successful will be rewarded by seeing

> * * * the scaffold untrodden and mouldy, I see no
> longer any axe upon it,
> I see the mighty and friendly emblem of the power
> of my own race, the newest largest race.

Whitman seems to say that the poet of the broad-axe must ignore his tool's destructiveness. But if he lets himself see only the beautiful forms and denies those which are "terrible" and "rude," he risks being merely the poet of "grace" and "delicatesse." On another level, his denial of the axe's destructiveness threatens to eliminate further insight, which might enhance the poetic process by destroying inhibiting illusions and defenses. It is a dilemma Whitman was never fully to resolve. He ends "Broad-Axe Poem" with a series of more or less protective affirmations:

The axe leaps!
The solid forest gives fluid utterances,
They tumble forth, they rise and form,
Hut, tent, landing, survey,
Flail, plough, pick, crowbar, spade.

The axe comes to be used to create everything from a hut
to the Manhattan steamboat. As the vision progresses, the
"shapes arise" from the "using of axes," and Whitman gives
us a long list of users of the axe and then, in section ten, of
things made by the axe. The shapes become increasingly
humanized: a coffin, a bride's-bed, a cradle, a floor, a home;
then the things made for people leading "normal" lives give
way to things for irregular lives: the "prisoner's place in
the court-room," the medicine boxes, the "liquor-bar," "the
shamed and angry stairs, trod by sneaking footsteps," an
adulterous settee, a gambling board, a gallows—and the
sheriff. The ideals of America's revolutionary beginning
have become fully as perverted as those of any European
civilization. But instead of demanding another revolution,
Whitman presents a series of new shapes—doors, "the exquisite flexible doors" to the uterus out of which arise "the
shapes of full-sized men!"

Men tactiturn yet loving, used to the open air, and
the manners of the open air,
Saying their ardor in native forms, saying the old
response,
Take what I have then, (saying fain,) take the pay
you approached for,
Take the white tears of my blood, if that is what
you are after.

America needs not political revolution, but biological
evolution and the love of fathers for their sons and wives
that overcomes taciturnity with ardor and generates yet
newer shapes. The violent rape with which "Broad-Axe
Poem" began evolves into this intensely gentle image of

155

semen, "the white tears of my blood," as the taciturn men fulfill the demand made by the women of Whitman's fantasies. Immediately,

> Her shape arises!
> She, less guarded than ever, yet more guarded than
>   ever,
> The gross and soiled she moves among do not make
>   her gross and soiled,
> She knows the thoughts as she passes, nothing is
>   concealed from her,
> She is none the less considerate or friendly therefore,
> She is the best-beloved, it is without exception, she
>   has no reason to fear, and she does not fear,
> Oaths, quarrels, hiccuped songs, smutty expressions,
>   are idle to her as she passes,
> She is silent, she is possessed of herself, they do not
>   offend her,
> She receives them as the laws of nature receive them,
>   she is strong,
> She too is a law of nature, there is no law greater
>   than she is.

The woman, now satisfied, can be "less guarded than ever," yet more protected. Perhaps sheer pregnancy guards this woman's movements through an offensive world. Who is the poet in this world? The fathering men? One of those whose coarseness might offend? Both, perhaps, but also, one who is yet to be born.

> His shape arises!
> Arrogant, masculine, naive, rowdyish,
> Laugher, weeper, worker, idler, citizen, countryman.

Edwin Miller describes the self-portrait that follows as "self-mockery which militates against the self-aggrandisement."[3] But the self-portrait is also a protective device: if

[3] *A Psychological Journey*, p. 137.

156

the poet himself is the first to mock and scorn, he may vitiate the force of others' mockery.

> Ample-limbed, a good feeder, weight a hundred
> and eighty pounds, full-blooded, six feet high,
> forty inches around the breast and back,

> ❀   ❀   ❀

> Voluptuous, inhabitive, combative, conscientious,
> alimentive, intuitive, of copious friendship,
> sublimity, firmness, self-esteem, comparison,
> individuality, form, locality, eventuality,
> Avowing by life, manners, works, to contribute
> illustrations of results of The States,
> Teacher of the unquenchable creed, namely,
> egotism,
> Inviter of others continually henceforth to try their
> strength against his.

Painting the paternal and maternal portraits in sections ten and eleven leads Whitman too close to a prime psychological ambivalence he cannot directly confront; to retreat, he disguises himself with this comic self-portrait. "Broad-Axe Poem" ends not in the powerful confrontation that concludes "Poem of Many In One," but in a familiar assertion that the shapes will unite themselves in a vast similitude, "bracing the whole earth, and braced with the whole earth."

III. *"Crossing Brooklyn Ferry"*

In 1856, in "Poem of Many In One" and "Broad-Axe Poem," Whitman explored in greater depth the function and responsibility of the American bard first described in the 1855 Preface. Whitman had hoped that the first *Leaves of Grass* would establish relations between himself and the world. In its Preface he depicted himself the leader of a nation of latent poets who would follow the bard's example and spring into song. The "America" he conceived was one in which the external and internal worlds were more or less united. The "Americans" of his mythic vision were ideal

157

readers who accepted the bard and were thereby reborn by the shock of bardic electricity. In a less conscious manner, Whitman used words like "America," "The States," and "These States" to combine perceptions of things and of myths with corresponding unconscious images. The combination sometimes permitted Whitman to fantasize the restoration of infantile security. Whitman's partly conscious myth of "America" is finally inseparable from a less conscious world-view in which earth, air, fire, and water symbolize important superego imagoes. Using these symbols Whitman could express internal conflicts without full or conscious acknowledgment. In his search for a benign superego, Whitman created his ideal American readers.

In fact, Whitman's superego was far from benign. For all the force of will Whitman brought to his poetic explorations, unconscious distortions and conflicts remained so threatening that he was never to directly approach, in consciousness, the psychologically determining sexual confusions. Identifications made in infancy with his mother and father changed very little as Whitman grew older. To the extent that he remained his father he saw himself a rapist, isolated and incapable of either worldly success or human intimacy, unanswerably oppressed by Louisa Whitman's well-meant dominance. To the extent that he remained his mother he resented his father's harshness, the consistent failures in the world, and the persistent taciturnity at home. The result was an inevitable diffusion of sexual identity and a retreat into autoerotic fantasy, the only sexual expression that did not bring greater anxiety than abstinence brought.

Among the short poems of 1856 are two that suggest the ramifications of Whitman's diffused sexual identity and the morbidity that followed from his lack of sexual identity. In "Bunch Poem" (later called "Spontaneous Me"), Whitman proceeds through a "bunch" of images to celebrate autoerotic sexuality in one of his most effective lyrics. The spontaneity of "Bunch Poem" is matched by that in "This Compost," which takes a remarkably direct look at the hard facts of mortality and which ends by affirming nothing but

the biological continuity of life.[4] The directness of these
two poems is as uncharacteristic for Whitman in 1856 as in
1855.

With few exceptions the new poems of 1856 succeeded
when Whitman could keep his residual sexual conflicts
buried. The most celebrated poem of the second edition is
"Crossing Brooklyn Ferry," to which we now turn. "Sun-
Down Poem" (as Whitman called "Crossing Brooklyn
Ferry" in 1856) answers the question of mortality presented
in "This Compost." In "Brooklyn Ferry" Whitman finds a
remarkably apt metaphor for a familiar defensive illusion.
The womb Whitman wants to inhabit is symbolized by the
boat. During the journeys back and forth across the water
(while the poet peers, Narcissus-like, at his own image reflected in the water), Whitman suspends the old conflicts
between the maternal sea and the paternal land. He re-
gresses to a time before he was specifically aware of sexual
urges. The unusually clear and precise imagery in "Brooklyn Ferry" derives from the comfort Whitman takes from
his central metaphor.[5] By means of an act of faith the poet
can plunge very deeply into his unconscious and still look

---

[4] The psychological movement of "This Compost" is typical for
Whitman until the end. Repulsed at the thought of touching the
sea and land, which are filled with corpses, the poet is flooded with
thoughts of disease and death. His preoccupation is relieved in an
atypical manner when he perceives an orderly family:

> The he-birds carol mornings and evenings,
>   while the she-birds sit on their nests,
> The young of poultry break through the
>   hatched eggs.

In this poem Whitman can endorse biological continuity and believe
that if animals can fulfill their roles without anxiety, perhaps man
can also. Later this embryo evolved into "Out of the Cradle," in
which the she-bird's disappearance destroys the family's attunement
with the universe.

[5] As Stanley Coffman has noticed, the earlier catalogs in "Crossing Brooklyn Ferry" have little of the evasive disorganization and
vagueness typical of Whitman; see " 'Crossing Brooklyn Ferry': A
Note on the Catalog Technique in Whitman's Poetry," *Modern
Philology*, 2 (1954), 225-32.

outward. Again we see that in order to make his poetic method succeed, Whitman must coordinate a dynamic sense of his inner topography with reflexive perceptions of the changing external world. In "Brooklyn Ferry" the precise imagery defines the poet's relation to the external world. Away from the shore and protected from the water around and below, Whitman can afford to identify the face reflected by the perilous water.

> Flood-tide of the river, flow on! I watch you,
>   face to face,
> Clouds of the west! sun half an hour high! I see
>   you also face to face.
>
> Crowds of men and women attired in the usual
>   costumes, how curious you are to me!
> On the ferry-boats the hundreds and hundreds that
>   cross are more curious to me than you suppose,
> And you that shall cross from shore to shore years
>   hence, are more to me, and more in my
>   meditations, than you might suppose.

For once we know precisely where Whitman is: he is looking westward at the setting sun and clouds as the ferry makes its crossing. We do not know whether he goes to Brooklyn or Manhattan, because his present sense of well-being depends on the continuation of his motion and might be jeopardized by destination. To remain free from conflict he must stay away from the shore and the things it symbolizes. His freedom enables him to look outward at the landscape and the other passengers. Yet even on the ferry his interest in the other passengers is sharply limited: he wants them to be curious about and interested in him. They must acknowledge the silent watching man as their creator.

Section two describes "The impalpable sustenance of me from all things at all hours of the day." Consciously Whitman probably refers to the air he breathes, but the logic of the ferryboat metaphor suggests that what sustains him "at all hours of the day" is autonomic umbilical feeding. To assure continued sustenance he affirms "The simple, compact, well-joined scheme." The "scheme" requires the abolition of identity (which, by definition, separates individuals). If Whitman can believe in the "scheme," the location of his body matters little, for disintegration implies immortality. Believing in immortality he can identify the space his body occupies and imagine the "current rushing so swiftly, and swimming with me far away." In the unified vast similitude neither he nor his fellow passengers will suffer the fate of the "beautiful gigantic swimmer" in "The Sleepers." All may enter the "gates of the ferry, and cross from shore to shore." Safe during their passage from threats to their narcissism, they may enjoy the sunset.

The assurance beginning section three, that time and place avail not, depends on the poet's belief that he can "project myself, also I return—I am with you, and know how it is." He "knows" the universality of the oceanic ecstasy and invites his fellow passengers to look into the river with him: "I too saw the reflection of the summer-sky in the water."

> Had my eyes dazzled by the shimmering track of
>   beams,
> Looked at the fine centrifugal spokes of light round
>   the shape of my head in the sun-lit water.

The highly organized catalog that follows the perception of his own image confirms his confidence that he can make specific external perceptions and organize them coherently without fearing that external reality threatens the security of his inner world. For once Whitman coordinates the external and internal. The half-hour remaining before sundown corresponds to the half-hour of the passage. We may say that in Whitman's elemental symbolism, where fire (the sun) usually represents sexual impulses, the metaphor of the safe ferry crossing protects against unconscious anxiety. Ogiastic images in this section,

161

> The round masts, the swinging motion of the hulls,
>   the slender serpentine pennants,
>
>   ✧   ✧   ✧
>
> The white wake left by the passage, the quick
>   tremulous whirl of the wheels,
>
>   ✧   ✧   ✧
>
> On the neighboring shore the fires from the foundry
>   chimneys burning high and glaringly into the
>   night,
> Casting their flicker of black, contrasted with wild
>   red and yellow light, over the tops of houses,
>   and down into the clefts of streets,

give focus and organization to the perceptions but diffuse the underlying sexuality. When the whole world is orgiastic, Whitman's fantasies are objectified and guilt is ameliorated. The poet can safely regress to a pre-genital life in which he can fantasize sexual fulfillment without fearing retribution or obligation.

In section four the movement back and forth between reality and the unconscious gives assurance that, should reality threaten, a safe retreat awaits. By "projecting" himself Whitman can "tell" his poems to the city and its people. But if the world has become a version of Whitman's orgiastic fantasies, his awareness that other people exist leads to a question, "What is it, then, between us? What is the count of the scores or hundreds of years between us?" The question first means "What connects us?" but its secondary meaning, "What separates us?" emerges as the section continues. Speaking of himself as if long dead, Whitman "recalls" having "lived," "walked the streets of Manhattan Island," "felt the curious abrupt questionings stir within me":

> In the day, among crowds of people, sometimes
>   they came upon me,
> In my walks home late at night, or as I lay in my
>   bed, they came upon me.

In this instance, no loving bedfellow comes to Whitman's side; the "questionings" arise when the poet examines his memories and finds past anxieties renewed.

> I too had been struck from the float forever held in
>   solution,
> I too had received identity by my body,
> That I was, I knew was of my body, and what I
>   should be, I knew I should be of my body.

He sets the recollection in terms that indicate a thing of the past. A list follows of doubts and guilts, the depression and agonies of old. In the past, separated from the womb-like security of the ferry, he felt himself merely equivalent to his body, bound to judge himself evil because of his body's demands:

> I too knitted the old knot of contrariety,
> Blabbed, blushed, resented, lied, stole, grudged,
> Had guile, anger, lust, hot wishes I dared not
>   speak,
>
>   ✼   ✼   ✼
>
> Refusals, hates, postponements, meanness, laziness,
>   none of these wanting.

But now, protected by the poem's basic metaphor, he feels himself saved from these "evils," including his auto-erotic response to sexual impulses.[6] The call of "young men as they saw me approaching or passing," potential ideal readers, led to the deep inner change Whitman feels has occurred; Whitman identifies the change with his new bardic role "that is what we make it, as great as we like, or as small as we like, or both great and small."

The recollection of his "calling" brings Whitman back, in section seven, to his concern that he and his reader share the protection of the "necessary film," the amnion that "en-

---

[6] Edwin Miller points out the autoerotic meaning of knitting "the old knot of contrariety" (*A Psychological Journey*, p. 206).

velops all, and envelops the soul for a proper time." Whitman feels a flood of bardic electricity as he promotes narcissism for the masses:

> We understand, then, do we not?
> What I promised without mentioning it, have you
>   not accepted?
> What the study could not teach—what the preaching
>   could not accomplish is accomplished, is it not?
> What the push of reading could not start is started
>   by me personally, is it not?

Nothing can excel such works as these. These poems are
not meant to preach, nor even to be read, but to infuse the
reader extra-linguistically—or so Whitman must believe to
sustain the ecstasy of his ferry passage. "Flow on, river!"
says Whitman, for the flood cannot harm those in his boat.
The river reflects back a single dazzling face from its sunlit
surface:

> Diverge, fine spokes of light, from the shape of my
>   head, or any one's head, in the sun-lit
>   water!

>   ✿   ✿   ✿

> Burn high your fires, foundry chimneys, cast black
>   shadows at night-fall! cast red and yellow light
>   over the tops of the houses!

>   ✿   ✿   ✿

> You necessary film, continue to envelop the soul!

But as the poem concludes, Whitman's assurances become diffused, his perceptions disordered.

> We descend upon you and all things, we arrest you
>   all,
> We realize the soul only by you, you faithful solids
>   and fluids,
> Through you color, form, location, sublimity,
>   ideality,

Through you every proof, comparison, and all the
    suggestions and determinations of ourselves.

You have waited, you always wait, you dumb
    beautiful ministers! you novices!
We receive you with free sense at last, and are
    insatiate henceforward,
Not you any more shall be able to foil us, or
    withhold yourselves from us,
We use you, and do not cast you aside—we plant
    you permanently within us,
We fathom you not—we love you—there is
    perfection in you also,
You furnish your parts toward eternity,
Great or small, you furnish your parts toward the
    soul.

The "dumb beautiful ministers" are the river, the earth,
the film, the air, the fellow passengers, all things that enhance Whitman's sense of immortality. Everything is perceived as part of the internal world of the poet's regressive
vision. It is catharsis and the narcissistic vision itself that
Whitman loves.

At the end of the poem Whitman seems to sense some
incompatibility between his unconscious vision and the
world outside. When he retreats from the external world
at the conclusion, he shows less confidence in the security
of his inner world than he had at the beginning. Perhaps he
loses confidence merely because faith, like logic, cannot
stand for long on an analogy. The recapitulation in section
nine carries less conviction than similar statements had at
the beginning of the poem:

Flow on river! Flow with the flood-tide, and ebb
    with the ebb-tide!
Frolic on, crested and scallop-edged waves!

                    *   *   *

Stand up, tall masts of Manahatta!—stand up,
    beautiful hills of Brooklyn,

                    *   *   *

165

Suspend here and everywhere, eternal float of
    solution!
Blab, blush, lie, steal, you or I or any one after us!
Gaze, loving and thirsting eyes, in the house or street
    or public assembly!
Sound out, voices of young men! loudly and
    musically call me by my nighest name!
Live, old life! play the part that looks back on the
    actor or actress!
Play the old role, the role that is great or small,
    according as one makes it!
Consider, you who peruse me, whether I may not
    in unknown ways be looking upon you!
Be firm, rail over the river, to support those who
    lean idly, yet haste with the hasting current!

✿   ✿   ✿

Diverge, fine spokes of light, from the shape of my
    head, or any one's head, in the sun-lit water!

The line in which he urges the "rail over the river" to "Be
firm" implies that a doubt not previously apparent now nags
him. Perhaps the doubt results from some not quite explicit
awareness that there is a contradiction between the repetition of old imagistic formulas and the sense that no matter
how often he repeats them, the eternal float cannot be suspended. The former images have become "magic words" to
him, as if the mere speaking assured his mastery of the
things he names. Because the security of the ferry-as-womb
analogy is dubious, Whitman must retreat from the danger
that the rail might collapse. The sense of movement—even
the back and forth crossing of the ferry—is suspended or
forgotten at the end of the poem. As often happens, Whitman stops writing when he senses an unresolvable psychological conflict. Each time a poem ends it appears that
he has given up trying to find solutions by means of poetry.
Yet he keeps on writing new poems.

At least for a time. In the eight months following the
issuance of the second *Leaves of Grass* Whitman wrote at

least sixty-eight new poems. Although most of the successful poems of 1856 tended to skirt the poet's underlying sexual confusions, the new poems included many that were to find their way into the "Calamus" and "Enfans d'Adam" clusters of 1860, whose explicit subjects were "adhesive" and "amative" love. On the poetic journeys represented by the new poems, Whitman met unconscious insistences he could neither deny nor easily answer. The increasing strength of conflicts and ambivalences soon caused a crisis of sufficient magnitude to threaten Whitman's psychological gains with reversal. It is this period of crisis that we must now examine.

3

**The Third
Leaves of
Grass and
After**

A Biography of an Imagination:
III

WHITMAN worked on the third *Leaves of Grass* in spurts of activity interrupted by periods of despair, for in the years between the second and third editions (1856-1860) he passed through a major psychological crisis. His depression apparently derived from psychosexual conflicts manifest in the poet since the time of his adolescent story "My Boys and Girls." Many scholars have sought to explain Whitman's crisis by supposing that he had an unhappy love affair. I believe that the principal manifestation of the crisis was not a love affair, but something more important to history: Whitman nearly abandoned his poetic vocation, a move that would have deprived the world of "Out of the Cradle," "As I Ebb'd," "Calamus," "Children of Adam," and "When Lilacs Last in the Dooryard Bloom'd." The poetic triumphs in the 1860 *Leaves of Grass* grew from Whitman's relentless confrontation with his conflicts, from transforming unconscious explorations into poetic form.

Yet the victory of 1860 was also an ending, the end of personal explorations, the end of Whitman's great poems. After the third *Leaves of Grass* came the Civil War, when Whitman became the wound dresser, the good gray poet. The poet of *Drum-Taps* imitated the poet of *Leaves of Grass*

171

with occasional success but frequent failure. The crisis of wartime America justified the poet's suppressing his continuing crisis within. Finally, the last great poem, "Lilacs," product of a public outrage and a private grief, declared that energy formerly directed toward personal exploration would henceforth be reserved for a ripped world that needed the idea of a bard more than the work of a poet.

The creative surge that resulted in the first two editions did not expend itself until Whitman had written at least a hundred poems, sometime before June 1857. At that time he complained to his friend, Sarah Tyndale:

"Fowler & Wells are bad persons for me. They retard my book very much. It is worse than ever. I wish now to bring out a third edition—I have now *a hundred* poems ready (the last edition had thirty-two)—and shall endeavor to make an arrangement with some publisher here to take the plates from F. & W. and make the additions needed, and so bring out the third edition. F. & W. are very willing to give up the plates—they want the thing off their hands. In the forthcoming Vol. I shall have, as I said, a hundred poems, and no other matter but poems—(no letters to or from Emerson—no notices, or any thing of that sort.) I know well enough, that *that* must be the *true* Leaves of Grass—I think it (the new Vol.) has an aspect of completeness, and makes its case clearer. The old poems are all retained. The difference is in the new character given to the mass, by the additions." [1]

But for the next three years, until the spring of 1860, Whitman's work toward the third edition suffered major interruptions that nearly destroyed the psychological gains implied by the existence of the first two books. It was midway in 1857 when the commitment Whitman had finally made to his vocation threatened to reverse itself. The poems written in fits and starts between 1857 and 1859 reveal the crisis that directly and specifically involved Whitman's newly won confidence in his poetic vocation. The interruptions

[1] *Corr.*, I, p. 44.

themselves, just as much as the material in the poems, indicate how serious was the crisis.

Although we have very few historical facts about Whitman's outward life in these years, Fredson Bowers' examination of Whitman's manuscripts of the period yielded two important discoveries: that "Calamus" grew out of a twelve-poem cluster Whitman called "Live Oak, with Moss" in a fair copy inscribed about March 1859, and that one of the "Enfans d'Adam" poems, "Once I Pass'd through a Populous City," referred in manuscript to a male, rather than female, lover.[2] The homosexual implications of "Live Oak, with Moss" and the alteration in the other poem led Bowers, Gay Wilson Allen, Edwin Miller, Roger Asselineau, and many others to argue anew the old contention that an unhappy homosexual affair about 1858 precipitated Whitman's crisis.[3] Readers accepting this contention approach the 1860 poems with mistaken assumptions. Critics who assume that Whitman was consciously and overtly homosexual tend to find their assumptions confirmed when they discuss "Calamus," "Out of the Cradle," and "Enfans d'Adam" and to complain (though the complaint is rarely explicit) that Whitman's covertness about homosexuality hypocritically betrayed the deepest aspect of his affectional life.[4] I ask that

[2] *Whitman's Manuscripts: "Leaves of Grass" (1860)* (Chicago, 1955), p. 64.

[3] As mentioned in Chapter 3, note 9, Edwin Miller (*A Psychological Journey*, p. 175) observes that even if such an affair could be proved, its significance would lie in something we already know: that the loss of love reactivated the sense of loss Whitman felt in infancy at the separation he experienced from his mother. However, ascertaining a middle-aged homosexual affair would also prove something Miller takes for granted: that Whitman was consciously homosexual and much more aware of his sexual confusions than I believe was the case. Miller's further speculation that the death of Whitman's father may have been a significant factor in the crisis appears to be confirmed by my reading of the symbolic substructure of such poems as "As I Ebb'd" and "Out of the Cradle."

[4] See, for example, one of the most perceptive readings of "Calamus": "When Whitman sought to treat comradeship philosophically in 1860, his work became thin and scratchy, about as abstract

my reader consider the biographical discussion and the interpretations of the poem I will present with quite a different hypothesis in mind.

It seems to me that historical and poetic evidence point to a Whitman very different from the poet described by most preceding scholars. I believe that Whitman regarded himself as sexually "normal," but that about 1856-1857 he began to be almost conscious of homosexual impulses, which he found abhorrent. In order to continue writing poetry that threatened to expose unconscious impulses, yet to continue the repression of such impulses, he developed an elaborate mystique of non-sexual masculine brotherhood (supported by the phrenological concept of "adhesiveness"), which justified his preoccupation with the subject. The psychological defense embodied in this mystique was only partly effective. As Whitman tried to continue composing poems, the regressive aspects of his creative process constantly threatened to make conscious homosexual wishes unacceptable to his ego ideals. This dilemma caused Whitman's work toward the third edition to progress erratically rather than in the spontaneous flood of creativity that yielded the first two books.

The most important events of 1856-1859 occurred within the privacy of Whitman's fantasy world, and their nature would not necessarily be evident even if we had many more historical facts than we do. As I will show, the "Live Oak" poems reveal the struggle of a poet on the verge of rejecting his vocation. An important piece of historical evidence tends to support the hypothesis I have presented and leads to a view of Whitman as a man whose motives and intentions were less conscious and more confused than has generally been assumed.

---

and implausible as the heterosexual poetry had been"; Clark Griffith, "Sex and Death, The Significance of Whitman's *Calamus* Themes," *Philological Quarterly*, 39 (1960), 38. The thinness, scratchiness, abstractness, and implausibility tend to vanish if one assumes that "Calamus" and "Enfans d'Adam" are about sexual fantasy, rather than homo- or heterosexual affairs.

In 1872 Whitman received an extraordinary letter from one of his first English admirers, John Addington Symonds (which I quote at length because I will later show that Whitman responds to the letter's tone as much as to its substance). After acknowledging a letter from Whitman, Symonds described his consuming interest in "passionate friendship," which he had traced "through Greece, Rome, the medieval and the modern world." Symonds continued:

"It was while engaged upon this work (years ago now) that I first read Leaves of Grass. The man who spoke to me from that Book impressed me in every way most profoundly —unalterably; but especially did I then learn confidently to believe that the Comradeship which I conceived as on a par with the sexual feeling for depth and strength and purity and capability of all good, was *real*—not a delusion of distorted passions, a dream of the Past, a scholar's fancy —but a strong and vital bond of man to man.

"Yet even then how hard I found it—brought up in English feudalism, educated at an aristocratic public school (Harrow) and an over refined University (Oxford)—to winnow from my own emotion and from my conception of the ideal friend all husks of affectations and aberrations and to be a simple human being! *You* cannot tell quite how hard this was, and how you helped me.

"I have pored for continuous hours over the pages of Calamus (as I used to pore over the pages of Plato), longing to hear you speak, burning for a revelation of your more developed meaning, panting to ask—is this what you would indicate?—are then the free men of your land really so pure and loving and noble and generous and sincere? Most of all did I desire to hear from your own lips—or from your pen —some story of athletic friendship from which to learn the truth. Yet I dared not to address you or dreamed that the thought of a student could abide the inevitable shafts of your searching intuition.

"Shall I ever be permitted to question you and learn from you?

"What the love of man for man has been in the Past I

175

think I know. What it is here now, I know also—alas! What you say it can and shall be I dimly discern in your Poems. But this hardly satisfies me—so desirous am I of learning what you teach.

"Some day, perhaps—in some form, I know not what, but in your own chosen form—you will tell me more about the Love of Friends. Till then I wait. Meanwhile you have told me more than any one beside.

"I have been led to write too much about myself, presuming on what you said, that you should like to know me better. . . .

"That you may know my face I enclose two portraits. The little girl in one of them is my youngest child.

"I am your ever grateful and indebted

"John Addington Symonds."[5]

Among the many implications of this letter, the following seem most striking: Symonds hints at his own homosexuality ("What the love of man for man [is] now, I know also—alas!"); he invites Whitman to join him in a passionate friendship ("I dared not to address you or dreamed that the thought of a student could abide the inevitable shafts of your searching intuition. / Shall I ever be permitted to question you and learn from you?"). He presents his credentials as a member of the English one per cent (Harrow and Oxford), hinting that he is in a position to further Whitman's literary fame in England if allowed to become one of the disciples that "Calamus" demands. Finally, the remarks at the end suggest that he will be discreet, should Whitman return him a similar confession or a favorable response: Symonds is married, and has children; he has adjusted to the heterosexual world.

It appears probable that Whitman more or less understood the implications I have described, as well as Symonds' tone.[6] What may be deduced from a conversation about

[5] Traubel, *With Walt Whitman in Camden* (Boston, 1906), i, pp. 75-76.

[6] That Symonds' admiration for his "Master" was slighter than may be apparent from the letter quoted in my text is implied in a

Symonds and from Whitman's reply to the letter eighteen
years later makes Whitman's reaction seem as extraordinary
as the letter itself. On 27 April 1888 Whitman showed the
letter to Horace Traubel, who recorded the following
discussion:

"Talked an hour or more about Symonds. W. very frank,
very affectionate. 'Symonds is a royal good fellow—he
comes along without qualifications: just happens into the
temple and takes his place. But he has a few doubts yet to
be quieted—not doubts of me, doubts rather of himself.
One of these doubts is about Calamus. What does Calamus
mean? What do the poems come to in the round-up? That
is worrying him a good deal—their involvement, as he sus-
pects, is the passional relations of men with men—the thing
he reads so much of in the literatures of southern Europe
and sees something of in his own experience. He is always
driving at me about that [that is, Symonds had written further letters to Whitman, after the first letter of 7 February
1872]: is that what Calamus means?—because of me or in
spite of me, is that what it means? I have said no, but no
does not satisfy him. But read this letter—read the whole
of it: it is very shrewd, very cute, in deadliest earnest: it
drives me hard—almost compels me—it is urgent, persistent: he sort of stands in the road and says: "I won't move
till you answer my question." You see, this is an old letter—
sixteen years old—and he is still asking the question: he
refers to it in one of his latest notes. He is surely a wonder-
ful man—a rare cleaned-up man—a white-souled, heroic
character. Look at the fight he has so far kept up with his
body—yes, and so far won: it is marvellous to me, even. I
have had my own troubles—I have seen other men with
troubles, too—worse than mine and not so bad as mine—
but Symonds is the noblest of us all.' This had all been

letter Symonds wrote to Swinburne on 8 December 1872: "I sent
Walt Whitman the [poem] called 'Love & Death,' & he graciously
accepted it as a tribute to the author of Calamus. Yet no one on
whose critical faculty I could rely has judged them" (quoted in
Corr., II, 158, n. 43).

called out by an old Symonds letter which he had been reading and which he gave to me. 'You will be writing something about Calamus some day,' said W., 'and this letter, and what I say, may help to clear your ideas. Calamus needs clear ideas: it may be easily, innocently distorted from its natural, its motive, body of doctrine.'

[Traubel here reprints the letter quoted above.]

"Said W.: 'Well, what do you think of that? Do you think that could be answered?' 'I don't see why you call that letter driving you hard. It's quiet enough—it only asks questions, and asks the questions mildly enough.' 'I suppose you are right—"drive" is not exactly the word: yet you know how I hate to be catechised. Symonds is right, no doubt, to ask the questions: I am just as much right if I do not answer them: just as much right if I do answer them. I often say to myself about Calamus—perhaps it means more or less than what I thought myself—means different: perhaps I don't know what it all means—perhaps never did know. My first instinct about all that Symonds writes is violently reactionary—is strong and brutal for no, no, no. Then the thought intervenes that I maybe do not know all my own meanings: I say to myself: "You, too, go away, come back, . . . study your own book, see what it amounts to." Sometime or other I will have to write him definitely about Calamus—give him my word for it what I meant or mean it to mean.' "[7]

Why Whitman should have been so upset by this letter, and why, under Traubel's disingenuous questioning, he should have so eulogized Symonds, calling him "heroic" for "the fight he has so far kept up with his body," are unclear, to say the least, but I will hazard a few guesses. When Whitman remarks that "Calamus" means perhaps more or something different from what he had intended, he seems to me to express genuine bewilderment; in this context he unmistakably invited Traubel to look for fugitive meanings. Whitman must have been convinced that his intention—to celebrate pure (unsexual) masculine love—would be revealed by such an examination. Quite apart from being a

[7] Traubel, I, pp. 73-77.

challenge to Whitman's belief in his own sexual normalcy, Symonds' letter must have been irritating in its subtle presumptuousness: Symonds says that he has Whitman figured out. With a bit more sensitivity, Symonds might have understood that Whitman's frequent statements that he cannot be easily known expressed a strong aversion to being known. Whitman's poetic invitations to intimacy are invariably followed by warnings against attempts at intimacy: "Put me down, and depart on your way."

Whitman's applause for Symonds' "heroism" seems to have been a reaction against the irritation he felt toward the letter and its writer. If Whitman could rarely express personal antipathy as condemnation, he could damn with mixed praise. His eulogy of Symonds seems to say: I applaud a man cursed with a perverse nature, who, by marrying, triumphed over that nature. Whitman probably unconsciously identified with Symonds, seeing himself also as one who had triumphed over abnormal impulses. The force of the eulogy emphasizes Symonds' abnormality rather than his heroism. Symonds' artfulness was a poor match for the intuitive shafts from the poet of American naïveté.

Whitman finally wrote Symonds definitely about "Calamus" on 19 August 1890, more than two years after the conversation with Traubel. Until then his letters had ignored Symonds reiterated questions about the poems. Whitman's reply is, in part, a self-conscious parody of the original catechism (which Symonds repeated in a letter of 3 August 1890):

"Y'rs of Aug: 3d just rec'd & glad to hear f'm you as always—Abt the little portraits, I cheerfully endorse the Munich reproduction of any of them you propose or any thing of the sort you choose—(I may soon send you some other preferable portraits of self)—Suppose you have rec'd papers & slips sent of late—Ab't the questions on Calamus pieces &c: they quite daze me. L of G. is only to be rightly construed by and within its own atmosphere and essential character—all of its pages & pieces so coming strictly under *that*—that the calamus part has even allow'd the possibility of such construction as mention'd is terrible—I am fain to hope the pages themselves are not to be even mention'd for such gratuitous and quite at the time entirely undream'd & unreck'd possibility of morbid inferences—wh' are disavow'd by me & seem damnable. Then [sic] one great difference between you and me, temperament & theory, is *restraint*—I know that while I have a horror of ranting & bawling I at certain moments let the spirit impulse, (?demon) rage its utmost, its wildest, damnedest—(I feel to do so in my L of G. & I do so). I end the matter by saying I wholly stand by L of G. as it is, long as all parts & pages are construed as I said by their own ensemble, spirit & atmosphere.

"I live here 72 y'rs old & completely paralyzed—brain & right arm ab't same as ever—digestion, sleep, appetite, &c: fair—sight & hearing half-and-half—spirits fair—locomotive power (legs) almost utterly gone—am propell'd outdoors nearly every day—get down to the river side here, the Delaware, an hour at sunset—The writing and rounding of L of G. has been to me the reason-for-being, & life comfort. My life, young manhood, mid-age, times South, &c: have all been jolly, bodily, and probably open to criticism—

"Tho' always unmarried I have had six children—two are dead—One living southern grandchild, fine boy, who writes to me occasionally. Circumstances connected with their benefit and fortune have separated me from intimate relations.

"I see I have written with haste & too great effusion—but let it stand."[8]

Scholars seeking fruitlessly for one—let alone six—of Whitman's progeny have failed to notice that Whitman's whopper parallels the end of Symonds' letter, in which the

---

[8] *Corr.*, v, 72-73. In his book, *Walt Whitman, a Study* (London, 1893), Symonds accepts without visible reservation Whitman's word about the meaning and intent of "Calamus," equivocating only to the extent of saying that some readers may be misled into thinking of a less pure sentiment.

Englishman spoke of his family to suggest his heterosexual adjustment. I doubt whether Whitman intended to mock Symonds, but the effect was to imply that a charade of marriage was meaningless.

Further, I think there is another meaning in Whitman's letter that carries a psychological truth. In Chapter One I discussed "My Boys and Girls," the adolescent fantasy Whitman wrote in 1836, which tells of the bachelor author's "several girls and boys." These children—Mary, Hannah Louisa, George Washington, Thomas Jefferson, and Andrew Jackson—were Whitman's sisters and three of his brothers. When we include Edward with the others we have the "six children" Whitman claimed. Two "children" were dead in 1890, the infant sister, and Andrew. Whitman's "lie" had an unconscious meaning, that the poet sublimated his homosexual sensibility by means of the paternal role he played in his parents' family. He was not being merely disingenuous when he protested against Symonds' inferences of homosexuality in "Calamus" and told Traubel, "Perhaps ["Calamus"] means more or less than what I thought myself—means different." The sublimation I have described would have left Whitman quite unaware of such latent meanings.

How else can we account for the exceptionally prolonged effect on Whitman of Symonds' catechizing? Even the fact that the Englishman reiterated his questions several times over the next eighteen years does not explain very much, for Whitman could have broken off the correspondence at any point. If Whitman had been aware of having a strong homosexual inclination and had consciously rejected this aspect of himself, he would surely have understood more readily the interpretation Symonds (and others) made of "Calamus"; and if he wished to keep this tendency secret, he could have censored such material. Similarly, he could have found some more convincing and more prompt rebuttal to the hints in Symonds' letters. On the other hand, were Whitman consciously homosexual and his protestations to the contrary merely attempts to escape Victorian censure, he would hardly have been as upset by Symonds' hints as he was. It seems likely that Whitman thought Symonds a sensitive reader who was deeply moved by the poems, but who misconstrued them to accord with his own experience. It was essential to Whitman that *Leaves of Grass* express abhorrence for no man or woman. In keeping with his principles, Whitman let the correspondence continue, but did so at some cost: Whitman had to permit Symonds to nag at an acute psychic vulnerability. To judge from the conversation with Traubel, Whitman nursed a private sense of irritation at the nagging for nearly two decades.

A parallel situation evidently existed during the years between the second and third editions of *Leaves of Grass*, fifteen years before the first letter from Symonds. By June 1857 Whitman had written several poems that hint strikingly at something that looks very much like homosexuality (including the seventeenth, twenty-second, and twenty-sixth "Calamus" poems of 1860). The date is significant because it marks the end of the activity that produced the first and second editions as well as another sixty-eight poems. Afterwards, Whitman had more difficulty writing, and the writing he did was often closely associated with periods of depression or "stagnation." As we shall see from the poetry, a major cause of the "stagnation" was the threat that deeply repressed material relating to homosexual impulses might reemerge into consciousness as a by-product of the poetic process. Finally the threat overwhelmed Whitman and the poet ceased making significant poems.

NINE

Leaves of Grass, 1860

ALTHOUGH it would be too simple to say that the chief subject of the 1860 *Leaves of Grass* is the poetic process, virtually all the best poems of the third edition enlarge our understanding of the process. The he-bird's song awakens the "outsetting bard of love" to his own sexuality, and thereby, "from that hour," awakens the bard's songs as well. When the poet ebbs, his despair comes as much from the real ME's mockery of his songs as from the more general mockery of himself and his wish to earn immortality. The heterosexual—"amative"—impulses that are the putative subject of "Enfans d'Adam" are justified not only by procreativity but also by poetic creativity. The "Calamus" lovers commune by means of the poems that create them.

Whitman's poetic identity emerged as a substitute for a sexual identity that remained latent. Yet the substitution could not resolve the confusion underlying Whitman's need for public acknowledgment that *Leaves of Grass* surpassed the work of all past bards, that it infused a flagging democracy with new breath and hope, and that it created by example a nation of poets and tenderest lovers. Neither love nor poetry erased Whitman's fear that love between himself and another actual person might jeopardize, rather than confirm, the fantasy of restoring infantile omnipotence.

Poetry might after all be "only a language experiment" rather than evidence of divine grace.

After 1856 Whitman increasingly thought of his work as metaphysically inspired. About the spring of 1857 he noted to himself: "The Great Construction of the New Bible. Not to be diverted from the principal object—the main life work—the three hundred and sixty-five.—It ought to be ready in 1859."[1] Thinking about his work as the creation of a "New Bible" did not help its progress. That this note and the letter to Mrs. Tyndale were apparently written about the same time suggests that Whitman's intentions remained as contradictory as when a similar ambivalence led to "Poem of Many In One" and "Broad-Axe Poem." At one moment he regarded his "new Vol." as complete, wanting only a publisher; at the next moment the third edition was a "New Bible" needing two hundred and sixty-five more poems. It seems less likely that the quarrel with Fowler and Wells, the publishers of the second *Leaves of Grass*, impeded the poet's progress than that the impediment was within Whitman himself. A phrase in the letter to Mrs. Tyndale (quoted at the beginning of the preceding chapter) hints at an important confusion within Whitman: "I think it (the new Vol.) has an aspect of completeness." To conceive of poetry as an organism, processive and progressive, excludes the idea of "completeness," for an organism is complete only when it dies. Whitman's preoccupation with his work's reception inevitably led him to look forward to public acclaim, which could not come until the work was done. His desires that his poems live and yet be complete echoed a more important contradiction within his poetic process: he felt most vital while writing poems, yet wanted his painful task to be at an end. Inevitably the conflicts led to periods of paralysis; the poet's fluctuations determined the shape and subject of the new poems.

It is therefore important to trace Whitman's halting steps toward the third *Leaves of Grass*. As I have said, historical

[1] Quoted in Bowers, *Whitman's Manuscripts*, p. xxxv. Dr. Bucke dated this note June 1857.

184

and poetic evidence suggests that Whitman's work proceeded in four surges of activity that we can somewhat reconstruct and roughly date. The first phase continued the work that produced the second edition and apparently ended shortly before Whitman wrote to Mrs. Tyndale; it yielded at least sixty-eight new poems. I infer from the Tyndale letter that the idea of arranging poems into clusters had not yet occurred to Whitman: "The old poems are all retained. The difference is in the new character given to the mass, by the additions." Half a list of titles survives, the titles numbered thirty-three to seventy-two, which Bowers related to the planned one-hundred-poem edition. In an important manuscript known as Valentine-Barrett, Whitman gave some of the poems numbers that correlate approximately with the numbered titles. The correlation implies that the list was made about the time Whitman wrote Mrs. Tyndale. Through the summer of 1859 (when the Valentine MS was finished), the list represented Whitman's plan for the third edition.[2] The numbering of poems in the manuscript allowed Bowers to continue the list in presumed accord with the lost second page of titles (numbered seventy-three to one hundred).

By studying Bowers' work one can define the four phases leading to the third *Leaves of Grass*:

I. Bowers enables us to learn that in the first phase—ending, let us say, 20 June 1857—Whitman had written various poems that, in the fourth phase, he would place in the major clusters of 1860 ("Calamus," "Enfans d'Adam," "Chants Democratic," and "Leaves of Grass").[3]

---

[2] Bowers, pp. xxxvii-xxxix.

[3] These include eleven of the 1860 "Calamus" poems (nos. 2, 16, 17, 21, 22, 25, 26, 27, 30, 41, 45); three of the 1860 "Adam" poems (nos. 7, 8, 10—not including nos. 3, 4, and 5, published in 1855 and 1856); nine of the 1860 "Chants Democratic" (nos. 4, 7, 12, 13, 16, 17, 18, 19, 20—not including nos. 1, 2, 3, 6, and 15, published in 1855 and 1856); and eight of the 1860 "Leaves of Grass" poems (nos. 13, 15, 16, 17, 18, 19, 21, 22—not including nos. 2, 3, 4, 5, 6, 7, 8, 9, 11, 12, and 14, published in 1855 and 1856).

185

II. The second phase probably ended about March-April, 1859.[4] The importance of this phase rests in the twelve Roman-numbered poems called "Live Oak, with Moss," the progenitor of "Calamus," written in this period. As I will later demonstrate, this group of poems tells of a profound crisis in Whitman's attitude about continuing to write poetry.

III. The third phase ended with the completion of the Valentine MS, about August 1859.[5]

IV. The last phase is the period between August 1859 and mid-May 1860, when the third *Leaves of Grass* was printed in Boston.[6] During this fourth phase, Whitman organized his poems into clusters, wrote or completed at least twenty-eight new poems (including "As I Ebb'd" and "Out of the Cradle"), and considerably revised many of the poems written earlier.

On 10 February 1860 Messrs. Thayer and Eldridge of Boston wrote Whitman that they wanted to "be the publishers of Walt Whitman's poems—Leaves of Grass." In mid-March Whitman went to Boston, met Emerson (who advised against publishing the "Adam" poems), and personally supervised the typesetting of his new book, which appeared two months later. Whatever conflicts hindered Whitman's earlier efforts to publish this third edition no longer operated in the winter of 1859-1860. The intention of two years earlier for the third *Leaves of Grass* to have an "aspect of completeness" and make "its case clearer" implies weaknesses Whitman sensed in the first two editions. Over-

[4] Bowers, p. xxix.

[5] Bowers, p. xxxiv. Among the 1860 poems first evident in this MS are the following: ten of the 1860 "Calamus" poems (nos. 1, 12, 15, 18, 31, 37, 38, 39, 40, and 44); two of the 1860 "Adam" poems (nos. 1 and 9); and four of the 1860 "Chants Democratic" (nos. 8, 9, 10, and 11).

[6] The following cluster poems are not evident before August 1859: eleven "Calamus" poems (nos. 3, 4, 5, 6, 13, 19, 24, 28, 29, 33, 35); seven "Adam" poems (nos. 2, 6, 11, 12, 13, 14, 15); three "Chants Democratic" (nos. 5, 14, and 21); and five "Leaves of Grass" poems (nos. 1, 10, 20, 23, and 24).

coming the weaknesses and resolving at least one profound personal conflict occupied Whitman during those two years. The Valentine manuscript, as well as the poems of 1860, permits us to understand something about both of these matters; the place to begin is with the "Live Oak" cluster.

I. *"Live Oak, with Moss"*

The twelve poems of "Live Oak, with Moss" present a coherent narrative, which develops as follows: the threat of being consumed by the flames of sexual impulses leads the poet to compare himself to the self-sufficient live oak tree and to recognize his own lack of self-sufficiency. Recognition leads to fantasies of intimacy (not necessarily sexual) with a male companion, and the importance of companionship momentarily supplants the importance of being America's bard. But even in fantasy Whitman cannot escape fears of abandonment and loss of love, to which intimacy makes him vulnerable. In response to these fears, he converts the fantasies of intimacy into the "dream of a city" where all men are "robust friends." This "dream" gives way to a vaguer dream of companions protected by distance and silence from "terrible" feelings in the poet that seem "ready to break forth." Finally, silence becomes everything; it defines the loving friends.

Much of the narrative emerges through the elemental symbolism that evolved in the earlier editions. The first "Live Oak" poem, "Not Heat Flames Up,"[7] presents a famil-

---

[7] I use the more familiar 1891-1892 titles for the "Live Oak" poems, but quotations are taken from the manuscript versions published by Bowers unless otherwise indicated. Arabic numbers in the following list indicate the location of the poem in the 1860 grouping; capital B followed by a page number indicates the reference to Bowers. i. "Not Heat Flames Up" (14; B, p. 92); ii. "I Saw in Louisiana a Live-Oak Growing" (20; B, p. 100); iii. "When I Heard at the Close of the Day" (11; B, p. 86); iv. "This Moment Yearning and Thoughtful" (23; B, p. 106); v. "Long I Thought That Knowledge Alone Would Suffice" (8; B, p. 80); vi. "What Think You I Take My Pen in Hand" (32; B, p. 116); vii. "Recorders Ages Hence" (10; B, p.

iar unconscious pattern in familiar terms: the heat "flames up and consumes," "the sea-waves hurry in and out," "white down-balls of myriads of seeds" are borne on the air. For this moment, at least, the poet expects to find his "lifelong lover," his hope warding off the potential anxieties that usually attend awareness of the fire inside. Because the poet identifies with the sea ("I, hurrying in and out"), we may presume that the identification supports his feeling of hope. The absence from this poem (and the next poem as well) of any perception of the earth facilitates the identification and hopefulness. Whitman's anxieties are often evoked by symbolic conjunctions of earth and water because his simultaneous and approximately equal identifications with both his mother and father make it impossible for him to embrace one identification fully without feeling he is rejecting the other and thereby rejecting a major part of himself. Whitman builds "Live Oak" on the expectation that the conflict may be resolved or evaded if he can give himself to a loving masculine friendship of which the maternal sea will not disapprove.

In "Live Oak" II, "I Saw in Louisiana a Live-Oak Growing," the poet identifies with a solitary tree hung with moss. Whitman contrasts his admiration for the tree's splendid isolation with his doubts that he could survive such loneliness.

> Without any companion it grew there, glistening out
>   joyous leaves of dark green,
> And its look, rude, unbending, lusty, made me think
>   of myself;
> But I wondered how it could utter joyous leaves,
>   standing alone there without its friend, its
>   lover—For I knew I could not;
> And I plucked a twig with a certain number of
>   leaves upon it, and twined around it a little

---

84); viii. "Hours Continuing Long" (9; B, p. 82); ix. "I Dream'd in a Dream" (34; B, p. 114); x. "O You Whom I Often" (43; B, p. 120); xi. "Earth, My Likeness" (36; B, p. 114); xii. "To a Western Boy" (42; B, p. 118).

moss, and brought it away—And I have placed
it in sight in my room,
It is not needed to remind me as of my friends,
(for I believe lately I think of little else than
of them,)
Yet it remains to me a curious token—it makes me
think of manly love,
For all that, and though the live oak glistens there
in Louisiana, solitary in a wide flat space,
uttering joyous leaves all its life, without a
friend, a lover, near—I know very well I
could not.

As James Miller notes, branches pulled off a tree is a
"very typical" dream symbol for masturbation.[8] The phallicism many critics have noticed in this tree has less to do
with genital masculinity than with another aspect of life
that to Whitman is definitively masculine, a man's work, his
professional commitments and identity. The unconscious
context out of which the live oak symbol grew parallels the
determinants that led Whitman, in "Song of Myself," to
identify with the "friendly and flowing savage." To Whitman, the savage, like the oak, is free from the agonizing introspection that prevents the poet's regenerating himself in
polymorphous androgyny. Whitman feels himself inescapably identified with the island, incessantly nagged by the
sea, isolated from all, unloved, and alien.

"Live Oak" III, "When I Heard at the Close of the Day,"
rejects the former ideal of "affectionate" absorption by the
poet's nation in favor of an anticipated union with the
friend who is to arrive that night. Whitman imagines himself reposing by his lover's side: "In the stillness his face
was inclined towards me, while the moon's clear beams
shone,/ And his arm lay lightly over my breast—And that

[8] *Walt Whitman,* p. 173; Miller cites Freud's *General Introduction to Psycho-Analysis,* Lecture x (*Standard Edition,* xv, 149-69).
The observation supports my general argument that the sexuality of
"Live Oak" (as well as of "Calamus" and "Adam") is autoerotic,
rather than heterosexual or homosexual.

night I was happy." What had formerly been an autoerotic fantasy gives way to a fantasy of nirvana-like peace and sleep, the ideal of the "vast similitude" that in "Clef Poem" led the poet to say, "This night I am happy" (see Chapter 3). In "The Sleepers" the fantasy of sexual union leads to morbid identification with the aging and dying woman before the awakening of dormant Oedipal conflicts. In "Live Oak" III Whitman seems unwilling to reenter that part of his unconscious world, seeking instead the "congratulations" of the sea for the friendship he has found. Once again the actual work of being a poet appears to conflict with the ideals Whitman has for his poetry: to work he must have a sense of professional identity and accept aloneness; yet he tries to write poems that restore infantile security and wordless communion. In part, Whitman seeks not "regression in the service of the ego," but rather the suspension of identity in service to regression. (These are the times Whitman seems most nearly to verge on schizophrenia.)

The next several "Live Oak" poems attempt to explore the possibilities of living exclusively within the regressive fantasy world of the vast transcendental similitude, which promises unchanging friendship. "Live Oak" IV, "This Moment Yearning and Thoughtful," projects the poet's mood and vision to foreign lands and concludes by asserting an international brotherhood of the lonely: the "Yearning and pensive" become "wise, beautiful, benevolent, as any in my own lands; O I think we should be brethren—I think I should be happy with them."

"Live Oak" V, "Long I Thought That Knowledge Alone Would Suffice," recounts with despair Whitman's efforts to cope with his identity crisis and concludes with an outright rejection of his poetic vocation.

> Long I thought that knowledge alone would suffice
>   me—O if I could but obtain knowledge!
> Then the Land of the Prairies engrossed me—the
>   south savannas engrossed me—For them I
>   would live—I would be their orator;

Then I met the examples of old and new heroes—I
  heard of warriors, sailors, and all dauntless
  persons—And it seemed to me I too had it in
  me to be as dauntless as any, and would be so;
And then to finish all, it came to me to strike up
  the songs of the New World—And then I
  believed my life must be spent in singing;
But now take notice * * *
            * * * that you all find someone else that
  he be your singer of songs,
For I can be your singer of songs no longer—I have
  ceased to enjoy them.
I have found him who loves me, as I him, in
  perfect love,
With the rest I dispense—I sever from all that I
  thought would suffice me, for it does not—it is
  now empty and tasteless to me,
I heed knowledge, and the grandeur of The States,
  and the examples of heroes, no more,
I am indifferent to my own songs—I am to go with
  him I love, and he is to go with me,
It is to be enough for each of us that we are together
  —We never separate again.

If we assume that the "knowledge" referred to in the first
line denotes self-knowledge as well as intellectual learning,
we may view the first part of this poem as a résumé of
"Song of Myself," while the second half rejects the poetic
identity to which Whitman aspires. The uses of this identity
have become "empty and tasteless" to a poet grown "indifferent" to his songs. Although Whitman had previously seen
his poetry as a sublimation of his sexual desires, he now
wants to reverse the process. The references to the lover in
this poem have a certain ring of specificity, as if Whitman
indeed waited for some actual person. Perhaps he did, but
the relationship he anticipated is conceived of as "perfect,"
implying little latitude for human mutability. "Perfection"
stands as remote from human reality as the symbiotic rela-

tions Whitman has otherwise sought in the master-disciple fantasies underlying so many other poems.

Apparently Whitman recognized the impossibility of the position he creates for himself, for he again becomes the poet in the sixth poem, "What Think You I Take My Pen in Hand." Instead of continuing to regard himself as the poet of "battle-ships" and "the splendors of the past day" or the night or the "glory and growth of the great city spread around me," he will be the poet who sings of

> * * * the two men I saw today on the pier, parting
> the parting of dear friends.
> The one to remain hung on the other's neck and
> passionately kissed him—while the one to
> depart tightly prest the one to remain in his arms.

This is the nearest Whitman will come in "Live Oak" to representing a sexual embrace between his fantasized lovers. The passionate kiss is imaginable to Whitman only because it is a parting kiss and imminent separation precludes its leading to intercourse. Like the parting kiss bestowed by the master on the wayfarer ("Song of Myself," section forty-six), and the kiss Whitman symbolically implored from his father (in "As I Ebb'd"), the kiss signals the end of a relationship. In the remainder of "Live Oak" Whitman increasingly imagines love as undemonstrated and finally as silent.

In "Live Oak" VII, "Recorders Ages Hence," the overt homosexual fantasy diminishes and Whitman resumes the bardic role.

> You bards of ages hence! when you refer to me,
> mind not so much my poems,
> Nor speak of me that I prophesied of The States
> and led them the way of their glories,
> But come, I will inform you who I was underneath
> that impassive exterior—I will tell you what to
> say of me,
> Publish my name and hang up my picture as that
> of the tenderest lover,

The friend, the lover's portrait, of whom his friend,
  his lover, was fondest,
Who was not proud of his songs, but of the
  measureless ocean of love within him—and
  freely poured it forth * * *

The oceanic feeling of love poured forth in poetry takes
the place of the kiss, for in poetry the threat of rejection
may be avoided. The poet can cope with his loneliness by
imagining himself to be one who gave up love for the sake
of his art:

Who pensive, away from one he loved, often lay
  sleepless and dissatisfied at night,
Who, dreading lest the one he loved might after all
  be indifferent to him, felt the sick feeling—O
  sick! sick!
Whose happiest days were those, far away through
  the fields, in woods, on hills, he and another,
  wandering hand in hand, they twain, apart
  from other men.
Who ever, as he sauntered the streets, curved with
  his arm the manly shoulder of his friend—while
  the curving arm of his friend rested upon him
  also.

The possessive exclusiveness of this friendship would
lead Whitman into the same psychological tautology that
he previously sought to escape (in "Song of Myself"); by
sending his disciple away, he leaves them both free to engage the external world. If, in "Live Oak" VII, Whitman
cannot contemplate the immediate abolition of his fantasy,
he has left himself a way out of the trap, reverting to an alternate fantasy of receiving the attention of future bards.

In "Live Oak" VIII, "Hours Continuing Long," Whitman
permits himself a final indulgence of grief at losing his fantasy of love. As in "Live Oak" IV, he projects a community
of rejected lovers and, despite being ashamed of himself,

seems to hope that his lost lover shares his agony. The homosexual fantasy has been completely abolished here in favor of preoccupation with his grief and sense of loss. Edwin Miller has noticed the similarity in tone between "Live Oak" VIII and journal entries made thirteen years later:[9]

"✸ ✸ ✸ cheating, childish abandonment of myself, fancying what does not really exist in another, but is all the time in myself alone—utterly deluded & cheated by *myself*, & my own weakness—REMEMBER WHERE I AM MOST WEAK, & most lacking. Yet always preserve a kind spirit & demeanor to 16. But PURSUE HER NO MORE."

"A cool, gentle (*less demonstrative*) *more* UNIFORM DEMEANOR—give to poor—help any,—be indulgent to to the criminal & silly & to low persons generally & the ignorant—but SAY little—make no explanations—*give no confidences*—never attempt puns, or plays upon words, or utter sarcastic comments, or, (under ordinary circumstances) hold any discussions or arguments."

June 17   good! July 15

"*It is* IMPERATIVE, that I obviate & remove myself (& my orbit) *at all hazards* from this *incessant enormous* & PERTURBATION

"Congress adjourned in great excitement War is said to be declared in Europe 2½ P.M.————I am writing in the office, not feeling very well————opprest with the heat
July 15—1870

"TO GIVE UP ABSOLUTELY & *for good, from this present hour*, this FEVERISH, FLUCTUATING, *useless undignified pursuit of* 164————*too long,* (*much too long*) persevered in,————so humiliating————*It must come at last* & had better come now————(*It cannot possibly be a success*) LET THERE FROM THIS HOUR BE NO FALTERING, NO GETTING————*at all henceforth,*

---

[9] *A Psychological Journey*, p. 158.

(NOT ONCE, *under any circumstances*)————*avoid seeing her, or meeting her, or any talk or explanations*————*or* ANY MEETING WHATEVER, FROM THIS HOUR FORTH, FOR LIFE."

July 15, '70[10]

It seems irrelevant whether "164" refers to someone like Peter Doyle or to an unknown "*her*." The evidence—including the crypt and the pronoun—confirms what Whitman himself suggests: that his "abandonment" is "all the time in myself alone"; that he is "utterly deluded & cheated by *myself*, & my own weakness"; and that he can defend himself against the ravages of such fantasies only when he can "REMEMBER WHERE I AM MOST WEAK, & most lacking." Such a fantasy-relation is clearly regressive and almost certainly Oedipal in character. Regression may well serve the ego, but it may just as certainly result in a pathogenic defense that excludes current reality. For the object, "164," "her," would seem to be nothing more than a surrogate for an unconscious image formed by the infant Whitman of both his mother and father. Where Whitman, in 1870, felt himself "MOST WEAK, & most lacking" was the same place as in 1857 or 1855: the emptiness he sought to fill by the creation through and by his poetry of fantasized relationships. Yet "Live Oak" VIII testifies as eloquently as anything Whitman ever wrote to the failure of such idealizations to gratify his needs, and, what is more important, to the psychological consequence of lingering too long in such a fantasy world: "*It is* IMPERATIVE, that I obviate & remove myself (& my orbit) *at all hazards* from this *incessant enormous* & PERTURBATION." (Unless my ear deceives me, there is a "Freudian" slip in this elliptical sentence, a noun having been omitted following "*enormous*." As it stands, the phrase "& PERTURBATION" seems to be in the place where Whitman may have intended to specify the alternative to remaining "perturbed"; however, the way the

[10] Quoted in Allen, *The Solitary Singer*, pp. 421-22.

195

sentence was actually written suggests that a word that sounds like "PERTURBATION"—namely, "masturbation" —was in the back of Whitman's mind. All of this tends to confirm what I have hypothesized about the implications of Whitman's autoeroticism.)

The perturbation expressed in Whitman's journal pervades "Live Oak, with Moss." In "Live Oak" VI, Whitman envisions the male lovers' parting kiss; in "Live Oak" VII, they hold hands, off by themselves, excluded from the rest of the world. "Live Oak" IX, "I Dream'd in a Dream," tries to restore the image of the lovers holding hands as they walk through a city "where all men were like brothers," a "city of robust friends—Nothing was greater there than manly love—it led the rest." In the city, another version of Whitman's America, the "brothers" and "robust friends" form the ideal American reader Whitman has repeatedly imagined. In place of Oedipal loss and rejection (mourned in "Live Oak" VIII) he seeks the mythical kingdom of manly love. Early in "Live Oak, with Moss" Whitman excludes references to the earth and father, and to the sea, maternity, and women in general. From "Live Oak" IX to the end only the earth and the fire are represented. Increasingly the "subtle electric fire that for your sake is playing within me" ("Live Oak" X) must be kept secret, and in XI we find as clear a statement as Whitman will ever make in support of secrecy:

> Earth! Though you look so impassive, ample and
>   spheric there—I now suspect that is not all,
> I now suspect there is something terrible in you,
>   ready to break forth,
> For an athlete loves me,—and I him—But toward
>   him there is something fierce and terrible in me,
> I dare not tell it in words—not even in these songs.

The terrible secret can hardly be homosexual attraction, since the poet has been explicit in eulogizing "manly love," kisses between men, men holding hands, and so on. The secret, "fierce and terrible in me," has something to do with

196

the earth to which the poem is addressed. The earth—the father—is somehow to be feared in the context of these feelings and poems; its mere presence evokes fierce and terrible responses in the poet's feelings. We can only assume that the poet expects to be rejected yet again by his father and that this anticipation leads to feelings too terrible to express. In this context, the ambivalence of the final poem is reasonably clear:

> To the young man, many things to absorb, to
>   engraft, to develop, I teach, that he be my eleve,
> But if through him speed not the blood of friendship,
>   hot and red—If he be not silently selected by
>   lovers, and do not silently select lovers—of what
>   use were it for him to seek to become eleve
> of mine?

What use indeed? Will the poet fail his "eleve" as his father failed him? Will the "eleve" fail the master, leaving yet more agonies of rejection and abandonment? Or is the reiterated demand for silence a hedge against this possibility? For if the relationships exist in fantasy only, the terrible rage resulting from frustration may be forestalled or eliminated. Even the fantasies of demonstrative love have vanished at the end of "Live Oak, with Moss." Passions and desperate ambivalences seem safely contained within an envelope that isolates them from the actuality they threaten to disrupt. With such protection Whitman will try a little longer to be the poet of the body as well as the poet of the soul.

II. *From "Live Oak" to "Calamus"*

"Live Oak, with Moss" moves away from love in the body and finally away from mortal communion; the poem idealizes escape from the pulse of the blood, from earthly mutability, and even from human speech. "Calamus" is Whitman's most highly developed effort to explore disembodied love. Seeing himself the poet of bodily love and mortal life, Whitman sought in his "New Bible" to reconcile the body to spiritual love. "Calamus" and its companion cluster, "Enfans d'Adam," explicitly and elaborately attempt to achieve a reconciliation.

In Emersonian terms, love may enable people to move toward communion that supersedes language, toward the mystical merging of individuals in the oversoul where communion is intuitive. As "Calamus" develops, Whitman's lovers become increasingly silent and intuitive. But this development leaves the needs for non-mystical communication as strong as ever. The "Adam" poems justify the need: procreation is biologically valuable. Yet Whitman excludes women and woman-love from the higher communion attainable by men with men. The compulsions of physical sexuality do not distract manly comrades from liberating the god within them.

If this is a compromise, it works heavily in favor of disembodiers and against celebrators of the body. Indeed, a "compromise" so unbalanced satisfies Whitman neither well nor long. If Whitman's interest in philosophy seems slight, if he appears anti-intelletual or anti-rational, it is because neither philosophy nor rationalism as Whitman knew them spoke to the fantasies underlying his poetic impulses. Whitman's fear of abandonment or rejection merges with a compensatory oral fantasy of restoring infantile symbiosis. This fantasy, its icon a detached breast, is autistic in its ultimate implications and it denies individuation. With the regression of the fantasy comes a feeling of infantile omnipotence, leading Whitman to insist "I alone would expect to be your God, sole and exclusive." By his fantasy the poet becomes the prophet who administers immortality.

The conscious form of Whitman's fantasy was commonly expressed in the romantic image of the Æolian Harp, through which the winds of heaven played the music of the spheres; by virtue of his mystical attunement the artist could hear the music and present it to less fortunate mortals. The unconscious form rests in the assumption of infancy that one's wishes are equivalent to realities. The regressive fantasies underlying "Calamus" emerge in a disguised form as the ideal of Calamus friendship. The manly comrades resemble latency-period companionships that have specific importance to Whitman, not merely because sexuality spontaneously sublimates itself in latency, but especially because such companionships echo Whitman's relations with his brothers and sisters. The unconscious fantasies intersect with each other and with the conscious fantasies and ideas, creating the world of "Calamus." In the last half of "Calamus" Whitman presents fantasies of a universe of democratic lovers and of two comrades fleeing from society to a privacy in which other people cannot disrupt their communion. The contradiction between the two views of the world is ameliorated (but not removed) by the condition of silence imposed on the lovers.

Beginning with the first "Calamus" poem, Whitman's subject is poetry and the making of poems.

> In paths untrodden,
> In the growth by margins of pond-waters,
> Escaped from the life that exhibits itself,
> From all the standards hitherto published—from
> the pleasures, profits, conformities,
> Which too long I was offering to feed to my Soul;
> Clear to me now, standards not yet published—
> clear to me that my Soul,
> That the Soul of the man I speak for, feeds, rejoices
> only in comrades;
> Here, by myself, away from the clank of the world,
> Tallying and talked to here by tongues aromatic,
> No longer abashed—for in this secluded spot I can
> respond as I would not dare elsewhere,
> Strong upon me the life that does not exhibit itself,
> yet contains all the rest,
> Resolved to sing no songs to-day but those of manly
> attachment,
> Projecting them along that substantial life,

Bequeathing, hence, types of athletic love,
Afternoon, this delicious Ninth Month, in my
    forty-first year,
I proceed, for all who are, or have been, young men,
To tell the secret of my nights and days,
To celebrate the need of comrades.

Whitman hints at a mostly unconscious conjunction of orality, phallicism, the poetic process, and comradeship, together with fantasies of escaping "published" standards and secluding love from worldly intrusions. He regards his poems as seminal essences that do "not exhibit" themselves yet contain "all the rest" that he projects through that "manly attachment," the penis, in order to bequeath "types of athletic love."[11] If "manly attachment" implies connection (not necessarily genital) between two men, the idea that the manly attachment refers to the genitals implies solitude; the explicit meaning of "attachment" is negated by an underlying ambivalence. The title symbol, the calamus reed, supports the underlying meaning: the reed resembles both the penis and the pen that writes the poems. By the "tongues aromatic" singing in paths untrodden, Whitman celebrates not comradeship but "the need of comrades."

The ambiguous "need of comrades" leads Whitman to conjoin love and death in the second poem. As elsewhere in Whitman the conjunction implies evasiveness rather than sexual phobia, for the poet is trying to protect his fantasy world from destructive consciousness.

Scented herbage of my breast,
Leaves from you I yield, I write, to be perused best
    afterwards,
Tomb-leaves, body-leaves, growing up above me,
    above death,
Perennial roots, tall leaves—O the winter shall not
    freeze you, delicate leaves,

[11] I am grateful to Mr. Paul Sanders for helping me interpret this poem.

Every year shall you bloom again—Out from where
   you retired, you shall emerge again;
O I do not know whether many, passing by, will
   discover you, or inhale your faint odor—but I
   believe a few will;
O slender leaves! O blossoms of my blood! I permit
   you to tell, in your own way, of the heart that
   is under you,
O burning and throbbing—surely all will one day
   be accomplished;
O I do not know what you mean, there underneath
   yourselves—you are not happiness,
You are often more bitter than I can bear—you
   burn and sting me,
Yet you are very beautiful to me, you faint-tinged
   roots—you make me think of Death,
Death is beautiful from you—(what indeed is
   beautiful, except Death and Love?)
O I think it is not for life I am chanting here my
   chant of lovers—I think it must be for Death,
For how calm, how solemn it grows, to ascend to
   the atmosphere of lovers,
Death or life I am then indifferent—my Soul
   declines to prefer,
I am not sure but the high Soul of Lovers welcomes
   death most;
Indeed, O Death, I think now these leaves mean
   precisely the same as you mean.

   This poem, written about 1856-1857, has obvious connec-
tions to some of Whitman's earliest themes: its basic image
recalls section six of "Song of Myself," the answer to the
child's question, "What is the grass?":

And now it seems to me the beautiful uncut hair
   of graves.

Tenderly will I use you curling grass,
It may be you transpire from the breasts of young
   men,

It may be if I had known them I would have loved
them.

In "Scented Herbage" Whitman has become the young
man whose decomposing body grows up in the grass of his
grave. Yet the metaphor acquires another meaning in
"Calamus": the heart out of which the scented herbage
grows generates Whitman's poetry. The poet's concern over
those coming later who may inhale the "faint odor" refers
to future readers of *Leaves of Grass*. The poet must permit
the poems "to tell, in your own way, of the heart that is
under you." Whitman refers to the resistance he finds in
himself against revealing deeply ambivalent, "bitter," burning, stinging fantasies, a concern expressed elsewhere in the
1860 edition. In "Proto-Leaf" (later called "Starting from
Paumanok"), Whitman urges:

> Creeds and schools in abeyance,
> Retiring back a while, sufficed at what they are,
>   but never forgotten,
> With accumulations, now coming forward in front,
> Arrived again, I harbor, for good or bad—I permit
>   to speak,
> Nature, without check, with original energy.

Deep within the poet lies "Nature"—what is innate, the
compost out of which the poems grow. Whitman must suspend judgments of conscience so that the poetic process can
overcome resistance against bringing dark fantasies into the
light.

As a result of feelings in such conflict, death seems beautiful to Whitman. The most convincing assurance of immortality Whitman can find accompanies the idea that the
poet's soul can merge with the poems and thus outlive the
body. To the extent of Whitman's belief in this possibility,
he is strongly motivated to make himself conscious of his
hidden self. At the same time death promises him relief
from various guilts about the perversities uncovered during

poetic journeys—and so he falls half in love with death's easefulness.

The rest of "Scented Herbage" hints at feelings expressed in "As I Ebb'd":

> Emblematic and capricious blades, I leave you—
>   now you serve me not,
> Away! I will say what I have to say, by itself,
> I will escape from the sham that was proposed to
>   me,
> I will sound myself and comrades only—I will
>   never again utter a call, only their call,
> I will raise with it, immortal reverberations through
>   The States,
> I will give an example to lovers, to take permanent
>   shape and will through The States.

In "As I Ebb'd," Whitman discovers that his past poems were "insolent" mockeries, before which the "real ME still stands untouched, untold, altogether unreached." The "emblematic and capricious" aspects of these earlier "blades" seem to Whitman evasions of some inner reality—"reality" and "the real ME" are the fantasies at the core of his sense of self. The burden of "Calamus" is to tell more truly the "real ME."

My sense of the strengths and weaknesses of "Calamus" derives from my understanding of the central fantasy to which Whitman's poems most frequently return. In this fantasy Whitman can take momentary comfort by imagining his return to an oral, pre-Oedipal phase prior to the conflicts with young and old men, prior to the separation from his mother. On this fantasy rests the great majority of poems written through 1860.

In such earlier poems as "Song of Myself" the fantasy assumes an explicitly psychosexual form:

> The atmosphere is not a perfume . . . . it has no taste
>   of the distillation . . . . it is odorless,

It is for my mouth forever . . . . I am in love with it,
I will go to the bank by the wood and become
    undisguised and naked,
I am mad for it to be in contact with me.

Often, in later poems, Whitman expresses the fantasy as a utopian vision of universal brotherhood and immutable love, as he does in "Calamus" 22:

Passing stranger! you do not know how longingly
    I look upon you,
You must be he I was seeking, or she I was seeking,
    (it comes to me, as of a dream,)
I have somewhere surely lived a life of joy with you,
All is recalled as we flit by each other, fluid,
    affectionate, chaste, matured,
You grew up with me, were a boy with me, or a
    girl with me,
I ate with you, and slept with you—your body has
    become not yours only, nor left my body mine
    only,
You give me the pleasure of your eyes, face, flesh,
    as we pass—you take of my beard, breast,
    hands, in return,
I am not to speak to you—I am to think of you when
    I sit alone, or wake at night alone,
I am to wait—I do not doubt I am to meet you
    again,
I am to see to it that I do not lose you.

Although the orality as such is less obvious in the "Calamus" poem than in the passage from "Song of Myself," the wish to merge, which occurs in both quotations, is essentially similar. In "Song of Myself" the atmosphere seems vaguely maternal, capable of enveloping the poet and also of being ingested by him. In the "Calamus" poem the "passing stranger" seems to be a brother or sister who has shared a mother with the poet.

The oral roots of this fantasy are remarkably visible at

times. Consider the following descriptions of the moon
(from "Out of the Cradle") as images of a nursing breast:

> From under that yellow half-moon, late-risen, and
>   swollen as if with tears,

❖   ❖   ❖

> *Low-hanging moon!*
> *What is that dusky spot in your brown yellow?*
> *O it is the shape of my mate!*
> *O moon, do not keep her from me any longer.*

❖   ❖   ❖

> *Carols of lonesome love! Death's carols!*
> *Carols under that lagging, yellow, waning moon!*
> *O, under that moon, where she droops almost down*
>   *into the sea!* ❖ ❖ ❖

> The yellow half-moon, enlarged, sagging down,
>   drooping ❖ ❖ ❖

Both in and out of context these images suggest that the
mother has chosen to withdraw her breast, leaving her child
to sing carols of lonesome love; the child's "mate" is not a
lover (in the adult sense) but rather is his connection to
infantile security, the nipple, *"that dusky spot in your
brown yellow."*

Consider again that the "discovery" of "death" as the
word out of the sea constitutes an evasive action. In addition to refusing to recognize the sexuality implied by "the
fire, the sweet hell within, / The unknown want, the destiny
of me," the poet tries to evade the anger he feels toward the
withdrawing mother. It is mother's fault that the poet also
feels rejected:

> Never more the cries of unsatisfied love be absent
>   from me,
> Never again leave me to be the peaceful child I
>   was before ❖ ❖ ❖.

Any unconscious hope that early security might be restored
depended on his maintaining the best possible relations

with his mother. A psychologically archaic condition motivates and shapes continuing fantasies and the poems that grow from the fantasies.

In this light the third "Calamus" poem becomes increasingly clear. Like so many other Whitman poems it begins with an obscure question which is never explicitly answered:

> Whoever you are holding me now in hand,
> Without one thing all will be useless,
> I give you fair warning, before you attempt me
>   further,
> I am not what you supposed, but far different.

The reader may want to know what the "one thing" is, without which "all will be useless," but the poem gives only warnings and coy promises. If one would become the poet's disciple, he must prepare to give up all else and go off in "stealth." Since even these tactics cannot guarantee against failure or destruction, the reader is urged at the end, "Therefore release me, and depart on your way." The nature of the "one thing" is hinted at in the fifth stanza:

> Or, if you will, thrusting me beneath your clothing,
> Where I may feel the throbs of your heart, or rest
>   upon your hip,
> Carry me when you go forth over land or sea;
> For thus, merely touching you, is enough—is best,
> And thus, touching you, would I silently sleep and
>   be carried eternally.

If we understand this stanza, the preceding warnings and promises begin to make sense. The poet demands nothing less than that his reader become his mother. Superficially, Whitman means that his book will be carried "beneath" his reader's clothing, but the reader is unlikely to forget Whitman's famous admonition, "Who touches this book touches a man." The sheer impossibility of Whitman's unconscious wish to be physically carried forces him to cloak his request in metaphors and warnings, preparing himself for inevitable rejection. To establish and maintain control he initiates the rejection himself: "Therefore release me, and depart on your way."

There can be no answer to Whitman's recurring dilemma save that offered by creative regressions. In the primary process assumptions of poetry, the hermaphroditic calamus reed (like the live oak) becomes an example to be poetically translated into human language. "Calamus" lovers may alleviate their loneliness by building self-sufficient fantasy worlds in which painful actualities are temporarily forgotten.

Whitman's isolated men, grieving over lost love, carry within themselves the "long-dumb voices" that the "outsetting bard of love" wishes to liberate. But they must share with the poet his vow of silence if Whitman is to avoid risking an irreversible breach with the source of maternal nurture. In short, "Calamus" sets out to establish the terms by which a secret society will exist. One condition for becoming a "disciple" of Whitman is sharing his attitude toward withdrawn maternal comfort. A disciple must also be silent and yield control to the master, who will incorporate individual myths into his poetic myth. Thus there are those curious warnings which recur throughout "Calamus":

Who would sign himself a candidate for my
    affections? Are you he?
The way is suspicious—the result slow, uncertain,
    may-be destructive;
You would have to give up all else—I alone would
    expect to be your God, sole and exclusive,
Your novitiate would even then be long and
    exhausting,
The whole past theory of your life, and all
    conformity to the lives around you, would have
    to be abandoned;
Therefore release me now, before troubling yourself
    any further—Let go your hand from my
    shoulders,
Put me down, and depart on your way.

207

Warnings like this are central to the fantasy-substructure of "Calamus," the part in which the poet is least certain about his motives. If Whitman fears that his poems can harm his readers, his fear must originate in a sense of infantile omnipotence; he confuses his power in fantasy with his power in reality.

The original forms of Whitman's "Calamus" fantasies occasionally become almost explicit, as in the thirty-eighth poem:

> Primeval my love for the woman I love,
> O bride! O wife! more resistless, more enduring
>   than I can tell, the thought of you!
> Then separate, as disembodied, the purest born,
> The ethereal, the last athletic reality, my consolation,
> I ascend—I float in the regions of your love, O man,
> O sharer of my roving life.

The first two lines hint at a love Whitman would indeed have felt to be archaic or "primeval"—that first love-affair with his mother. Its recurrence irresistibly dominates his fantasies until he learns to convert it into a less direct and less disturbing form. In the secondary fantasy, he feels himself "disembodied" and thus he desexualizes his feelings for "the woman I love"; at this point, the fantasy turns into one of reinstituting the sorts of friendships that occur in the preadolescent period of sexual latency—"Calamus" friendships.

Finally "Calamus," as its last two poems suggest, is an attempt to bring up-to-date (1860) the explorations begun in "Song of Myself." In 1855, "Song of Myself" ended mysteriously:

> Failing to fetch me at first keep encouraged,
> Missing me one place search another,
> I stop some where waiting for you[.]

The casual ambiguity of these lines is by no means clarified in the ending of "Calamus":

208

When you read these, I, that was visible, am
    become invisible;
Now it is you, compact, visible, realizing my
    poems, seeking me,
Fancying how happy you were, if I could be with
    you, and become your lover;
Be it as if I were with you. Be not too certain but
    I am now with you.

As always with Whitman we must begin by abandoning hope for resolution or reconciliation. We can have no clearer idea at the end of "Calamus" than we had at the end of "Song of Myself" whether the poet hopes to continue being "with us" through his poetry, through metempsychosis, or through Emersonian transcendence; what is clear is his uncertainty. Yet in other respects, "Calamus" differs strikingly from "Song of Myself." It is much less randomly explorative, much more clearly focused; nearly all of the "Calamus" poems express either Whitman's primary fantasy of pre-Oedipal regression or the secondary form of this fantasy, "we two boys together clinging." At the same time, the extraordinary energy and power that explodes from time to time in "Song of Myself" is almost entirely absent from "Calamus"—a change of tone that parallels a change occurring in Whitman's psychological structure. The forms Whitman's fantasies take in "Calamus" are much more limited than in earlier poems. Gone almost entirely are the polymorphous orgiastic fantasies in their seemingly infinite variety; in their place are occasional allusions to orgies, a parting kiss, and the mute holding of hands. By comparison to earlier poems, "Calamus" seems profoundly constricted, as if Whitman can no longer freely express or even perceive the fantasies that earlier had burst from his primordial self, like eruptions from a long-dormant volcano.

When we reexamine the twenty-second "Calamus" poem (quoted above) we see that it contains most of the elements developed in the whole cluster. The opening salutation sug-

209

gests the promiscuity many readers have called sexual. But Whitman's subject is the dream-like nature of his fantasy.

> Passing stranger! you do not know how longingly
>   I look upon you,
> You must be he I was seeking, or she I was seeking,
>   (It comes to me, as of a dream,).

Whitman longs to restore the polymorphous pleasures of infancy (the time when he did not need to distinguish between man or woman). The fantasy is a profoundly passive dream of being no longer alone. When read in the context of Whitman's familial relationships, the next four lines seem to have a clear biographical specificity:

> I have somewhere surely lived a life of joy with you,
> All is recalled as we flit by each other, fluid,
>   affectionate, chaste, matured,
> You grew up with me, were a boy with me, or a girl
>   with me,
> I ate with you, and slept with you—your body has
>   become not yours only, nor left my body mine
>   only.

The "somewhere" of the poet's "life of joy" where he ate and slept and grew up is the infant world that still exists in unconscious memory. Where time has no authority, Whitman perceives as coexisting in the womb brothers and sisters who came serially. Boundaries between brothers, sisters, and self collapse, relieving anxiety about mortality (time) and dissolving childhood rivalries.

The poet's attention turns from expression of fantasy to unconscious strategies for maintaining the comfort fantasy grants. Whitman disguises the regressive nature of the fantasy: "You give me the pleasure of your eyes, face, flesh, as we pass—you take of my beard, breast, hands, in return." The touching changes the previously "chaste" character of the infants, and the mention of the poet's beard and breast shifts the time from infancy to the physical present. If the fantasy is sustained in its pure form for long, its infantile and incestuous aspects will become conscious. Whitman overcomes the danger by changing the scene to the temporal present. But activity, including sexual activity, carries a threat of restoring former existential and psychological anxieties that requires a modification of strategy. The poet retreats into the silence and postponement which concluded "Live Oak, with Moss."

> I am not to speak to you—I am to think of you
>   when I sit alone, or wake at night alone,
> I am to wait—I do not doubt I am to meet
>   you again,
> I am to see to it that I do not lose you.

As in "Live Oak," the impulse that leads to this retreat from fantasies of physical intimacy to fantasies of intuitive communion seems nearly autistic: it appears that Whitman would abolish actual social exchanges altogether in order to protect an all too vulnerable fantasy world. Yet two aspects of the "Calamus" vision operate against the autistic impulse. First, the sheer fact that these fantasies are expressed in poetry intended for the widest possible audience implies a strong counter-balancing impulse toward communication by manifest rather than intuitive means. Second, the considerations against which Whitman wants to protect his fantasy world seem to be realistically perceived: he appears to recognize that he cannot actually get what he wants through intuitive companionships (and thus he seeks to protect the fantasy by refusing to test it—the fantasy itself yields some gratification). The point here is that the reality-testing activities of Whitman's ego kept on operating at full strength even when the world being perceived promised cold comfort. By now it should be apparent that the most important thing in Whitman's life was the set of fantasies his poems directly and indirectly express. Yet by tenaciously clinging to a reality that jeopardized his fantasy world, Whitman avoided being seduced into autism.[12] The

---

[12] Emily Dickinson, whose psychological patterns strikingly resemble Whitman's, apparently responded to similar stresses by falling into

same ego that kept Whitman in touch with external realities also found the most graceful and elegant solution to this multitude of psychic conflicts, the writing of poems.

Once again we see that Whitman accepts death only when the anxiety surrounding the idea of death is overbalanced by even greater anxiety surrounding his sexual impulses. Whitman is no closer to accepting the difficult existential facts than he was at the end of the first *Leaves of Grass*. Because Whitman was deflected from the initial goal, the ambivalence in his earlier search begins to yield to a single-minded pursuit of a role that permits him to continue life without changing or seriously confronting the personal conflicts that made him a poet. By no coincidence, the fluidity and lack of external structure of the first two editions give way in 1860 to a set of more or less unsatisfactory structural divisions. Whitman tries to compartmentalize the various aspects of his fantasy world into "Chants Democratic," "Enfans d'Adam," "Calamus," "Leaves of Grass," "Thoughts," "Says," etc. By separating potentially conflicting elements, he may assure himself that the earlier conflicts are gone forever. Adopting the role of a bard who contains multitudes and happily contradicts himself promises the poet relief from the bitter, burning, throbbing, stinging process of making new journeys into chaos. The day of Whitman's great poems fades into a night that obscures hard dialectics. The friction of the old opposites can often create poems of rare authenticity, for the conflicts are as authentic as the fantasies and ideals. When fantasies continue but do not conflict in the poems, evasiveness is no longer an adjunct to the creative process but its reason for being.

III. *Children in Paradise*

The "Enfans d'Adam" cluster of 1860 descends as directly from "Live Oak, with Moss" as does "Calamus." Moreover,

---

a prolonged schizophrenic episode; see John Cody's excellent psychoanalytic study, *After Great Pain* (Cambridge, Mass., 1971).

the successes and failures of "Enfans d'Adam" significantly reflect the triumphs and failures of the entire 1860 venture. This cluster of fifteen poems is at once the most deliberately constructed of the 1860 clusters and the most tenuously unified. The problems complicating our attempts to read these poems range from the general to the particular, but all have large implications. For example, is the substitution in the ninth poem, "Once I Pass'd through a Populous City," of a woman-lover for the man mentioned in the manuscript version meant to disguise the content of this poem about homosexuality?[13] Or does the change mean that the sex of Whitman's lover mattered little to him? Is the narrator of the cluster the Adam of Genesis, or the American Adam of Emerson's "party of hope," or a new Adam of Whitman's own devising? The second "Adam" poem, "From Pent-up Aching Rivers," seems intended to establish a program for the cluster and should help us understand what Whitman meant to do. Yet the poem merely reiterates themes and concerns familiar since the first *Leaves of Grass,* saying little about the new Adam, the new version of paradise, or the poet's willingness to "court destruction" in order to experience "one brief hour of madness and joy."

Since as many unconscious as conscious motives stand behind the "Adam" cluster, Whitman probably could not have stated his full intention, nor have told us clearly how to read these poems. Bowers quotes two notes in Whitman's hand that indicate something of the poet's conscious intent:

"A string of Poems, (short etc.) embodying the amative love of woman—the same as *Live Oak Leaves* do the passion of friendship for man." (p. lxxiii.)

"Theory of a Cluster of Poems the same *to the passion of Woman-Love* as the *Calamus-Leaves* are to adhesiveness,

[13] See, again, Griffith, note 4, Chapter Seven, above. In *Whitman's Drama of Identity* (East Lansing, Michigan, 1973), E. Fred Carlisle notes in passing the autoerotic quality of Whitman's "Adam" poems, pp. 117, 121.

manly love. Full of animal fire, tender, burning.—. . . .
Adam, as a central figure and type." (p. lxxiv.)[14]

Few readers have taken Whitman's word as definitive,
because much of the substance of these fifteen poems stands
apart from the poet's attempt to embody "the amative love
of woman": the electrical storm, the central metaphor of the
sixth poem; "the midnight orgies of young men" in the
eighth; and the equation of "the new garden" with the modern city in the eleventh. The relation between the poet's
concern for the poetic process, evident in most of the
poems, and "the amative love of woman" is not clear. Nor
is it clear whether the lovers Whitman imagines are men or
women. Just as it is profoundly misleading to read
"Calamus" as a celebration of homosexuality, so do we over-
simplify "Enfans d'Adam" if we expect it to resolve Whitman's feelings about woman-love. As in "Live Oak, with
Moss," the primary subject of "Adam" and "Calamus" is the
relation between sexual feelings and poetic activity. In both
clusters Whitman expresses autoerotic rather than hetero- or
homosexuality.

Assurances in "Adam" and "Calamus" that the poet is
loved and lovable remain secure only in the context of the
primary process. Whitman may hedge against disillusion-
ment by making poetry itself his chief concern, implicitly
returning to the ambience of "Poem of Many In One,"
where he hoped to earn love by his genius. The question of
woman-love, so fraught with threats to Whitman's sense of
adequacy and to his lingering Oedipal guilt, compounds the
poet's insecurity. If we understand that deep regressions ac-
company Whitman's acknowledgments of heterosexual passion, the notes about the intent for "Adam" make more
sense. But in context, the word "Enfans" becomes more important than the word "Adam." Only through poetry is this
Adam the father of mankind. Otherwise, he is a child whose
lover must become childlike also—the Eve in the first poem,

[14] Bowers' version of the second note differs in form from the
version in *The Complete Writings*, IX, 150.

behind, beside, ahead of the poet, as the two children explore an imaginary paradise. Even this camaraderie cannot last long. In most of these poems, Adam is as painfully alone as Walt Whitman himself, torn between his fear of loneliness and his fear of intimacy.

Despite the aptness of the Adam and Eden metaphor, and despite Whitman's efforts to control the structure, the unity of "Enfans d'Adam" remains labored and tenuous because so much anxiety inevitably attends Whitman's efforts to explore sexual impulses. "I Sing the Body Electric" and "A Woman Waits for Me" attempt to justify heterosexual impulses on the grounds that procreation continues—and improves!—the species. "Spontaneous Me" has almost nothing to do with "woman-love." Its images progress through "friendship" to sexually undifferentiated explorations of bodies, to an act of masturbation, to children who magically appear after the poet feels "the souse upon me of my lover the sea, as I lie willing and naked." The images finally return us to Whitman's usual ambivalence: "The great chastity of paternity, to match the great chastity of maternity, / The oath of procreation I have sworn." That the defenses in these poems overwhelm the insights Whitman seeks reveals the unconscious resistance hindering the poet's conscious desires. To a considerable extent, such resistance inhibits the development of the cluster and determines the successes and failures Whitman meets when he tries to confront his unconscious attitudes and assumptions about woman-love.

Whitman's concern with woman-love does not seem to have influenced significantly the Valentine manuscript version of the first "Adam" poem, "To the Garden the World," in which Eve appears to be an afterthought.

"Leaves-Droppings"

In the garden, the world, I Adam, again wander,
Curious, here behold my resurrection after ages of
    slumber,

215

The revolving cycles in their wide sweeps having
    again brought me—I return the same,
All beautiful to me—all wondrous—I am myself
    most wondrous,
I exist—I peer and penetrate still,
Content with the present, content with the past,
By my side Eve following, and I following her just
    the same.—[15]

Since this manuscript version, long preceding the idea of
a cluster of woman-love poems, regards Eve not as a lover
but as another child in the garden, Whitman can evade fantasies of adult sexuality and thus feel contentment. Apparently Whitman originally intended to affirm the widespread
nineteenth century conceit of America as a new Eden.
Whitman's introduction of "amativeness" into the poem
does not effectively alter the poem's fantasy structure.

To the garden, the world, anew ascending,
Potent mates, daughters, sons, preluding,
The love, the life of their bodies, meaning and
    being,
Curious, here behold my resurrection, after slumber,
The revolving cycles, in their wide sweep, having
    brought me again,
Amorous, mature—all beautiful to me—all
    wondrous,
My limbs, and the quivering fire that ever plays
    through them, for reasons, most wondrous;
Existing, I peer and penetrate still,
Content with the present—content with the past,
By my side, or back of me, Eve following,
Or in front, and I following her just the same.

As in the manuscript version, the narrator and Eve seem
to be brother and sister, rather than lovers, children of
Adam, as much as Adam and Eve. It is not clear that Eve
has anything to do with the "quivering fire that ever plays

[15] Bowers, p. 59.

through" the narrator's limbs; the sexuality of the narrator and his "Potent mates, daughters, sons" remains autoerotic. Heterosexual fantasies continued to require Whitman to convert his lovers into pre-adolescent children whose walled garden excludes adult sexuality.

Adam and his garden disappear after the first poem until, in the sixth, a clear associative line begins to unite the last ten poems with the first. Excluding poems two to five, the narrative of "Enfans d'Adam" develops as follows: (1) Adam regains paradise, recognizes his sexuality, and finds Eve. (6) Adam associates cathartic ecstasy felt in electrical storms with his return to paradise; he will "court destruction" in order to experience "one brief hour of madness and joy." (7) Paradise, analogous in the sixth poem to cathartic ecstasy, becomes regressive escape from human mortality (when the lovers become fishes, rocks, trees, minerals, etc.); in other words, Whitman sometimes experiences deep regressions as "Paradise" or catharsis. (8) The regressions described in the seventh poem are now called "Native moments" (the time of birth); Whitman imagines the "Native moments" to be polymorphously orgiastic and defines for himself a role as poet of "shunned persons": he fantasizes watching from a safe distance the "orgies of young men," loving a prostitute, and taking for his friend some "low" person. (9) The poet recalls passing through a "populous city" where he loved "a woman I casually met there, who detained me for love of me"; in this city of orgies and love *en masse,* the paradise of democracy, Adam finds himself restored to the garden. (10) The movement toward a "brief hour of madness and joy," toward the "transmutation" of the lovers into non-human things, toward the "Native moments" and the populous city, must pass through the "house of maternity" on its way to the world; yet the confused voyager stands as far from his destination as when he began. (11) Whitman identifies the garden with the city and projects the journey into the future as well as the past, seeking "you, born years, centuries after me." (12) Whitman makes the familiar equation between poetic and sexual cre-

217

ativity, asserting that through poetry he may escape time and sexuality. (13) The act of faith attempted in the eleventh and twelfth poems fails, leaving the poet feeling tantalized and threatened by marriage, virginity, and death; the "brief hour" has gone and the destruction courted by the poet seems at hand. (14) The attempted subordination of sexuality to poetry has failed; the poet aches with love, feels attracted and attracting, but remains inexorably afraid of his body. (15) The cluster ends where it began: Adam, awakening "refreshed" from his long sleep outside the garden, once again implores himself and others to "be not afraid of my body."

The journey of "Enfans d'Adam" begins with the distant apprehension of conflict, explores regressive sexual fantasies, and concludes with the conflicts unresolved but more fully perceived. At the end, Whitman reiterates his determination to believe that being a poet will help him survive the storms, the orgies, and the lapses from cathartic ecstasy. And yet the promises of poetry cannot altogether comfort Whitman for renouncing his search for a brief hour of madness and joy.

The following psychological interpretation of the narrative just described seems sound and accurate: the "Adam" cluster means Whitman assumed that being a poet excluded him from physical life and love (this meaning, directly connects "Adam" to the "Live Oak" crisis). Yet the clarity of this meaning depends on omitting the second, third, fourth, and fifth poems, and the last three of these are the best and most celebrated in the cluster. Restoring the four excluded poems distorts the cluster's structural integrity but adds three excellent poems to an otherwise undistinguished lot. The problem of "Enfans d'Adam" is that by late 1859 Whitman had already begun to sacrifice the unconscious sources of his poetry to didactic and defensive purposes. Because of his confusions about "woman-love," he had to approach the subject indirectly. The conscious intention of the "Adam" cluster—to celebrate heterosexuality—made indirectness difficult.

218

To understand the problem of "Enfans d'Adam" we must review the history of its composition.

1855, "I Sing the Body Electric" (EA no. 3) published.

1856, "A Woman Waits for Me" (EA no. 4) and "Spontaneous Me" (EA no. 5) published; "Body Electric" reprinted, its ending revised and expanded.

1857, Tyndale letter reveals that the "Adam" poems in the Valentine MS (nos. 1, 7, 8, 9, 10) existed.

Between August, 1859 (when the Valentine MS was completed), and March, 1860, the rest of the "Adam" poems (nos. 2, 6, 11, 12, 13, 14, 15) were probably composed.

Allusions in the second poem, "From Pent-up Aching Rivers," to the first, third, sixth, seventh, eighth, and ninth poems suggest that the second poem was intended to offer Whitman's reader a guide to the rest of the cluster.[16] The absence of allusions to the last five poems implies that Whitman had not written these poems when he compiled "From Pent-up Aching Rivers."

Based on Whitman's "Theory of a cluster," these poems have a didactic tone largely set by the poet's evident determination, in "From Pent-up Aching Rivers," to move cheerfully over the surface of old conflicts. He may have wanted, consciously, to write about woman-love, but his didactic purpose required him to avoid significant confrontation with Oedipal conflicts. Whitman's renewed caution leaves "Enfans d'Adam" a cluster of poems with intellectual rather than "felt" unity.

If Whitman still knew, in 1859, that regressive journeys into times past may enhance times future, he could not give up his hope that past, present, and future may be united in a timeless return to the rocked cradle. The poet's defenses against ambivalence began to change. In the past the pro-

---

[16] *Leaves of Grass* (1860), p. 289. Line 28 refers to the first "Adam" poem ("My limbs and the quivering fire,") and to the auctioneer's inventory in the third poem; line 29 refers to poem six; line 33 refers to poem seven; line 34 refers to poems six and eight; line 35 refers to poem nine. Other allusions are scattered throughout "From Pent-up Aching Rivers."

cess by which Whitman made poems had sometimes enabled him to contend with neurotic conflicts and desperate loneliness. But as he concluded the third *Leaves of Grass* he hoped that writing these poems secured him a place in the world's attention. In his remaining thirty-two years Whitman was unable to continue exploring the chaos within; increasingly, he turned to revising old poems and organizing them into new clusters. To write poems was

> To drive free! to love free! to dash reckless and
>   dangerous!
> To court destruction with taunts—with invitations!

Yet to write poems also required resignation to the consequences:

> To be lost, if it must be so!
> To feed the remainder of life with one
>   hour of fulness and freedom!
> With one brief hour of madness and joy.

TEN

A Biography of an Imagination:
IV

HISTORICAL information about Whitman's life after 1860 offers extensive confirmation of my hypotheses about the psychological patterns described and traced throughout this study. As the poet increasingly sought to fulfill in "real life" the ideals and fantasies underlying his poetry and adolescent fiction, his creative excursions into the regressive, unconscious world, the source of his poetic power, became fewer and more superficial. The central event in the period yet to be studied (1860-1865) appears, from the standpoint of a psychoanalytic investigation, to be the illness Whitman suffered in 1864 following eighteen months of intensive volunteer service in Washington military hospitals. This chapter seeks to examine the event in the context of Whitman's personal and poetic activities in order to draw inferences about the illness and its relation to the poetic process.

In mid-December 1862 George Whitman, who had enlisted at the beginning of the Civil War, was reported wounded. The poet left immediately for Washington, and on 29 December he wrote Jeff that George's wound was harmless. Deciding to remain in Washington, Whitman got work with the army paymaster and wrote Emerson to ask for letters recommending him for employment by the Departments of State and Treasury. Whitman probably intended to send newsletters about the war to New York papers, feeling that despite his age (forty-three) he should share George's peril. The letter to Emerson hints that the war offered a means of honorable escape from personal problems associated with home.

"Breaking up a few weeks since, and for good, my New York stagnation—wandering since through camp and battle scenes—I fetch up here in harsh and superb plight—wretchedly poor, excellent well, (my only torment, family matters)—realizing at last that it is necessary for me to fall for the time in the wise old way, to push my fortune, to be brazen, and get employment, and have an income—determined to do it, (at any rate until I get out of horrible sloughs) I write you, asking you as follows [i.e., for letters of introduction]." (*Corr.*, I, 61.)

Whitman's embarrassment at having to make this request probably accounts for the odd tone of the letter. If his "only torment, family matters" refers to George's injury, it is strange that Whitman did not support his request by specifying that his brother had been honorably wounded defending the Union, and that Whitman himself proposed to employ his pen in the cause. He probably had in mind less mentionable problems with two other brothers. Andrew, dying of drink and a tubercular infection, would within the year leave his streetwalker wife to bear his posthumous child; Jesse, syphilitic and increasingly difficult, would have to be confined to an asylum within two years. Yet family problems were so chronic that it seems unlikely that they alone could have caused the "New York stagnation," the "horrible sloughs." These phrases may refer to something Whitman discussed previously with Emerson, possibly in a lost letter or in their Boston meeting eighteen months before. Among other things Whitman's depression may have been related to increasing difficulty in writing poetry. Whitman may have hoped that going off to war would change his mode of life and thereby reactivate his creative processes.

A few days after writing Emerson, Whitman described to Jeff's wife the beginnings of his new life.

"O my dear sister, how your heart would ache to go through the rows of wounded young men, as I did—and stopt to speak a comforting word to them. There were about 100 in one long room, just a long shed neatly white-washed inside. One young man was very much prostrated, and groaning with pain. I stopt and tried to comfort him. He was very sick. I found he had not had any medical attention since he was brought there—among so many he had been overlooked. So I sent for the doctor, and he made an examination of him—the doctor behaved very well—seemed to be anxious to do right—said that the young man would recover—he had been brought pretty low with diarroeha and now had bronchitis, but not so serious as to be dangerous. I talked to him some time—he seemed to have entirely give up, and lost heart—he had not a cent of money—not a friend or acquaintance—I wrote a letter from him to his sister * * * I gave him a little change I had—he said he would like to buy a drink of milk, when the woman came through with milk. Trifling as this was, he was over-come and began to cry." (*Corr.*, I, 63-64.)

Whitman aroused exceptionally strong affections in the soldiers he nursed. His relationships with several of these men lasted for many years, mainly through correspondence. In these relationships Whitman could play the parental role long fantasized in his poems and fiction and express some aspects of his homosexual sensibility in a context that did not require recognition of sexual implications. As noted above, Whitman's friendships with the New York stage-drivers began an experiment in making real the "Calamus" fantasies; the nursing experiences in Washington were a further and more complicated stage in the experiment.

In the spring of 1863 Whitman began especially intense relationships with Thomas Sawyer and Lewis Brown. The

erotic implications of these relationships, however visible
to us, probably remained hidden from Whitman himself.
Yet no matter how unconscious, such implications evidently
generated enough vague anxiety to cause Whitman to become seriously ill. Without exception, Whitman's correspondence and recorded statements to friends and ac-
quaintances indicate that he did not regard himself as
sexually unusual, certainly not as homosexual. Yet he could
write sentences like the following (in a letter to Sawyer,
21 April 1863):

"I was at the armory last evening, saw Lewy Brown, sat
with him a good while, he was very cheerful, told me how
he laid out to do, when he got well enough to go from hospital, (which he expects soon), says he intends to go home
to Maryland, go to school, and learn to write better, and
learn a little bookkeeping, &c.—so that he can be fit for
some light employment. Lew is so good, so affectionate—
when I came away, he reached up his face, I put my arm
around him, and we gave each other a long kiss, half
a minute long." (*Corr.*, I, 91.)

Sentences like the last must mean either that Whitman
freely shared the secret of his homosexuality with his cor-
respondent, or that, with startling innocence, Whitman was
quite unaware of erotic implications in a half-minute kiss.
It appears that the latent eroticism threatened to break into
consciousness as Whitman spent hours every day, month
after month, nursing his hospitalized friends. After eighteen
months of such labor, Whitman became so ill that he
had to return to his mother's home for six months of
recuperation.

In January 1865 the poet returned to Washington, carry-
ing warnings from his family not to go "too strong" in his
hospital work. Taking this advice seriously, he returned to
Brooklyn late in March to visit and to arrange the printing
of *Drum-Taps*, his Civil War poems. He left a Washington
alive with rumors of plots to assassinate or abduct the President. Whitman was still in Brooklyn on April 9th when Lee

surrendered and on the 13th when Lincoln was shot. News of the assassination reached Brooklyn the morning of the 14th, Good Friday, and Whitman immediately returned to the capital, perhaps seeking the companionship of his intellectual friends, O'Connor and Burroughs. I can find no allusion whatever in Whitman's writings of this period to any of the rumored political plots that filled Washington— for example, that the assassination had been plotted by Secretary of War Stanton and that Vice President Johnson had been a passive conspirator. It is understandable that Whitman may have needed to believe that the political situation was more stable than it appeared; at this time Whitman was composing his "Sequel" to *Drum-Taps*, which psychologically connects the health of the nation to his own health and that of his family.[1] After the assassination, some of the earlier *Drum-Taps* poems, with their jingoistic patriotism and fervor for war, must have seemed embarrassingly naïve to the poet. The bardic image he cultivated among his soldier-sons required him to be balanced, calm, and rational, and to reassure others (as well as himself) that when the chaos was sorted out, an essential political sanity would be seen to prevail.[2]

The *Drum-Taps* poems reveal that those changes in Whitman's conception of his poetic processes described in

[1] As Kenneth Burke explains in "Policy Made Personal," *"Leaves of Grass" 100 Years After*, Milton Hindus, ed. (Stanford, 1955), pp. 74-108.

[2] Another event of this year probably contributed to Whitman's impulse toward moderation. Whitman himself was personally affected by Washington's post-assassination hysteria. An Iowa Methodist, Senator James Harlan, became Secretary of the Interior on 11 May and immediately ordered loyalty reports on all employees in the department. Someone brought to the Secretary's attention the fact that one of his clerks was author of the notorious *Leaves of Grass*. On 30 June Whitman was dismissed because of his "moral character." William O'Connor went to a friend, J. Hubley Ashton, Assistant Attorney General, to make such a scene that the next day Whitman was transferred to the Office of the Attorney General, where he worked without incident until his paralyzing stroke of 1873.

regard to "Enfans d'Adam" continued to inhibit the poet's creativity. The tendency toward didacticism increased, for the war called forth simplifications and an end to ambivalence. War justified young men making clean breaks with their families (as Whitman and his brothers had been unable to do). War justified expressing the violent feelings civilization otherwise suppressed. War brought men together in the most intense, yet least sexual, of intimacies, enhancing the prophecy of "Calamus." Most important, the war gave Whitman a less personal subject than "oneself" at a time when the former sources of his poetry had become inaccessible. When Whitman told O'Connor that *Drum-Taps* had a more "simple & winning" subject than *Leaves of Grass*, the poet apparently meant that his own attitudes toward the war and the nation coincided with the attitudes of the moderate Northern public (in contrast to the "egotism" he had had to defend in his earlier poems). But he meant something more ominous as well. He went on in that letter: "Still Leaves of Grass is dear to me, always dearest to me, as my first born, as daughter of my life's first hopes, doubts, & the putting in form of those days' efforts & aspirations—true, I see now, with some things in it I should not put in if I were to write now, but yet I shall certainly let them stand, even if but for proofs of phases passed away—" (*Corr.*, I, 247). The "things" he "should not put in" *Leaves of Grass*, were he writing it in 1865, were those originally unconscious images whose implications became psychologically threatening with their increased visibility after 1860. The return of repressed material endangered the structure of Whitman's ego defenses, causing, for example, his difficulties in completing the third *Leaves of Grass*. The "phases" that had "passed away" were not the old conflicts that *Leaves of Grass* expressed; Whitman had lost his ability to explore the conflicts. Whitman's new defenses required that he see the conflicts as resolved and himself as elevated to the position fantasized in 1856 (and even earlier—in "Lingave's Temptation"). The attitudes and stances expressed in almost all the poetry Whitman wrote after 1860 were fit for a poet laureate.

Having studied "Song of Myself," "Poem of Many in One," "Song of the Broad-Axe," and "Calamus" in chronological order, a reader might expect the Civil War to have inspired Whitman to his very greatest poetry. Whitman had long made an unconscious, as well as a conscious, identification with his nation, seeing himself as a new Adam who, by expressing America, could teach the citizens to sing. As we have seen, the psychological conflicts within the poet had social, political, economic, and moral analogs in the issues that split the nation: slavery, misuse of economic potential, a lawless frontier, Jacksonian values in conflict with those of the Southern Whigs, the spirit of Manhattan challenging the spirit of Boston, and much more. In 1860 the nation elected a Whitmanian rough for its President. The war itself offered a unique opportunity for young soldiers to develop Calamus comradeships and to imitate the Revolutionary War heroes celebrated in Whitman's early fiction and in *Leaves of Grass*.

In fact, the war had a reductive effect on Whitman's poetry. Far from inspiring further explorations of the unconscious, the war drove Whitman to celebrate slogans and affirm a national unity rarely evident in those troubled times. The best *Drum-Taps* poems were spoken not by the broad-axe poet, nor the poet of many in one, nor yet the "Calamus" lover, but by the sleeper who wandered "lost and confused" by the bedsides of the wounded. Probably the dreadful external reality of the war amplified Whitman's continuing fear of analogous conflicts still emerging from his internal reality. From his identification with the nation came personal terrors. The public image Whitman presented to post-Civil War America was not the radical, rude, savage poet of old, but "The Good Gray Poet," radiating benign geniality (even Christlikeness, according to William O'Connor, who coined the nickname). Until the culminating shock of Lincoln's assassination, Whitman's private explorations and personal voice had been silent.

The suppressed poetic potential is evident from the beginning of *Drum-Taps*. The first poem ("Drum-Taps") depicts "Manhattan" leading the nation to respond to attack: young soldiers-to-be leaving home, women volunteering as nurses, the city and army camps alive with excited anticipation. Whitman ignores the ambiguity latent in his title, "taps" being a funeral dirge played either by drum or bugle. Instead he celebrates, without complication, "Mannahatta a-march!—and it's O to sing it well!"—a celebration that ignores the draft riots that had recently torn the same Manhattan. In 1855 the maternal sea had been held accountable for the fears Whitman associated with sexuality and violent death, but the poet approves as the maternal city of *Drum-Taps* smiles "with joy" to send her young men off to be killed. In peace the cruel and capricious sea dashed the beautiful, gigantic swimmer against the rocks; in war Whitman accepts as justified maternal caprice. The poet seems to feel that the nation needs an example of unity from its largest city and its largest bard. He responds by turning away from his private world and affirming an imaginary political similitude.[3]

Whitman's evasion, not only of psychological conflicts but also of his basic poetic material, is even more pronounced in "1861," a poem that epitomizes the crossed purposes of *Drum-Taps*. The catalog describing the "year of the struggle" carries an impulse to celebrate violent phallicism, but the poem begins and ends with judgments of conscience: the year is terrible, hurrying, crashing, sad, and distracted. Earlier, ambivalence and equivocation contributed to poetic intensity when Whitman tried to confront conflicts between the internal and external worlds, but in "1861" he stifled and dissipated the conflicts. The political requirements of the nation at war justified the poet's understandable inclination to avoid introspection. Whitman seems to

[3] Whitman's wartime renunciation of "egotism" is reflected in the poet's uncharacteristic failure to publicize *Drum-Taps* and its sequel.

associate the effeminate "poetling" "lisping cadenzas piano" with his own tendency toward introspection and self-doubt. Conditions in the world demanded silence from the inner voice.

The inner voice speaks in *Drum-Taps* only after Whitman becomes "The Wound Dresser," who can ignore the propagandistic requirements of the world because the nursing service he performs justifies his poetic vocation. As wound dresser he can loosen the reins that normally check his impulses toward intimacy. When he encourages the impulses, unconscious fantasies may interact with perceptions of external events, permitting Whitman to renew his commitment to the projections of his dreams:

> While the world of gain and appearance and mirth
>   goes on,
> So soon what is over forgotten, and waves wash
>   the imprints off the sand,
> In nature's reverie sad, with hinged knees returning,
>   I enter the doors—(while for you up there,
> Whoever you are, follow me without noise, and
>   be of strong heart.)

The "you up there," the same phantom who haunted Whitman's steps in "As I Ebb'd" and thus devalued poetic achievements as mere insolent blab, is curtly silenced, for the poet has valuable work to do. With a tone rare to *Drum-Taps* Whitman describes the soldiers' horrible wounds, neither cajoling the reader to patriotism nor trying to shock him into bloody awareness:

> From the stump of the arm, the amputated hand,
> I undo the clotted lint, remove the slough, wash off
>   the matter and blood;
> Back on his pillow the soldier bends, with curv'd
>   neck, and side-falling head;
> His eyes are closed, his face is pale, he dares not look
>   on the bloody stump,
> And has not yet looked on it.

Not since "Faces" (1855) has Whitman presented such horrific images in a tone and context so compassionately personal. In "The Wound Dresser" (as in "Faces") the subject is the poet's attitude toward the wounds and wounded. With wonder he watches his own outward calmness and competence while a natural sense of horror cries within. Whitman sees himself become the calm and ministering father-mother he has long idealized, justifiably proud that he rises above temptations to withdraw or reject the grotesque and defective. The "Calamus" lover has adopted the medical ethic, which demands loving compassion for patients and judges repugnant or morbid any selfish lust or desire. Whitman prevents lust from attending compassion by casting the nursing life into a dream vision and by casting himself as a grandfatherly bard with the passions of youth long behind him. Rejecting youthful fantasies of bravery, Whitman projects the dream of the nurse, the dream nourished since adolescence. In *Drum-Taps* as in "Calamus," he rejects the role of lover to become the bard of lovers and heroes.

Yet the horrors of the hospitals had effects on Whitman that the role of bard could not neutralize. About the time he was trying to arrange the publication of *Drum-Taps*, Whitman suffered the first serious illness of his life. The apparently psychogenic nature of this illness links it to the poems he had been writing, to his hospital duties, and to the last great poem he would write, "When Lilacs Last in the Door-Yard Bloom'd," composed shortly after his recovery. The illness is described in a series of letters. On 18 May 1864 he began a letter to his mother with an uncharacteristic complaint: "my head feels disagreeable, from being in too much." He added in the same letter, "I expect one of these days, if I live, I shall have awful thoughts & dreams." On 7 June he continued, "Mother, I have not felt well at all the last week—I had spells of deathly faintness, and bad trouble in my head too, & sore throat ° ° ° My head was the worst, though I don't know, the faint weak spells were not very pleasant—but I feel so much better this forenoon I believe it has passed over" (*Corr.*, I, pp. 223, 224, 241). But "it" did not "pass over." He repeated his complaint on 10 June, and on the 14th he wrote: "I am not feeling very well these days—the doctors have told me not to come inside the hospitals for the present—I send there by a friend every day, I send things & aid to some cases I know, & hear from there also, but I do not go myself at present—it is probable that the hospital poison has affected my system, & I find it worse than I calculated—I have spells of faintness & very bad feeling in my head, fullness & pain—& besides sore throat—my boarding place, 502 Pennsylvania av, is a miserable place, very bad air—But I shall feel better soon, I know—the doctors say it will pass over—they have long told me I was going in too strong—some days I think it has all gone & I feel well again, but in a few hours I have a spell again" (*Corr.*, I, 233).

In context, Whitman's complaints about the "boarding place" seem either a subtle request for Louisa Whitman to come down and take care of her son or his attempt to persuade himself that he ought to return to Brooklyn; he ends that letter, "Mother, I want to see you & Jeff so much—I have been working a little at copying, but have stopt it lately." Nothing could be more reasonable than Whitman's wanting the comfort of his family at such a time; but it is less understandable that he could not express his feelings more directly. On 17 June he has made up his mind to go home: "this place & the hospitals seem to have got the better of me—I do not feel so badly this forenoon—but I have bad nights & bad days too, some of the spells are pretty bad—still I am up some & around every day—the doctors have told me for a fortnight I must leave, that I need an entire change of air, &c." But even yet he is ambivalent about coming home: "I think I shall come home for a short time, & pretty soon—(I will try it two or three days yet, though, & if I find my illness goes over, I will stay here yet awhile—all I think about is to be here if any thing should happen to George)." Whitman then postscripted, "Mother, if I should come I will write a day or so before" (*Corr.*, I, 234). We do not know whether he wrote again, but on the 22nd he left for Brooklyn, where his health seemed to improve immediately—at least according to a letter to Eldridge dated 28 June. The remission was temporary. On 5 July he wrote O'Connor of having had "three or four pretty bad days & nights ° ° ° bad spells of weakness with heavy aching head —I think the throat is no worse, but it is not well yet" (*Corr.*, i, 235-36). Apparently the symptoms showed gradual improvement over the summer, for he wrote O'Connor on 11 September, "My health is quite reestablished, yet not exactly the same unconscious state of health as formerly" (*Corr.*, i, 241). But Whitman did not return to Washington until late the following January.

On 11 July 1864 Whitman wrote to one of his hospital friends, "This is the first sickness I have ever had & I find upon trial such things as faintness, headache & trembling & tossing all night, & all day too, are not proper companions for a good union man like myself" (*Corr.*, i, 238). This posture is consonant with the image Whitman always projected of his bursting good health and vitality; yet in a letter of 30 May 1864 Whitman told his mother, "my head begins to trouble me a little with a sort of fullness, as it often does in the hot weather" (*Corr.*, i, 228). The last remark may refer to a chronic sinus condition that Louisa Whitman knew about. It also may entitle us to doubt that Whitman had always "unconsciously" assumed his own good health; and it suggests the possibility of psychogenic allergies, for hot weather brings pollination. The possible allergy, the statement by the doctors that Whitman was "going in too strong" with the hospital work, and Whitman's remarks about his dreams may mean that the poet's illness grew, at least in part, from emotional sources.[4]

---

[4] "After reading this portion of my manuscript, John Cody, M.D., Medical and Administrative Director of the High Plains Mental Health Center, Hays, Kansas, offered the following analogical corroboration: "I once was consulted by a male college student who had recently taken a job as an orderly in a hospital. Soon after, he developed headaches, faintness, severe free-floating anxiety and insomnia. He had

At the time the illness began, Whitman was completing *Drum-Taps*, poems that reveal that the poet's hospital experiences had been introjected into his pre-conscious and unconscious. Later, fragments of these percepts returned to consciousness as Whitman went through the process of writing the poems. As I have reiterated, the process of making poetry may have either adaptive or maladaptive effects. It appears that in relation to *Drum-Taps* regressions toward unconscious material increased rather than decreased conscious psychic conflict; the conflicts were manifested in Whitman's "faintness, headaches & trembling & tossing all night, & all day too." The temporary relaxation of ego defenses, which was necessary to the creation of poetry, evidently paralleled a prolonged general weakening of the defenses. When the assassination of Lincoln led Whitman to write his last great poem, the unconscious burden of that poem was the poet's announcement that exploratory journeys through an interior world had ended when the search for psychosexual identity was abandoned.

---

first noticed these symptoms following the hospitalization of one of his classmates for a herniorraphy. He prepped the young man for surgery matter-of-factly and later provided post-op care. He had no conscious emotional response to any of this but whenever he went near the patient he experienced an intensification of his symptoms. Later, in therapy, he remembered that at the sight of his patient's naked body during the administration of an enema he had experienced a feeling of sexual arousal. At this point in therapy the patient became panicky and expressed the fear that he was homosexual. When he finally accepted the fact that, while he may have some impulses of this kind, one swallow doesn't make a summer, his symptoms dramatically subsided" [personal communication].

If this patient's experience is analogous to Whitman's, certain things may be inferred: in order to generate such psychosomatic symptoms, Whitman must have been either unaware of homosexual impulses in himself (the effort required to keep such impulses repressed from consciousness causing the illness), or else he violently repudiated impulses that emerged partly into consciousness, hating this aspect of himself and making himself ill.

233

Epilogue

EPITAPH FOR FATHER AND MOTHER

WITH explicit symbolic patterns and formal interweaving of personal and public scenes, "When Lilacs Last in the Dooryard Bloom'd" evokes admiration from readers not often attracted to Whitman. The poet's subordination of "egotism" to an external subject is reflected in the control shown over the dithyrambic style and in tactful suppression of sexual obsessions. To those who admire *Drum-Taps*, "Lilacs" seems a suitably tragic and sublime sequel. But the language, the imagery, and even the structure link "Lilacs" much more closely to the 1860 *Leaves of Grass* than to *Drum-Taps* (whose sequel "Lilacs" heads). "Lilacs" follows directly from "Out of the Cradle Endlessly Rocking": while a lonely bird sings of its deprivation, the poet translates the bird's song into a carol to Death, "lovely and soothing Death," the "Dark Mother, always gliding near, with soft feet." As Kenneth Burke and Edwin Miller perceive, the relation between the poet and his subject resembles that of son to idealized father—not, to be sure, the tyrannical father of "There Was a Child," but the he-bird brother-father of "Out of the Cradle" or the symbolic father whose kiss Whitman implored in "As I Ebb'd." Burke and Miller both note a certain sexual ambiguity about the subject of the elegy; the perfume associated with the President is no less feminine than the western star which identifies Lincoln with Venus. When Whitman's later poems succeed, they do so because the poet has returned to the original sources of his creative energies. "Lilacs" brilliantly culminates the modes, processes, and themes of *Leaves of Grass*.

The opening lines show that "Lilacs" has as much to do

234

with the poet's attitude toward death as with Lincoln or the President's death.

> When lilacs last in the door-yard bloom'd,
> And the great star early droop'd in the western
>   sky in the night,
> I mourn'd . . . and yet shall mourn with ever-
>   returning spring.
>
> O ever-returning spring! trinity sure to me you
>   bring;
> Lilac blooming perennial, and drooping star in the
>   west,
> And thought of him I love.

The idea that spring is a time for mourning has very deep roots in *Leaves of Grass*. In spring, the new growths emerge from the compost of the dead, a fact that simultaneously elates and terrifies Whitman. If we understand the relationship of "Lilacs" to *Leaves of Grass*, then the "trinity" may suggest not only the dead President, the honoring thoughts, and the shrub, but also the trinity from "Out of the Cradle" (the he-bird, the she-bird and the child); "him I love" is not only Lincoln, but also the he-bird mourning his lost mate. It seems to me that this understanding begins to account for the sexual ambiguity of the imago "Lilacs" mourns.

There are many other links between "Lilacs" and "Out of the Cradle." In the earlier poem, the he-bird's carol blamed the elements for obscuring the sight of his mate; this theme is continued in "Lilacs":

> O powerful, western, fallen star!
> O shades of night! O moody, tearful night!
> O great star disappear'd! O the black murk that
>   hides the star!
> O cruel hands that hold me powerless! O helpless
>   soul of me!
> O harsh surrounding cloud that will not free my
>   soul!

Beyond this, one of the chief structural devices in "Lilacs" is the identification of the poet's song with the song of the isolated bird, who sings, like the other he-bird, because if he could not sing he would die.

In section four, as in "Out of the Cradle," Whitman identifies with the bird, his brother, for good reason. Like the speaker in "Calamus," the bird shuns settlements and withdraws to himself to sing of love. The poet abandons houses and rooms with the perfumes that (in "Song of Myself") would intoxicate him. Yet if "Calamus" taught Whitman anything, it was that he could not abandon the civilized world and survive the loneliness of the live oak. The role taken by the poet in "Lilacs" intercedes between the isolated hermit thrush and the world of farmyard, houses, and cities. "Lilacs" tries to make less alien the isolated world of the bird within the poet; his song correlates the world of unconscious vision to the external world, through which the coffin passes on its way to the catafalque. Sections three, five, and six integrate the journey of the coffin with the narrative of the lonely bird and with the lilac-bearing poet, merging Whitman's sensibility of 1865 with that of 1855. The landscape painted contains the elements familiar since the first *Leaves of Grass*: the earth, the air, the fire, the water, the changes of city and country, the relentless growth of the grass and wheat—mementos of human mortality.

In sections seven and eight, the ambiguity surrounding the subject of the poem is intensified by the poet's personal dirge. His is one of the mournful thousand voices "pour'd around the coffin":

> (Nor for you, for one, alone;
> Blossoms and branches green to coffins all I bring:
> For fresh as the morning—thus would I chant a
> song for you, O sane and sacred death.

The poet seems to address the dead President until the last words abstract the subject from the dead to death. The confusion of subject continues as the poet tells of covering not the dead man but death itself with roses, lilies, and lilacs. As Burke suggests, the perfumed flowers have feminine connotations in Whitman's poetry, and the coffin may represent the womb. Burke's interpretation leads me to detect a regressive aspect to Whitman's feelings about the man the poet mourns for; Whitman perceives the dead man in terms of infantile generalizations. The regressive aspects continue in the eighth section, where the "western orb" symbolizing the dead man suggests not only Venus, but also the breast-like moon, which sagged and drooped and touched the face of the sea in "Out of the Cradle." In "Lilacs," the poet recalls having wandered sleepless with the star through the "transparent shadowy night," the maternal and seductive night of "The Sleepers"; the star, the night, and the poet form another trinity of mother, father, and poet-child. The identities of all three merge in the last lines of section eight, as indicated by the grammatically singular "was" (instead of "were"):

> As I watch'd where you pass'd and [I] was lost in
>   the netherward black of the night,
> As my soul, in its trouble, dissatisfied, sank, as
>   where you, sad orb,
> Concluded, dropt in the night, and [I] was gone.

Following the merging with the dead and death, and with his father and mother, the poet answers a call from the bird:

> Sing on, there in the swamp!
> O singer bashful and tender! I hear your notes—
>   I hear your call;
> I hear—I come presently—I understand you;
> But a moment I linger—for the lustrous star has
>   detain'd me;
> The star, my comrade, departing, holds and detains
>   me.

The ambiguous "my comrade" may refer either to the bird or the star, for unconscious identifications begun earlier extend here to the bird who speaks for the poet's internal world. The new call echoes the threat felt in the preceding section of becoming "lost in the netherward black of the night": Death, mother, and the unconscious. Whitman's fear of submersion in regression and unconscious chaos lends force and intensity to the poetic process and requires the poet to explore the unconscious world (which he has resisted doing since 1860). The poet's ambivalence continues in section nine, where Whitman feels an impulse to linger in the external world with the lustrous star, while being irresistibly called by the bird to turn inward. However much the poet wants to integrate the conscious and unconscious worlds, he must suppress the conflicts bred by integration.

The conflicts return immediately in the next section, the language of which recalls poet and reader to "As I Ebb'd" as well as to "Out of the Cradle." In "As I Ebb'd" Whitman had symbolically demanded from his father a model by which to develop a sense of masculine identity: "I fear I shall become crazed, if I cannot emulate it, and utter myself as well as it"; and "Out of the Cradle" continued that same search for "The unknown want, the destiny of me." But in "Lilacs" (as in the war poems) the overwhelmingly tragic occasion lends support to Whitman's understandable reluctance to force another painful confrontation. In section ten Whitman concedes that he will settle for considerably less than his original goal.

> O how shall I warble myself for the dead one there
> I loved?
> And how shall I deck my song for the large sweet
> soul that has gone?
> And what shall my perfume be, for the grave of
> him I love?
>
> Sea-winds, blown from east and west,
> Blown from the eastern sea, and blown from the
> western sea, till there on the prairies meeting:

These, and with these, and the breath of my chant,
I perfume the grave of him I love.

Although Whitman's search for a way to "warble" himself shows that he has not entirely forgotten earlier goals, the urgency of his need to celebrate himself and escape the perfumed houses and rooms has diminished. The father escaped his son's demands by dying; when the son accepts the finality of his father's death, ten years later, he gives up hope for the masculine model he once thought would lead him beyond confusion. The poet-son himself becomes the bearer of perfume and (in the next section) the adorner of rooms and houses. Section ten shows Whitman renouncing forever his search for a way to express the fire within himself, taking his chief elemental identity from the mediating air which watches family conflicts from a careful distance. With his final resignation to his father's death, Whitman becomes conciliatory, seeking compromises by which to integrate the potentially conflicting earth, air, fire, water, phallic city, and maternal death.

O what shall I hang on the chamber walls?
And what shall the pictures be that I hang on the
    walls,
To adorn the burial-house of him I love?

Pictures of growing spring, and farms, and homes,
With the Fourth-month eve at sundown, and the
    gray-smoke lucid and bright,
With floods of the yellow gold of the gorgeous,
    indolent, sinking sun, burning, expanding the
    air.

The placidity of the next several sections comes from Whitman's acquiescence to, and even complicity with, his own symbolic castration: the elimination from himself of the fiery element formerly held responsible for continuing unconscious conflicts. In sections fifteen and sixteen the self-castration is symbolically identified with death (as in the end of "Out of the Cradle"):

> Then with the knowledge of death as walking one
>   side of me,
> And the thought of death close-walking the other
>   side of me,
> And I in the middle, as with companions, and as
>   holding the hands of companions,
> I fled forth to the hiding receiving night, that talks
>   not,
> Down to the shores of the water, the path by the
>   swamp in the dimness,
> To the solemn shadowy cedars, and ghostly pines so
>   still.
>
> And the singer so shy to the rest receiv'd me;
> The gray-brown bird I know, receiv'd us comrades
>   three;
> And he sang what seem'd the song of death, and a
>   verse for him I love.

The heart of the poem follows (in section sixteen), a song translated (as in "Out of the Cradle") from the language of the unconscious into English.

> Come, lovely and soothing Death,
> Undulate round the world, serenely arriving,
>   arriving,
> In the day, in the night, to all, to each,
> Sooner or later, delicate Death.
>
> Prais'd be the fathomless universe,
> For life and joy, and for objects and knowledge
>   curious;
> And for love, sweet love—But praise! O praise and
>   praise,
> For the sure-enwinding arms of cool-enfolding
>   Death.

Dark Mother, always gliding near, with soft feet,
Have none chanted for thee a chant of fullest
    welcome?
Then I chant it for thee—I glorify thee above all;
I bring thee a song that when thou must indeed
    come, come unfalteringly.

Approach, encompassing Death—strong Deliveress!
When it is so—when thou hast taken them, I joyously
    sing the dead,
Lost in the loving, floating ocean of thee,
Laved in the flood of thy bliss, O Death.

From me to thee glad serenades,
Dances for thee I propose, saluting thee—
    adornments and feastings for thee;
And the sights of the open landscape, and the
    high-spread sky, are fitting,
And life and the fields, and the huge and thoughtful
    night.

The night, in silence, under many a star;
The ocean shore, and the husky whispering wave,
    whose voice I know;
And the soul turning to thee, O vast and well-veil'd
    Death,
And the body gratefully nestling close to thee.

Over the tree-tops I float thee a song!
Over the rising and sinking waves—over the myriad
    fields, and the prairies wide;
Over the dense-pack'd cities all, and the teeming
    wharves and ways,
I float this carol with joy, with joy to thee, O Death!

As in "Out of the Cradle," the poet addresses the bird's
love song to the mother, Death, beside whose body he
gratefully nestles. The "enwinding," "enfolding," "encompassing" ocean of the "strong Deliveress" submerges the

putative subject of the poem. In "Out of the Cradle" (as in many earlier poems) Whitman's impulse to evade death, to develop his masculine strengths, and to escape from maternal identification rebelled against a willingness to be seduced and engulfed by maternal death. But the opposing impulses are quiet in "Lilacs"; the fratricidal war has taught the poet that there can be no triumph over the parts of himself that identified with his mother. The complementary activities of nurse and poet remain. In section eighteen Whitman recounts the "vision of armies" presented in *Drum-Taps*, and in section nineteen the vision of armies merges with the vision of night first presented a decade before in "The Sleepers." "Lilacs" ends as "The Sleepers" ended, with a sense of contentment at the conviction that "I will duly pass the day O my mother and duly return to you."

> Must I leave thee, lilac with heart-shaped leaves?
> Must I leave thee there in the door-yard, blooming,
>   returning with spring?
>
> Must I pass from my song for thee;
> From my gaze on thee in the west, fronting the west,
>   communing with thee,
> O comrade lustrous, with silver face in the night?

21

> Yet each I keep, and all;
> The song, the wondrous chant of the gray-brown
>   bird, I keep,
> And the tallying chant, the echo arous'd in my soul,
>   I keep,
> With the lustrous and drooping star, with the
>   countenance full of woe;
> With the lilac tall, and its blossoms of mastering
>   odor;
> Comrades mine, and I in the midst, and their
>   memory ever I keep—for the dead I loved so
>   well;

For the sweetest, wisest soul of all my days and
    lands . . . and this for his dear sake;
Lilac and star and bird, twined with the chant of
    my soul,
With the holders holding my hand, nearing the
    call of the bird,
There in the fragrant pines, and the cedars dusk
    and dim.

The questions asked in section twenty amount to: "Must
I die?"—the answer to which the poet has in advance.
Knowing that he must die, he retreats to the narcissistic
inner world of his earlier poetry in which he evades conflicts between his masculine impulses and his mother by
confining his masculinity to fantasy and by clinging to the
hands of Death, who walks on either side of him. This is the
evasion that ended "Out of the Cradle."

In retrospect, we may find this evasion confirmed by recalling Whitman's eulogy of his mother written ten years
after "Lilacs": "the most perfect and magnetic character,
the rarest combination of practical, moral and spiritual, and
the least selfish, of all and any I have ever known. . . ." This
sounds rather like "the sweetest, wisest soul of all my days
and lands," the last line in "Lilacs" which describes Lincoln.
But in the narcissistic inner world, the less distinction made
between fathers and mothers, the better, for all "others" are
ultimately united in fantasies of symbiosis. "Lilacs" signals
capitulation in the search for sexual identity begun a decade before. The conflicts made conscious by that search
have become insuperable and the poet resigns. The attacks
by the enemy, Whitman's own superego, have come in the
form of terrifying fantasies, anxieties, depressions, and
physical illnesses. These psychological assaults, together
with the experiences of the war, were too powerful and
confusing to be rendered in poetry with consistent success;
and the events immediately after the war ended Whitman's
ability to continue in his poetry the dynamic creation of a

mythic vision. The work that remained for Whitman's last twenty-seven years was the consolidation of his public identity as America's self-appointed poet laureate. O'Connor's title, "The Good Gray Poet," however inappropriate for the poet of the 1850's, fit him after the war like a comfortable cloak beneath which Whitman concealed his aging body and exhausted soul.

Bibliography

Allen, Gay Wilson. *The Solitary Singer: Walt Whitman.* New York: New York Univ. Press, 1967.

———. *Walt Whitman Handbook.* New York: Hendricks House, 1946.

Asselineau, Roger. *The Evolution of Walt Whitman.* 2 vols. Cambridge: Harvard Univ. Press, 1960, 1962.

Black, Stephen A. "Radical Utterances from the Soul's Abysms: Toward a New Sense of Whitman." *PMLA*, 88 (1973), 100-11.

———. "Walt Whitman and Psychoanalytic Criticism." *Literature and Psychology*, 20 (1970), 79-81.

———. "Whitman and the Failure of Mysticism: Identity and Identifications in 'Song of Myself.'" *Walt Whitman Review*, 15 (1969), 223-30.

Bowers, Fredson. *Whitman's Manuscripts: Leaves of Grass (1860).* Chicago: Univ. of Chicago Press, 1955.

Brenner, Charles. *An Elementary Textbook of Psychoanalysis.* Garden City, New York: Doubleday, 1957.

Brill, A. A. *Basic Principles of Psychoanalysis.* New York: Norton, 1949.

Burke, Kenneth. "Policy Made Personal." *"Leaves of Grass" 100 Years After.* Ed. Milton Hindus. Stanford: Stanford Univ. Press, 1955, pp. 74-108.

Bychowski, Gustav. "Walt Whitman, A Study in Sublimation." *Psychoanalysis and the Social Sciences*, 3 (1951), 223-61.

Carlisle, E. Fred. *The Uncertain Self: Whitman's Drama of Identity.* East Lansing: Michigan State Univ. Press, 1973.

Catel, Jean. *Walt Whitman, la naissance du poète.* Paris: Les Editions Rieder, 1929.

Chanover, E. Pierre. "Walt Whitman: A Psychological and Psychoanalytic Bibliography." *Psychoanalytic Review*, 59 (1972), 467-74.

Chari, V. K. *Whitman in the Light of Vedantic Mysticism.* Lincoln: Univ. of Nebraska Press, 1964.

Chase, Richard. " 'Out of the Cradle' as a Romance." *The Presence of Walt Whitman*. Ed. R. W. B. Lewis. New York: Columbia Univ. Press, 1962, pp. 52-71.

———. *Walt Whitman*. Minneapolis: Univ. of Minnesota Press, 1961.

———. *Walt Whitman Reconsidered*. New York: William Sloan, 1955.

Cody, John. *After Great Pain: The Inner Life of Emily Dickinson*. Cambridge, Mass.: Harvard Univ. Press, 1971.

Coffman, Stanley. " 'Crossing Brooklyn Ferry': A Note on the Catalog Technique in Whitman's Poetry." *Modern Philology*, 2 (1954), 225-32.

Crawley, Thomas E. *The Structure of "Leaves of Grass."* Austin: Univ. of Texas Press, 1970.

Crews, Frederick C. *The Sins of the Fathers: Hawthorne's Psychological Themes*. New York: Oxford, 1964.

Erikson, Erik H. *Childhood and Society*. New York: Norton, 1963.

———. *Young Man Luther*. New York: Norton, 1958.

Faber, M. D. "Analytic Prolegomena to the Study of Western Tragedy." *Hartford Studies in Literature*, 5 (1973), 31-60.

Feidelson, Charles Jr. *Symbolism and American Literature*. Chicago: Univ. of Chicago Press, 1953.

Fenichel, Otto. *The Psychoanalytic Theory of Neurosis*. New York: Norton, 1945.

Freud, Anna. *Normality and Pathology in Childhood*. New York: International Universities Press, 1965.

Freud, Sigmund. *The Standard Edition of the Complete Psychological Works of Sigmund Freud*. 24 vols. Ed. James Strachey. London: Hogarth Press, 1951-1974.

Fussell, Paul Jr. "Whitman's Curious Warble." *The Presence of Walt Whitman*. Ed. R. W. B. Lewis. New York: Columbia Univ. Press, 1962, pp. 28-51.

Griffith, Clark. "Sex and Death, the Significance of Whitman's *Calamus* Themes." *Philological Quarterly*, 39 (1960), 18-38.

Holland, Norman N. *The Dynamics of Literary Response*. New York: Oxford Univ. Press, 1968.

———. *Poems in Persons: An Introduction to the Psychoanalysis of Literature*. New York: Norton, 1973.

Jacobson, Edith. *The Self and the Object World*. New York: International Universities Press, 1964.

246

Jones, Ernest. *Hamlet and Oedipus.* New York: Norton, 1949.

————. *The Life and Work of Sigmund Freud.* 3 vols. New York: Basic Books, 1953-1957.

Kohut, Heinz and Philip F. D. Seitz. "Concepts and Theories of Psychoanalysis." *Concepts of Personality.* Ed. J. M. Wepman and R. Heine. Chicago: Aldine, 1963, pp. 113-41.

Kris, Ernst. *Psychoanalytic Explorations in Art.* New York: Schocken, 1964.

Kubie, Lawrence S. *Neurotic Distortion of the Creative Process.* New York: Noonday, 1961.

Lewis, R. W. B., ed. *The Presence of Walt Whitman.* New York: Columbia Univ. Press, 1962.

Malin, Stephen D. " 'A Boston Ballad' and the Boston Riot." *Walt Whitman Review,* 9 (1963), 51-57.

Miller, Edwin Haviland. "Introduction." *A Century of Whitman Criticism.* Bloomington: Indiana Univ. Press, 1969.

————. *Walt Whitman's Poetry: A Psychological Journey.* Boston: Houghton Mifflin, 1968.

Miller, James E. Jr. *A Critical Guide to "Leaves of Grass."* Chicago: Univ. of Chicago Press, 1957.

————. *Walt Whitman.* New York: Twayne, 1962.

Molinoff, Katherine. *Some Notes on Whitman's Family.* Brooklyn: Comet Press, 1941.

Pearce, Roy Harvey. *The Continuity of American Poetry.* Princeton: Princeton Univ. Press, 1961.

————. "Introduction." *"Leaves of Grass," Facsimile Edition of the 1860 Text.* Ithaca: Cornell Univ. Press, 1961, pp. viii-li.

Rieff, Philip. *The Triumph of the Therapeutic.* New York: Harper, 1966.

Rycroft, Charles. *A Critical Dictionary of Psychoanalysis.* Middlesex, England: Penguin, 1972.

————. *Imagination and Reality.* London: Hogarth Press, 1968.

Schyberg, Frederik. *Walt Whitman.* Trans. E. A. Allen, New York: Columbia Univ. Press, 1951.

Spitzer, Leo. *"Explication de Texte* Applied to Walt Whitman's 'Out of the Cradle Endlessly Rocking.' " *A Century of Whitman Criticism.* Ed. Edwin Haviland Miller. Bloomington: Indiana Univ. Press, 1969, pp. 273-84.

Strauch, Carl F. "The Structure of Walt Whitman's 'Song of Myself.' " *English Journal,* 27 (1938), 597-607.

Symonds, John Addington. *Walt Whitman, a Study*. London: J. C. Nimmo, 1893.

Traubel, Horace. *With Walt Whitman in Camden*. Vol. i, Boston: Small, Maynard, 1906. Vol. ii, New York: Appleton, 1908. Vol. iii, New York: M. Kennerly, 1914.

Waelder, Robert. "The Principle of Multiple Function." *Psychoanalytic Quarterly*, 5 (1936), 45-62.

Waskow, Howard J. *Whitman: Explorations in Form*. Chicago: Univ. of Chicago Press, 1966.

Whicher, Stephen. "Whitman's Awakening to Death." *The Presence of Walt Whitman*. Ed. R. W. B. Lewis. New York: Columbia Univ. Press, 1962, pp. 1-27.

Whitman, Walt. *The Collected Writings of Walt Whitman*. Gen. eds. Gay Wilson Allen and Sculley Bradley. New York: New York Univ. Press, 1961-

————. *The Complete Writings of Walt Whitman*. 10 vols. Ed. R. M. Bucke et al. New York: Putnam, 1902.

————. *The Correspondence*. 5 vols. Ed. Edwin Haviland Miller. *The Collected Writings of Walt Whitman*. New York: New York Univ. Press, 1961-1969.

————. *Drum-Taps*. New York [Bunce and Huntington], 1865.

————. *Drum-Taps and Sequel to Drum-Taps*. Washington, 1865-1866.

————. *The Early Poems and the Fiction*. Ed. Thomas Brasher. *The Collected Writings of Walt Whitman*. New York: New York Univ. Press, 1963.

————. *Leaves of Grass*. Brooklyn, 1855.

————. *Leaves of Grass*. Brooklyn, 1856.

————. *Leaves of Grass*. Boston: Thayer and Eldridge, 1860-1861.

————. *"Leaves of Grass": Comprehensive Reader's Edition*. Ed. Harold W. Blodgett and Sculley Bradley. *The Collected Writings of Walt Whitman*. New York: New York Univ. Press, 1964.

————. *Prose Works 1892*. Ed. Floyd Stovall. *The Collected Writings of Walt Whitman*. New York: New York Univ. Press, 1963.

————. *Specimen Days & Collect*. Philadelphia: David McKay, 1882-1883.

————. *Walt Whitman's Blue Book*. 2 vols. Ed. Arthur Golden. New York: New York Public Library, 1968.

248

Index

Library of Congress Cataloging in Publication Data

Black, Stephen Ames, 1935-
   Whitman's journeys into chaos.

   Bibliography: p.
   Includes index.
   1. Whitman, Walt, 1819-1892.   I. Title.
PS3231.B57   811'.3   75-2979
ISBN 0-691-06288-9